Anaïs Nin and the Remaking of Self

Anaïs Nin and the Remaking of Self

Gender, Modernism, and Narrative Identity

DIANE RICHARD-ALLERDYCE

Northern Illinois University Press

DeKalb   1998

Library of Congress Cataloging-in-Publication Data
Richard-Allerdyce, Diane.
Anaïs Nin and the remaking of self : gender, modernism, and narrative identity / Diane
Richard-Allerdyce.
            p.   cm.
Includes bibliographical references and index.
ISBN 0-87580-232-X (alk. paper)
1. Nin, Anaïs, 1903–1977—Criticism and interpretation. 2. Psychoanalysis and literature—
United States—History—20th century. 3. Women and literature—United States—History—
20th century. 4. Psychological fiction, American—History and criticism. 5. Modernism
(Literature)—United States. 6. Sex (Psychology) in literature. 7. Gender identity in literature.
8. Narration (Rhetoric). 9. Self in literature. 10. Fiction—Technique. 11. Lacan, Jacques,
1901– . I. Title.
PS3527.I865Z86   1997
818'.5209—DC21   97-14215
CIP

Excerpts from *Fire, From a Journal of Love* by Anaïs Nin (copyright © 1995 by Rupert Pole as
Trustee under the Last Will and Testament of Anaïs Nin); *The Diary of Anaïs Nin, 1931–1934*,
Volume I (copyright © 1966 by Anaïs Nin and renewed 1994 by Rupert Pole and Gunther
Stuhlmann); *The Diary of Anaïs Nin, 1934–1939*, Volume II (copyright © 1967 by Anaïs Nin
and renewed 1995 by Rupert Pole and Gunther Stuhlmann); *The Diary of Anaïs Nin, 1939–
1944*, Volume III (copyright © 1969 by Anaïs Nin); *The Diary of Anaïs Nin, 1944–1947*,
Volume IV (copyright © 1971 by Anaïs Nin); *The Diary of Anaïs Nin, 1947–1955*, Volume V
(copyright © 1974 by Anaïs Nin); *The Diary of Anaïs Nin, 1955–1966*, Volume VI (copyright
© 1976 by Anaïs Nin); *The Diary of Anaïs Nin, 1966–1974*, by Anaïs Nin (copyright © 1980
by Gunther Stuhlmann); *Henry & June: From a Journal of Love* by Anaïs Nin (copyright © 1986
by Rupert Pole as Trustee under the Last Will and Testament of Anaïs Nin), reprinted by permission of Harcourt Brace & Company and the Author's Representative, Gunther Stuhlmann.

Contents

Acknowledgments

I AM INDEBTED TO ELLIE RAGLAND, who introduced me to Lacan's work at the University of Florida during the mid-eighties. Her expert guidance and encouragement in the early stages of my Lacanian reading of Nin's work have continued to inspire. I am also grateful to Daniel R. Schwarz, director of a National Endowment for the Humanities Summer Seminar in which I participated in 1993 at Cornell University, for leading me to think critically about Nin's relation to Modernism, for suggesting I write this book, and for providing encouragement during the process. Several fellow participants in that seminar, "Theoretical and Critical Perspectives on the Modernist Tradition," offered important feedback on my original proposal and an early version of chapter 6: Winifred Bevilacqua, Joseph Heininger, Margaret Kouidis, Jayne Marek, and Daniel Morris. Valuable suggestions for improving the manuscript in its entirety came from Robert J. Anthony, acquisitions editor at Northern Illinois University Press, as well as two anonymous readers for the press. Susan Bean and Pippa Letsky provided expert editorial suggestions. Gunther Stuhlmann provided valuable feedback about publication history and other pertinent information about Nin's life and career. I am grateful as well to Jennifer Braaten and Judith Jones Walker at Lynn University, to Joel Blaustein for many thoughtful discussions about psychoanalysis, and to Jennifer Halpern, who read and helped to prepare for submission an early version of the

manuscript. I thank Debra, Avery, and Iris Allerdyce; Natalie Gilbert; Paul
Herron; Pamela Kovacs; John and Karen Patton; my parents, Victor and Joyce
Richard; and my brother, Daniel Richard, for their continued encouragement
during its writing.

For permission to quote from the Swallow editions of Nin's fiction and crit-
icism and to reprint material that originally appeared in *Anaïs: An
International Journal* 13 (1995), I thank Gunther Stuhlmann and the Anaïs
Nin Foundation.

I offer my deepest gratitude to my husband, John Pickering, and my children, James and Julia Allerdyce, whose unending support, patience, and love
have sustained me throughout this project and beyond.

Anaïs Nin and the Remaking of Self

Introduction

ANAÏS NIN (1903–1977) was a French-born naturalized American
of Cuban, Danish, and Spanish heritage.[1] Her story is one of uneven reception
and ostensibly conflicting allegiances. In terms of the serious recognition Nin
hoped her experiments in fiction would earn from the critical world, some
would say it is a story of failure. It is also one of strength and courage, a

narrative that calls into question tenets of Poststructuralist thought by tracing a process whereby writing can have real effects on both writer and the community created through readership, an idea that Nin emphasized in the last decades of her career. The relationship Nin asserted between literary and social change, for example, suggests the possibility that the interrelations of language, culture, and history can be grounded in a context that includes what has often been marginalized and uncanonized in literature, the personal, the feminine, the prosaic—a context that also allows for a belief in the value and meaning of life beyond the signifying system with which it is represented.

This book's particular focus is the way Nin's fiction, criticism, and diaries thematize her nearly lifelong struggle to resist the tendency toward despair and to use psychoanalysis in conjunction with writing in a process of "narrative recovery" in a way that establishes her as an important Modernist and feminist writer.[2] Nin employed literary form as a means to instill much-needed boundaries in her life, even as she developed a theory of literary creativity that allowed her to retain the elements of fluidity she associated with both a feminine principle and an understanding of the unconscious forces that shape humans' lives.

The present book is unique among book-length studies of Nin's work in several ways. In order to make her works accessible to the widest possible range of readers, I have provided here a unified view of Nin's oeuvre while also offering a title by title approach. To my knowledge, this book is the first full-length critical study of Nin's works to make use of the four volumes of previously expurgated portions of Nin's diaries that Harcourt Brace has published since 1986 as parts of Nin's "A Journal of Love."[3] The unexpurgated diary volumes have provided an important corrective to my relationship with Nin's works. I have also drawn upon works by the first biographers to have access to archived material, Noël Riley Fitch and Deirdre Bair.[4] Bair's Anaïs Nin: A Biography (1995), in particular, has allowed me to move beyond some of the early conjecture on which by necessity I based my early readings of Nin's writing.

This book's most important original contribution to Nin studies is its use of a narrative theory based largely on Lacanian psychoanalysis, with which I have gathered the disparate elements of Nin's life into a coherent whole, in a way that is compatible with Nin's own sense of the Modern self.[5] My approach is nonetheless pluralistic, combining close textual criticism of individual works with a theoretical cultural criticism that takes into account some of the aims and discontinuities of twentieth-century critical thought and the angst of the nuclear age. In her later work, Nin's focus widens from an emphasis on gender difference and the nature of the unconscious to include an interest in Modern art and the relationship between individual and society. This book also widens its scope as it progresses from an examination of Nin's place within contemporary debates on writing the body and on the effects of past trauma to consider such questions as how her work was informed by the necessities of the publishing world, for instance, and how it draws on the inspiration of Modernist painters and jazz musicians while it also anticipates a Postmodern emphasis on the permeable boundaries between art and life. Acknowledging the paradox that Modern literature can encompass both flux and boundaries was a cornerstone of Nin's own narrative theories. It is the Lacanian lens through which I have described these theories that provides the connective tissue among them.

Several existing studies employ psychoanalytic perspectives to explicate Nin's work.[6] Nin's own long-term involvement as an analysand with at least five therapists over the span of her adult life and her brief career as lay analyst under Otto Rank's direction in the mid-1930s make psychoanalytic readings of her work a natural fit. Nin referred to psychoanalytic ideas in almost all her writing and believed that psychoanalysis could provide the Modern artist with the integrative themes necessary for making sense of the images of fragmentation prevalent in twentieth-century literature, art, and popular culture.

The Lacanian perspective in this study complements and contributes to existing scholarship on Nin's relationship with psychoanalytic narrative thought in the following ways. First, Nin's self-mythologizing tendencies provide an exaggerated version of identity construction itself as described in Lacan's theory. The story Nin created about the origins of her nearly life-long diary—that she began it as a series of letters to the absent, adored father by whom she was abandoned—is especially pertinent within a Lacanian reading of paternal influence on identity and psychological structure.[7]

Second, Nin's own interest in psychoanalysis and Modernism highlights the relevance of both to an understanding of her work. I have found a natural affinity between Lacan's and the Modernists' emphasis on splitting and fragmentation, which I believe can shed reciprocal light on Nin's artistic and therapeutic aims. Nin's understanding of the self as fragmented finds its most artistic expression in passages where her own psychoanalytic insights aim to capture in language the perceptual multiplicity she admired in the work of Modernist painters. The Lacanian perspective that informs my reading is particularly compatible with the Modernist emphasis on a synchronic moment in art. Humanist critic Daniel R. Schwarz, for instance, describes Modernist artists' attempts to play off one perceptual mode against another in a way that highlights Nin's attempts in her later work to capture the rhythms of music. Nin also incorporated a link she saw between perception and a consciousness rooted in a somatic experience of language.

Third, Nin's attempts to formulate a theory of gender can be understood in terms of Lacan's ideas about feminine *jouissance*. In my view, gender is the most important element in the Lacanian account of the narrative myths people use to structure identities, as well as one of the most important in Nin's formal and theoretical fictions. Nin's relation to women's studies and her treatment of gender—because she made conscious the way gender was imbedded in her identity construction and thematized that issue in all her writing—is invaluable to an understanding of her work. Overall, Lacan's depictions of language and identity, of necessary limits and literary response, and of the anchoring of consciousness in a reality that lies beyond signifying systems provide a unique view of Nin's own attempts to theorize these very concepts.

As part of my focus on Nin's narrative recovery in terms of a Modernist perspective based on psychoanalytic principles, my explication emphasizes Nin's relationship to truth and her use of literary form as necessary limitation to chaos and to the endless stream of possibilities inherent in a purely relativistic view of humans' capacity for making meaning. Related to Nin's use of form as a structure within which to heal from trauma, Nin's foregrounding of the fictionality of experience and identity (within a frame comprised of the same materials) makes her thoroughly Modern. Nin's affinities with a psychoanalytically informed Modernism include her aesthetic resistance to "copy models" of reality, her attempts to challenge conventional narrative linearity through repetition, her belief in the importance of creating a personal mythology, and her interest in art's power to create a transpersonal realm.

The theme of gender runs throughout her work and throughout this discussion. For Nin, gender was inextricably part of a larger emphasis on women that makes her work important to women's studies. Throughout the present study, I shall treat gender—specifically Nin's notion of "the feminine"—as the most important thematic element of the self-mythology she developed to represent her notion of the Modern self in response to, and specifically to heal from, a devastating early life.

The relationship of truth to fiction embodied in her work—including the sometimes arbitrary nature of truth and its paradoxical relation to human or literary expression—is among her most challenging explorations. On one hand, Nin's writing stands as an assertion of her determination to convince herself that life is meaningful beyond the surface reality of everyday life and beyond the ways a society evaluates and represents that life. Truth, for her, lies in one's own ability to access an authentic relationship to one's fictions through the creative process. This meaningfulness, on the other hand, is complicated in Nin's case by her proclivity to lying, which thus undercuts her own concepts of an authentic self.

Charges of autobiographical dishonesty abounded after the unexpurgated diary volume *Incest* was published in 1992. Readers were understandably shocked to learn that Nin had sustained an incestuous affair with her father when she was thirty. It was a feeling of having been led on, however, that brought the most intense reaction to *Incest*'s revelations that the "stillbirth" she had written about so poignantly in *The Diary of Anaïs Nin, Volume 1 (1931–1934)* and in her short story "Birth" (see chapter 4) was really an abortion.[8] As a result, recent critics have joined those who argued earlier that Nin's *Diary* is largely fiction, a carefully constructed and falsified self-portrait of a woman who never moved past a crippling self-absorption in her writing or her life.[9] Bair has shown the degree to which Nin composed a life for herself in her diary from the age of ten or eleven, using so much embellishment to relate the events of her life that the result was, according to one of her contacts, more of a "liary" than a "diary" (Bair xvi). Yet, as Bair puts it toward the end of her expansive study, "One wonders why 'truth' is the primary criterion for judging diaries, especially those such as Nin's, which were intended from the beginning to represent one woman's view of herself and her life" (Bair 518).

The issue of autobiographical authenticity is further complicated by the narrative integrity that readers have often found between the lines of Nin's writing. The themes of incest and early wounding around the issue of the paternal, for instance, are among the most palpably present in Nin's fiction and expurgated diaries. Alice Miller has written about the way "'the works of writers, poets, and painters tell the encoded story of childhood traumas no longer consciously remembered in adulthood.'"[10] Nin's work resonates with her unsayable response to early paternal abuse (whether sexual or otherwise psychological and physical) and the "earth-shattering" effects of that violation on her later life, effects of the kind that feminist cultural critic Jane Caputi has compared with those of the atomic bomb (see chapter 1 for a fuller discussion of Caputi's work on the relationship between the effects of incest and nuclearism as it pertains to Nin's *House of Incest* and later work).

Nin's narrative recovery from the trauma of her early life depended on her being able to express the sense of fragmentation and shock that resulted from her father's emotional and physical abuse. She tried in many ways to say what she often did not even know she needed to say. One way was to create a series of selves in fiction and in her diary, asserting her right to do so even when confronted with the disparity between one version of herself and another. Another way was to find distancing techniques in categories of gender. By pitting the feminine against the masculine in her first book (the study of D. H. Lawrence she published in 1932), for instance, Nin devised a way to incorporate a psychoanalytic emphasis on self-exploration into an identification with a writer she could see as both masculine in his creative energy and feminine in his use of language. Setting Lawrence up as a literary father figure, she could potentially negate her own father's power over her identity.

Her needing several lovers as additional father substitutes and her wanting to play multiple roles with all of them, however, led Nin to lie, while she was working out alternatives to remaining identified with her father. Later, when she published the account of her relationship with Henry Miller, for example, she "lied" again to her readers by editing out the sexual nature of their relationship. Yet, once again, the issue is complicated by the narrative authenticity that resonates between the lines and by Nin's leaving a full record of her life for posthumous publication as an unexpurgated series of diaries.

For some readers, the status of Nin's written life story *as a story* that foregrounds the fictional nature of memory and arbitrary notions of gender roles is part of its value as Modernist women's autobiography. For others, Nin's problematic conception of truth constitutes grounds for dismissal.[11] The tension between these two views highlights one of the difficulties posed by a study of Nin's works in relation to her life—that a clear line cannot be drawn between her life and her art. The absence of this border is also one of the dominant themes of her work, appearing time and again in her diaries, essays, and fiction. Although Nin would try during the early decades of her career to establish a clear line between fiction and diary writing, she eventually came to embrace the idea that the boundary must be a permeable one, constructed of formal limits that are elastic enough to portray the flux of life.

Yet she needed a clear line, and she needed to draw it herself. This is why the theme of boundaries—tied inextricably with her Modernist and psychoanalytic perspectives and inseparable during several stages of her career from the issue of gender—is one of the most important motifs I consider within this study. It was boundaries that Nin sought to establish in writing, in part to compensate for the lack of a stable identity born of early wounding, in part to develop an artistic aesthetic in which form and content could be wed and, at the same time, distinguished. Literary form became her stay against confusion, her way of warding off her tendency to identify with the source of her emotional unease. The writing of fiction in particular provided her with a means for mourning the past, so that she could move beyond it, albeit not far beyond it nor for long at a time.

Nin herself believed, I think rightly, that her non-diary writings would provide the distance she needed to deal with some of the psychological damage she suffered during childhood—whether as the result of her father's abandonment of his family when Anaïs was a child, or (as Fitch has argued and Nin later believed [Bair 18; *Nearer the Moon* 207]) as the result of early sexual violation. She was never able to make the transition fully from diarist to fiction writer (see Bair 43), and she could not, of course, completely undo the effects of trauma. Still, her fictional works offer evidence of maturing artistry, and to some degree a lessening of affective pain. Unlike the prodigious, nearly boundary-less diary from which the *Diary* was drawn, the works Nin published as fiction and criticism provide a formal closure she was not able to achieve elsewhere.

In addition to her need for boundaries as a formal stay against chaos, Nin's affinities with a psychoanalytically informed Modernism included her aesthetic resistance to "copy models" of reality. Nin's aesthetics hinged on the difference she saw between literary realism and the reality lying at the core of an existence lived in harmony with natural principles. Evelyn J. Hinz, in *The Mirror and the Garden*, argues that an understanding of all Nin's work lies in her distinction between the artificial world of convention and surface appearances (as symbolized in Nin's work by the mirror) and the psychological realms wherein one can find a healthy and natural sense of self (which Nin represented in terms of the garden). Nin's need to draw lines between categories finds fulfillment, in part, in this distinction.

More important, her resistance to conventional modes of representation parallels her resistance to prefabricated roles that a woman, specifically a wounded daughter, must play. Her emphasis on a quest for an authentic self of one's own making rather than a self dependent on another's perspective becomes part of the creative process she then sets up as the opposite of artifice. As Suzanne Nalbantian has pointed out, Nin based her aesthetics on the notion of a composite self that eludes wholeness yet paradoxically finds permanence through artistic representation. This permanence satisfies and highlights Nin's need for a meaningful reality that is simultaneously created in a self-fulfilling creative project and anchored to something real lying beyond the self. Her belief in this anchor makes her a Modern, even as it points out the psychoanalytic basis of her thought.

While much of her fiction is in direct confrontation with conventional literary realism, Nin refused to relinquish reality itself, believing it a matter of psychological rather than external landscapes.[12] She expresses this concept in the title, themes, and characterizations of *Cities of the Interior*, her five-part "continuous novel" (1945–1961). Again, Nin is Modern in this regard, retaining her emphasis on a disciplined mastery of artistic technique while going beyond what Altieri, in *Painterly Abstraction in Modernist American Poetry*, has dubbed a "copy model of truth" (Altieri 428), or a Poststructuralist condensation of truth into a dichotomy of presence and absence. Altieri's point about many Modernists' loss of faith in mimetic principles—that it reflected not an argument with truth itself, "but with one particular technique for constructing truths, which they felt confined art to the domain of appearances" (Altieri 427)—well describes Nin's own emphasis in her culminating critical work, *The Novel of the Future* (1968). Nin's Lawrence book shows that her resistance to strictly empirical representations framed the whole of her writing career. "One aspect of her early affinity to Lawrence is that—according to her—he recognized the limited value of social criticism and consequently pursued more profound themes" (Hinz 33).

In her resistance to popular social realisms, Nin's work also corresponds with that of Proust and Woolf.[13] She shared Gertrude Stein's resistance to plot and narrative, as well as Stein's preference that art capture the intensity of an experience rather than relate its factual details.[14] Nin's belief in alternative representations parallels that of Joyce and Stevens as well. Like them, Nin found in the Modernist visual, musical, and architectural arts an adequate way of representing the twentieth-century fragmented self without rendering it meaningless.[15] The belief that representation could be based on non-empiricist models is among Nin's strongest affinities with Modernist visual artists such as Picasso and Duchamp, even as it defines her sense that psychoanalysis allowed one to access the truer truth of one's patterned relationships with the world and one's own fictional selves. Nin directly incorporated reference to Duchamp's *Nude Descending a Staircase* (1913) into her continuous novel *Cities of the Interior*, for example, as an image of the Modern self she wanted to portray.

As part of her challenge to conventional narrative linearity and realism, Nin used repetition in her work in ways that highlight both Modernist and psychoanalytic principles. She was not always successful in her use of repeated passages, symbols, and characterizations. Parts of *Cities of the Interior* as well as some stories in *Under a Glass Bell* (1944) break down, for example, because she refuses to relinquish her attachment to the conditions of her childhood abandonment in order to hold on to the image of her father through grief and she becomes overly repetitive. Nevertheless, repetitions provide part of the framework that calls attention to the author's and the works' attempt to rely on their own structuring principles to provide a reorientation toward loss—much as Altieri describes Stevens's ability to renegotiate loss by focusing the mind's relation to those losses and by using poetic repetitions as formal anchors to root perception in its own "needs, processes, and powers" (Altieri 27–28). Nin's work is equally concerned with—and designed specifically for—the purpose of negotiating the author's relationship with the terms of her own existence.

For Nin, as for Stevens, the work of art becomes both the act of acting upon and the object being acted upon. For Nin in particular, the self-referential and self-structuring properties of art were best explained through psychoanalytic concepts that describe how identification takes place. Yet her use of repeated scenes, images, and themes is less compatible with Freud's use of repetition as reenactment of unresolved psychic trauma than it is a "potentially revitalizing" technique such as that Stein advocated (Steiner 176). Nor does Nin use repeated passages in keeping with the mechanistically repeated images that (Steiner reminds us) were the hallmark of pop art during the 1960s.[16] For Nin, repetitions of phrases operated in literature as Duchamp's repeated images operated in *Nude Descending a Staircase*, as a way to indicate a deeper, more real reality. In *The Novel of the Future*, Nin writes that phrase repetitions "give the book the flow of water, the sea breaking and flowing, and the sea symbol is a good one for the background music of the book, . . . the long and short rhythms of failure and success as the incidents come and go" (*Future* 31–32).

Nin's interest in the power of art to create a transpersonal realm is another element that she based upon her understanding of Modernist art and her belief in psychoanalytic principles. The transpersonal properties that Nin made a cornerstone of her theories about art in general—and upon which she built her own aesthetics—are, paradoxically, a direct outcome of art's self-referentiality. Popular response to Nin's *Diary*, in particular, illustrates Altieri's idea that encountering the ways a work of art becomes its own subject suggests to readers that the artist has become his or her own maker, in a creative process they must at least potentially share. In her fiction, Nin uses self-referring repetition and form to enact the transpersonal principle she discusses in *The Novel of the Future,* that if one delves deeply enough into the personal, one reaches the universal. The quest toward psychological freedom thematized in *Cities of the Interior* was Nin's singular quest, but one with universal implications in that each person must, if he or she is to attain a similar freedom from painful patterns, pursue an equally singular path. By the time the first volumes of her *Diary* were published, in the late 1960s, she had found support for her philosophy of seeking the universal through the personal in hundreds of fan letters, which suggested that her personal issues were indeed shared by others.

Nin had begun her writing career exploring this transpersonality. *D. H. Lawrence: An Unprofessional Study* enacts the paradox that artistic creativity is · both an individual quest and a vehicle for reaching that which connects humans to one another. Hinz has placed Nin's response to Lawrence within a tradition of subjective criticism in which writers use others' fictions to delineate, restructure, and re-create their own personal theories (Hinz 31–32). Such is the nature of several Modernist writers' response to visual art, which Altieri discusses as part of his own emphasis on the transpersonal nature of response. For instance, Pater, writes Altieri, saw that "the writer's challenge is to capture the intricacies of one's sensibility . . . that is available, in different registers, to other temperaments" (24). For William Carlos Williams, the writer's intelligence responds not so much to the sensibilities evoked as to the structuring principles at work in the identification between artist and writer. This identification highlights the writer's "own compositional powers" as a means to reorganize one's own writerly relation to the world, much as Nin reinvented herself from unpublished writer to published author of psychological insight by writing her book on Lawrence. Altieri distinguishes Stevens's notion of the transpersonal function of art from Pater's and Williams's: for Stevens in *The Necessary Angel* the artistic act lies in focusing in on one's own powers to find a resolution in art and redefining the self accordingly (Altieri 25).

Nin devoted her adult life to pursuing such focus. She was often criticized for self-absorption, but both Williams and Stevens commented positively on her work. It was perhaps Nin's greatest weakness to continue seeking such recognition long after she had resolved that, as Stevens believed, one must focus on one's own reconstructive powers. In life, Nin never let go of the need for others' recognition. In her art, however, she attains and thematizes the self-referential nature of Modernist creativity.

Another primary part of her relation to literary Modernism and one that defines her place in women's studies curricula of the late twentieth and early twenty-first centuries is that of feminist self-making. The singularity of the experience she had as a woman connected her with other women who had recognized in her work their own relation to the overtly prosaic nature of many women's lives—lives historically rooted to bodily experience and often defined in terms of reproductive and familial roles. This singularity of female experience did not, in her mind, negate her ability in her work to access a universality beyond gender. Nin's treatment of gender is central to the literary reconstructions to which she devoted her life as a writer.

Nin was perhaps not intellectually disciplined enough to become a serious literary or cultural critic in the usual sense of the term "critic." She was nevertheless a prescient synthesizer of ideas, and thinker enough in her own right to provide what I believe are some important ideas, important not only for the study of gender and its relation to both identity and literary style but (most relevant to this study) also to an understanding of how a writer might access the body through literature in order to mourn his or her own bodily and psychological wounding. Nin laid the groundwork for this process in her study of Lawrence, which immediately precedes her beginning the process of writing fiction seriously as well as her involvement with psychoanalytic theory and practice.[17]

Her attempts to define gender in terms of social roles and core identity parallel her uneasy relationship with women's studies in general and with literary feminism in particular.[18] Nin's work does support a belief in a core identity grounded in self-knowledge and self-creation, but she is not the essentialist that several feminists, in spurning Nin's work, have described. I argue throughout this study that Nin's nearly lifelong effort to define writing in terms of gender places her within a tradition of *l'écriture féminine* at the same time that it distinguishes her theory from its most essentialist counterparts. Nalbantian goes so far as to suggest that—in Nin's refuting the chauvinism of male psychoanalysts who saw women's identity as pathological in itself and in her focus on women artists—Nin's feminism goes beyond even that of Virginia Woolf (Nalbantian 184). As Nin challenged her own role of seduced and seducing daughter, a role that Jane Gallop, in *The Daughter's Seduction,* argues traps female subjects in a vicious cycle of enticement by and of a "father" presumed to know the answers and to possess authority (70–71), she took part in a larger women's movement toward re-creating and redefining the female experience.

Nin's use of labyrinth and Minotaur imagery places her at a crossroads where a tradition of literary feminism meets Modernist emphasis on self-making. In *The Madwoman in the Attic: The Woman Writer and the Nineteenth-*

Century Literary Imagination (1979), Sandra M. Gilbert and Susan Gubar describe the importance of this theme to feminism, arguing that "the female monster" in traditional mythology "is a striking illustration of Simone de Beauvoir's thesis that woman has been made to represent all of man's ambivalent feelings about his own inability to control his own physical existence, his own birth and death, in essence, life's contingency" (Gilbert and Gubar 34).[19] Similarly, in her book on Lawrence and afterward, Nin presents the unconscious, as well as the realm that lies beyond even its grasp, as that which has been considered formidable but which, in reality, should be acknowledged despite the ego's attempt to cover it up.

Nin saw the monster not only as society's portraiture of women but also as one's own tendency to buy into that portraiture, a co-creation of the individual and of culture. Her labyrinth metaphor condenses her interest in psychoanalytic exploration with Modernist mythology such as Joyce's use of the Dedalus myth. Nin shared with Joyce an acknowledgment that one can all too easily become trapped into identifying with cultural seductions, an idea she expresses in the title of her fifth novel, *Seduction of the Minotaur* (1961). In this novel, "Lillian is able to identify the 'minotaur' at the heart of masochistic behavior patterns which dominate her life" (Henke, "Lillian Beye" 134). Nin also wanted to provide an alternative to flying out of the labyrinth. For Nin, labyrinth imagery represents the unconscious and life's complexity rather than a human-made trap from which one can escape. In Nin's mythology, it is only by confronting and prevailing against one's own unconscious entrapments and attachments and by realigning oneself in relation to cultural expectations that one can become free. This freedom involves distinguishing one's status as re-creative artist of one's own life, capable of drawing one's own self-portrait, from one's status as complicit pawn in others' vision of what one should be. Nin shared this goal with other feminists, although it is not an exclusively feminist concern. Nin's confrontation of the Minotaur is both feminist and Modernist, combining a belief in self re-creation, such as Altieri and Schwarz identify in Stevens's work, with her faith in psychoanalytic principles for delving into past patterns.

In a passage from Volume 2 of her published *Diary*, Nin emphasizes taking responsibility for one's own portrait: "the modern hero," she writes, is "one who would master his own neurosis so that it would not become universal, who would struggle with his myths, who would know that he himself created them, who would enter the labyrinth and fight the monster" (2: 347). We know that Joyce flew from the seductions of Irish Catholicism and Dublin provinciality. Whether Nin was as successful in resisting her own seducing monsters and in moving out of her role as seduced and seducing daughter is one of the questions debated in this book. I believe that, for the most part, she did.

At the heart of this book is my belief that Nin is an important Modernist writer, deserving recognition within the literary canon for her experiments in fiction and criticism and for her policy of eventual full disclosure in her unexpurgated diary.[20] Her narrative recovery from trauma and her relationship to her reading audience at the end of her life stand as important evidence that literature has a real effect beyond the signifying systems of language it uses as medium. Nin's writings have received less serious critical attention than have other Modernist works although they are essentially teachable in the university classroom and provide a great deal of interpretive food for thought. I believe critical close readings of the kind I offer here can reveal the value of Nin's works for canonical reassessment and can help in determining whether Nin's fictions are texts that, to use Dominick LaCapra's distinction, are not only worth "thinking about" (as LaCapra says all texts are) but also "thinking with."[21]

1

Narrative Openings

D. H. Lawrence and House of Incest

*[Lawrence] certainly never had before and probably will never have
again such an unambiguous relationship to women's literature as he
does in Anaïs Nin's texts.*

—Carol Siegel

*. . . the word she cannot utter against her father, she shouts in the
title of her first book [of fiction].*

—Noël Riley Fitch

ANAÏS NIN'S NARRATIVE RECOVERY from a traumatic
early life began in earnest with the writing of her first two books: a critical study
of D. H. Lawrence, published in 1932, and the work that eventually became
her first published book of fiction, the prose poem *House of Incest* (1936).[1] It is
no wonder, then, that when Nin edited the first volume of her *Diary*, published
in 1966, she chose to begin her life story with the events of 1931–1934 rather
than with the childhood diary she had begun at the age of eleven as a series of
letters to her absent father. Bair has attributed this choice to Nin's belief that she
could entice publishers and potential readers with her written portraits of famous others such as Henry Miller and Antonin Artaud (Bair 464).[2]

This entry point was a logical choice for thematically more significant reasons as well, for it was during this period that she really began to come of age
as a writer.[3] In addition, Nin began at this time to use several kinds of writing

as a tool for relinquishing the melancholy that Dominick LaCapra argues can block mourning, "insofar as the melancholic disavows loss, remains narcissistically identified with the loved other and is unable to affirm, empathize with and, in certain respects, take leave of the other as other" (*Representing the Holocaust* 213). Nin's first two books—one critical and the other fiction—represent the author's movement out of the melancholy of her childhood toward a recognition that a partnership between artistic and psychoanalytic processes might provide a way of thematizing and working through, rather than repressing and acting out, early issues. Writing *D. H. Lawrence: An Unprofessional Study* launched Nin on a lifelong quest to theorize and employ an aesthetics of recovery that she based upon psychoanalytic principles.[4] In particular, what she called the "texture" of Lawrence's writing inspired her to use her own fiction to capture a flesh-and-blood experience in language and to use that somatic vividness to express the real memory of past pain in order to heal.

Writing *House of Incest* was Nin's first coherent attempt to apply the theories she had begun to develop in her own fiction. She had failed at several early attempts to write fiction and had purposely set out to overcome that failure by writing the critical work. In the process, Nin learned to release some of her melancholic resistance to mourning by formulating her ideas about writing, especially its relation to physical reality and to the issue of formal literary boundaries, as a labyrinth for capturing one's monsters. To most of Nin's readers, the nature of her own monsters was, until recently, discernable only between the lines.

Because Nin purposely obscured many biographical facts about herself during her lifetime, the details were sketchy of her formative years as a writer and as a person deeply engaged in a process of mourning. They were available only through official biographical statements prepared by Nin and her publishers during her life and, afterward, through four volumes of *The Early Diary of Anaïs Nin,* published between 1978 and 1985. Even with the early diaries, critics found it difficult to unearth a straightforward story, for in these volumes, writes Gunther Stuhlmann in the introduction to *The Early Diary,* Volume 2, "As in all of Anaïs's diary volumes, the events jump rather than walk, explode rather than flower" (2: xiii). Bair's account in *Anaïs Nin* (1995) has allowed further understanding of the circumstances of her development as a writer who identified with the Modernist emphasis on self-making through art and who came to view psychoanalysis as a way to access her own artistry.

THE FIRST THIRTY YEARS

From the time of her birth in Neuilly-sur-Seine, a suburb of Paris, on February 21, 1903, Angela Anaïs Juana Antolina Rosa Edelmira Nin y Culmell experienced awful family turmoil (Bair 12). The fighting was nearly constant between her parents, Joaquín Nin y Castellanos (1879–1949) and Rosa Culmell y Vaurigaud (1871?–1954). That they were both musicians meant they were able, at least, to pass on to their daughter and her two younger brothers an appreciation for the arts. This was the one quality that made life bearable for the family otherwise traumatized by parental fighting and paternal violence. Anaïs's later emphasis on writing as well as the musical and visual arts as sources of comfort and structure finds its origin in this aspect of her childhood.

From the very beginning, Anaïs formed an identity in relation to the co-existence of artistry and violence in her father, Joaquín Nin, a talented, arrogant pianist of Spanish-Cuban birth. She also reacted to his frequent absence from the family as he undertook a series of concert tours and academic appointments away from home. In 1913, Joaquín abandoned the family for good, in part to stay in the good graces of a wealthy couple he had courted as his patrons (and with whose sixteen-year-old daughter he had become infatuated). By this time, his own daughter had experienced almost more than her fragile temperament would allow her to bear. Afterward, Anaïs was devastated and hysterical, clinging to her mother and grandmother, indeed developing separation anxiety in relation to them as well (Bair 24).

Rosa Culmell had an independent character that had often exacerbated her husband's violence, but which became a source of comfort and strength to her daughter after he was gone. Rosa was thirty-one in 1901, when she met the twenty-three-year-old Joaquín in a music store in Havana. (Joaquín had returned from Barcelona to his birthplace, Havana, having had to flee Spain, as Bair recounts, to extract himself from a sexual entanglement that had grown dangerous.[5]) Rosa's own mother had abandoned the family and left Rosa to serve as surrogate mother to several siblings. The occupation had prepared her well for what was to follow. As the daughter of a wealthy businessman, Rosa did not have to marry for financial security. So she married for love, or what she thought was love, and committed herself to the poor musician of minor Spanish nobility with whom she had become smitten at first sight (Bair 10).

When she gave birth less than eleven months later to Anaïs, Rosa found her husband was jealous of the attention she gave the new baby, whom he criticized from the start (Bair 12). Then each addition to the family was equally abused. After Thorvald was born in Cuba in 1905, and Joaquín in Berlin in 1908,[6] the senior Joaquín included them in regular beatings. He liked to torture Rosa by locking her up and beating the children so she could hear them screaming without being able to rescue them. He also tormented the children by following them around with his camera and photographing them, unexpectedly, after surprising them when they were naked and in the process of bathing or dressing (Bair 13–14). He told his daughter regularly that she was ugly, especially after a bout of typhoid fever at the age of two left her scrawny and weak.

The effect on all the children, of course, was serious. Thorvald withdrew and became a recalcitrant, resentful child. As an adult he became irreconcilably estranged from his sister, whom he hated and whose writing he detested because he felt it threw the family's image into its worst light. The youngest Nin child was subjected less to his father's abuse, if only because he spent fewer years with his father, but Joaquínito was certainly affected as well. Unlike his brother and despite several years of estrangement around 1940, Joaquín Nin-Culmell would remain Anaïs's friend and supporter throughout most of her life (Bair 570 n. 49). It was Anaïs who suffered the most, or perhaps the most openly, from her father's behavior. She strove for the rest of her life to overcome the effects of the early abuse and eventual abandonment by the man whom she feared, and yet adored beyond reason.

Nin's career as a writer was born of this trauma. Just before her father left the family permanently, in 1913, and ordered them to go to live with his parents in Barcelona, she had, ironically, become more attached to him than ever before. After a burst appendix, which almost killed her in October 1912, Anaïs remained deathly ill through January of the next year. Although it was Rosa who stayed at her bedside throughout the three-month ordeal, her father did rally for her, and her faith in his love had been restored, despite the early beatings and humiliating photography sessions.

Fortunately, the insightful Rosa encouraged her daughter to use her natural talent at storytelling to deal with her grief.[7] In Barcelona, Rosa presented Anaïs with a small writing journal, which she hoped would serve to distract the increasingly needy and emotional girl from her fixation on her father (Bair 29). Joaquín interfered with the distraction by sending his daughter a series of emotionally manipulative letters, which supported her fantasy that he would soon return, out of love for her (Bair 25). Nin's diary originated in this fantasy.

Later, when Nin created a story of the diary she began in the book her mother gave her, she placed its origins in the boat ride from Spain to New York—after Rosa, having finally given up trying to please her in-laws, accepted financial help from two of her sisters, on the condition that she join them in the States. Nin did write steadily in her diary during that seventeen-day trip in the summer of 1914. This series of letters from a young girl to an absent—but adored—father became, in truth, one of the most remarkable diaries of the century. The picture of the eleven-year-old Anaïs carrying her diary in a little basket as she disembarked with her mother and brothers in New York remains among the dominant images in her many volumes of self-writing, appearing not only in her published diary but also in her fiction, where the idea of diary as a "labyrinth of the soul" takes many forms.

Nin lived out her adolescence in New York.[8] The family stayed first with relatives, eventually moving several times around Manhattan until Rosa, with funding from her sisters, opened a boarding house on West Seventy-fifth

Street. Rosa had not been able to support herself and her family by singing, as she had hoped, but she became a businesswoman, investing in real estate and operating an international shopping service between New York and Cuba, which provided her with a good income until the collapse of the Cuban sugar industry in 1919. The brothers thrived during this time; but Anaïs developed habits that both worried her ever more indulgent mother and characterized Nin's behavior for many years afterward: stubbornness, loyalty to her father (to whom she still wrote avidly), impulsiveness, and lying. Rosa eventually allowed Anaïs to drop out of high school. By this time, Anaïs had decided she would become a writer, and she fully expected to become published and successful within the near-future. Unfortunately, although she would not recognize it until she was nearly thirty, "her obsession with refining the raw material of her life" for her diary "was so inhibiting that it interfered time and again with the creativity necessary for writing fiction" (Bair 40).

Eventually, Rosa's strength as a single parent and self-supporting woman, at a time when it was unusual for women to be either, began to decline. Rosa and her children would have some tight years. When financial necessity left them without a maid, for instance, Anaïs was assigned the housework while her mother went daily to her now quiet Manhattan office. The occupation of housekeeper at least left Anaïs free to write in her diary and to submit some poems to a journal. At seventeen, she chose English as the language she would write in for the rest of her life.[9] It was her third language, and she had resisted learning it for some time after arriving in New York. Her resistance stemmed in part from her father's letters, in which he disparaged English and asked her to renounce both it and Spanish in order to keep her French identity (Bair 34).[10]

After becoming an avid reader of English prose, however, the young Nin decided to emulate the writers she most admired.[11] Even at that time, she was defensive and rebellious about her writing, withdrawing into her diary almost completely when faced with a rejection from an editor. Anaïs also worked as a model for a time, to bring in some money. By the time her image appeared on the cover of the *Saturday Evening Post* in 1922, she had stopped modeling, after reporting to Rosa a series of inappropriate requests by her employers (Bair 54). Nin's experiences as a model were to inform her later stories, especially the erotica she wrote to order in the 1940s.

After Rosa had suffered a nervous breakdown in 1919 (Bair 38), she had decided that Anaïs would eventually have to be married in Cuba to a man of means. Her plan would come to fruition on March 3, 1923, when Anaïs was married to an American, Hugh Parker Guiler (1898–1985), in Havana. He would remain her legal husband for the rest of her life. Nin's relationship with Hugh, or Hugo, had begun in 1921. Because his Scottish family scorned the idea of his marriage to a poor Catholic girl and because of his tendency to hold his emotions in check, the courtship was a long one (Bair 56–62). Anaïs's Aunt

Antolina proceeded with her niece's debut in Cuba, where Hugh—eventually won over to the point that he was willing to face being disowned by his wealthy family (he was reconciled with his mother in late 1924, and with his father in 1925)—arrived to marry her in the spring of 1923. For the occasion, he converted to Catholicism, which he later renounced. He brought with him to Havana two tickets for the couple's trip back to New York, where he would work for the National City Bank.

Hugh was a devoted husband who, despite artistic yearnings of his own, remained a banker for over twenty-eight years in order to provide for his wife, his mother-in-law, and (until they were established) Thorvald and young Joaquín.[12] During their marriage, he would eventually finance some of Nin's writing projects and turn a blind eye when she used the money he gave her as a household allowance to subsidize not a few of her artist friends. Most famous of the writers whose careers his money helped to launch was Henry Miller, whom the Guilers met in Paris in 1931.[13] By the end of Hugh Guiler's life, he would depend on Anaïs's money, but she owed much of her exposure as a writer to her husband.

The early years of marriage were good for Nin's development as a writer, in several ways. As a graduate of Columbia University with a degree in English and economics, Hugh was a good critic of her style. For a time he offered useful advice about her constructions, including a never published autobiographical novel she was dabbling at writing, "Aline's Choice." He soon discovered that his advice was less welcome than his praise, however, and Bair reports he soon acquiesced to giving *only* praise. Later, he lauded nearly everything she did, including her experiments in sexuality. For a time he also kept a mutual diary with Anaïs and spent many an evening exchanging readings with her.

In 1924, Hugh arranged a transfer to Paris effective January 1925 (Bair 70), and the entire household began making arrangements to move. In the interval, Anaïs served as an intermediary in her parents' divorce, which was being finalized after ten years' separation, so that Joaquín Nin could marry Maruca, the girl whose parents had been his patrons when he first abandoned his family in 1913. Anaïs had taken her mother's side when her father tried in 1921 to initiate divorce proceedings—by charging Rosa, ironically, with abandonment (Bair 51–52). During the months preceding Anaïs's move to Paris, she wrote to both her parents, trying to serve as their diplomat.[14]

After arriving in Paris in 1925, Anaïs entered a depression that lasted about a year, a time during which Hugh tried to enhance their sex life by reading erotica and sexual how-to manuals (Bair 75).[15] Although within a few years their roles would reverse on this matter, she resisted his attempts to widen their horizons sexually. Hugh also encouraged his wife to branch out from the diary and become interested in a wider variety of endeavors. He was himself becoming more interested in his own work and in other artistic pursuits while at home in the evenings. Despite her intentions to write seriously, she continued to obsess over her diary and abandoned each alternative writing project, including a play and a novel, soon after beginning it (Bair 78). Her depression came to a close when the writer John Erskine, who had been Hugh's professor at Columbia, visited Paris in the mid-1920s and introduced the Guilers to Hélène Bousinescq, a teacher and translator who kept a literary salon and whose breadth and depth of literary knowledge inspired Anaïs to think about Modernism (Bair 78–79). As a result, Anaïs eventually overcame her prudish resistance to reading Freud and Proust, whose thought then became a model for her own.[16]

Throughout the 1920s, Nin's father continued to exert a psychological influence that his daughter had not yet fully acknowledged. One sign of this was her jealousy and sense of competition. Another was the promiscuity that would soon become an obsession. By Bair's account, Nin was, through the 1920s as well as afterward, more jealous of others' successes than inspired by them (80–81, 213, 234, 454). Her resentment of her father—from whom she had received a note upon her arrival with Hugh in Paris—surfaced when she began receiving social invitations that she knew depended on her status as the famous pianist's daughter. Dancing became her way to demonstrate an artistic success of her own.[17] She even convinced her young husband to join her in lessons, and the two gave a number of performances in full costume at their home.

It was not the obliging Hugh, however, that awakened the sexual interest that would dominate her life for at least the next two decades. Her "flirtations," writes Bair, "were adding up," from a serious exploration with the dance instructor, to "countless unnamed others with whom she flirted in various drawing rooms in Paris" (Bair 90).[18] It is by now fairly well known among Nin's readers that these "flirtations" would escalate into a series of affairs with several men: with Miller, with her analysts René Allendy in 1933 and Otto Rank from 1933 until early 1935, with her own father in 1933, with the Communist activist Gonzalo Moré from 1936 through 1944, briefly with Edmund Wilson in 1945, and others, before she settled into the sort of double marriage she sustained with both Hugh Guiler and Rupert Pole for the last decades of her life. She would also have a number of relationships of an uncertain nature with homosexual men—most famously the surrealist Antonin Artaud in 1933 and Gore Vidal in 1946—and with a string of young poets from 1945 through 1947. When her feelings for Erskine in 1929 did not lead anywhere, however, Nin entered another depression that lasted over a year (Bair 92),[19] which was intensified by the family's investment losses when the stock market crashed in October 1929. Lying low in bed following the crash, Nin read *Women in Love* and decided to write a book on D. H. Lawrence (Bair 94). Lawrence became Nin's first literary father substitute.

For the first time, Nin began to write daily in a disciplined way, submitting several stories to American publications and engaging Hugh in a sustained study of Lawrence's work. Though her stories were rejected, she achieved her first publication when the piece on Lawrence that she later revised as her first book was accepted as an essay by the *Canadian Forum*. What is most important about this time is that, according to Bair, she was for the first time working consistently at writing outside her diary. In addition, she was beginning to incorporate into her writing the psychoanalytic insights she would depend on throughout her career. She had not yet begun analysis herself, but, in addition to her reading in the twentieth-century science of the psyche, she was leaning toward accepting a suggestion by her favorite cousin, Eduardo Sánchez, that she consider seeing his analyst, René Allendy. She would do so in 1932.[20]

Released by Edward Titus in the spring of 1932 in an edition of just over five hundred copies, and reissued in 1964 by Swallow Press with an introduction by Harry T. Moore, *D. H. Lawrence: An Unprofessional Study* launched Nin's career in several important ways. By writing it, and especially with its publication, Nin acknowledged to herself, as well as publicly, several key ideas that would inform her later theories about the relationship between writing and gender, between literary style and psychological structure, and between writing and the therapeutic process. Lawrence provided her with a model for expressing psychoanalytic ideas in literature. His work also contained a quality she would call the "texture" of his writing, an aspect of language she would go on to imitate as well as to make a cornerstone of her later theories about writing. By naming and describing this quality in her first book, she was paving the way for her to write the fiction she knew she needed to write.

Nin's study of Lawrence served her well, although its initial critical failure would rankle until it was reissued in 1964 to a more positive reception.[21] Most important among the ideas she used Lawrence's work to formulate is the relation between literature and the body, which Nin, whether consciously or not, used as a springboard to begin mourning and to define the role of literary form in establishing psychological boundaries. As "a deeply personal text that tells as much about Nin's theories on everything from psychoanalysis to sex as about Lawrence's" (Bair 98), Nin's first book allowed her to formulate, for herself, a way to access unconscious memory and a way to come to terms with her own trauma through writing.

TEXTURE AND TEXT IN LAWRENCE'S WORK

Placing Nin's work on Lawrence within a tradition of subjective criticism, Evelyn Hinz, in *The Mirror and the Garden,* insists that it is "as the deliberate use of fiction to express a personal theory" that Nin's Lawrence book must be approached (31). As Hinz emphasizes, Nin's use of Lawrence was more an anticipation of her own later novels' characterizations and themes than it was a study of Lawrence's use of the unconscious (32).[22] Through Lawrence, Nin expressed her theory of art's transpersonal function, as well as a number of additional points she would pursue in her own writing career.

The idea expressed in the Lawrence book that was most important to Nin's own process of mourning her past is the notion that she, like Lawrence, could access the body's response to trauma through writing literature. Nin describes, for example, the process by which the body's "own dreams" can (according to Lawrence) "be evoked and made apparent and potent." By listening "attentively to these dreams," one could evoke the genie's power in language (*Lawrence* 19). Lawrence's fleshy, corporal language was the quality that Nin believed represented his ability to respond to a real center of existence. Early in the book, for instance, she writes that "to begin to realize Lawrence is to begin immediately to realize philosophy not merely as an intellectual edifice but as a passionate blood-experience" (13). The "feelings of the body" that Lawrence's writing captured for her represented a source of direct and thus authentic perception. Nin's emphasis on the power of Lawrence's writing to cultivate "the warm root of true vision" by making "a physical impression" (60) parallels the Lacanian notion of language's "materiality."

For Lacan, language makes this impression when a writer uses language to appeal to the inaccessible part of the unconscious that inhabits the spaces between words and their intended meanings, and thus to create effects in the reader. These effects can be reproduced when a writer employs writing as a permeable boundary between conscious and unconscious awareness and points—with language—to the existence of something real and palpable beyond language. For Lacan, the ability to do this was related to feminine *jouissance,* or identification through and beyond the physical body, to access a part of consciousness that exceeds physical boundaries. Throughout her study of Lawrence, Nin emphasizes a link between a feminine writing style and the somatic nature of his writing.

Nin's use of Lawrence's writing to theorize a link between a concept of "writing the body" and a writing style she considered feminine has unfortunately caused more resistance to her work among contemporary readers than perhaps any of her literary or critical weaknesses.[23] For example, in *Lawrence among the Women: Wavering Boundaries in Women's Literary Traditions* (1991), Carol Siegel depicts Nin as an essentialist, whose reductive view of gender limits her otherwise potentially valuable insights.[24] Nin's own wording on these issues often seems contradictory and is part of the reason her position is often read as rooted in a primary essentialism. For instance, she writes that Lawrence was criticized for his outdated vision of women, when his views "were not antediluvian, but again to be translated in terms of quintessences" (*Lawrence* 49). Nin considers that his ideas came from his quest for "the core of woman," which in Nin's opinion is to be found in "her relation to man" (49). Much feminist objection might well be made on these statements alone, especially if they are not considered in context of Nin's attempt to confront seemingly contradictory elements of a binary relation between men and women.

In order to formulate her own ideas, Nin highlights Lawrence's recognizing the social fictions about gender roles that are operative in culture. Neither the element in her writing that mirrored Lawrence's "texture" nor her whole-hearted praise of Lawrence's depiction of sexual difference positions Nin in a primarily essentialist position.[25] When Nin writes, for instance, that Lawrence hit the "center, the vulnerable center of our bodies with his physical language, his physical vision" (33), she links the materiality of language to a feminine principle, but she does so without linking the corporal basis of language to an exclusively female style.

Nin recognized Lawrence's writing as a "labyrinthian voyage" (28) that led her into her own psyche. According to Nin, Lawrence's expressing what he found in a personal labyrinth evoked readers' responses to their own unconscious memories rooted in the body, because the unconscious is universal although the journey there is an individual one. On this point Nin's interest in psychoanalytic explorations into the unconscious merges with her anticipation of Modernist concepts of the transpersonality of art. According to the Lacanian critic Ellie Ragland, it is in literature that the excluded parts of a writer's being return enigmatically through language as affect ("Magnetism" 384, 390–91), evoking in the reader "a shadow meaning" (404). "These evocations infer a dream-like quality to images, a Real power to words, and a concrete materiality to language" (404). Nin refers to both the enigmatic, evasive element behind language and to the evocative nature of its concrete materiality in her study of Lawrence when she links literary texture to reader response. She portrays Lawrence as a writer who exploited the material effects of language by using "word-shattering descriptions" and by giving his writing "sound, musicality, cadence: thus words sometimes used less for their sense than their sound" (63). Nin characterized her response to Lawrence as stemming from its concreteness, its ability to allow individual readers to access the universal through the personal by "pass[ing] through the channels of the senses" (63). As Hinz explains, Nin believed an artist's "'inward contemplation' is justified because—and when—it leads from the personal beyond to the universal and then back to the concrete (or personal) universal, the work of art" (Hinz 25).

"L'ÉCRITURE FÉMININE" AND ITS DISCONTENTS

Nin's *D. H. Lawrence* is, as the subtitle announces, "unprofessional."[26] However, Nin's Lawrence book provides some useful premises for negotiating current feminist debates on women's writing, particularly in terms of women's writing and its relation to what in recent feminist criticism has come to be known as *l'écriture féminine*. In studying Lawrence's work, Nin grappled with asymmetry between biological gender and creativity. "It is not the first time that artists and poets have come closer to the woman than other men have" (*Lawrence* 59), she writes, distinguishing on one hand between "artists and poets" and "the woman," while on the other hand acknowledging the categories as neither mutually exclusive nor evenly inclusive. "Of course, the woman-artist, who was herself an image maker, a pattern maker, made her own images and her own patterns. Georges [*sic*] Sand was Georges Sand all through. In fact, a revelation to man. So [were] Madame de Staël . . . Jane Austen and George Eliot, Amy Lowell, and so, today, is Ruth Draper" (50).[27] Here Nin refutes the overvaluation of male writers that is characteristic of literary history. She also avoids the reversal of this categorization. Rather than seeing Lawrence's "depiction of the superficial and material as 'man's world'—the outside—and the inner 'untouched core' of both individuality and artistic perception as female" (Siegel 124), Nin links the kind of knowledge associated with normative investment to the superficial and social.

Nin's statement that "Women are more closely bound to the earth. There is a secret, natural connection between them and elemental flows" (*Lawrence* 65) meant, not that women have a necessarily more direct connection to the unconscious than men have, but that, it seemed to Nin, women often resisted what she considered a masculine tendency toward rationalization through language. Nowhere, she writes in her diary, was this tendency more obvious than in some male writers' identification with notions of a paternalistic God. She found her male colleagues' identification with an autonomous creator presumptuous (*Diary* 2: 233–34) and believed a more fruitful attitude could be achieved by acknowledging the lack of autonomy central, in her view, to selfhood and to literary creativity.[28] Similarly, she attributes Lawrence's characterization of Hermione in *Women in Love* to Hermione's lack of understanding that knowledge is "on the outside, like a costume" (*Lawrence* 80). Hermione, unlike Lawrence, "thinks she is complete" (80).

Throughout her career, Nin would distinguish between knowledge used as a type of defense and knowledge based on the acknowledgment that there is no absolute universal truth or complete autonomy. According to Nin, Lawrence's "truth" was of the latter. For her, Lawrence's ability to identify with something beyond a culturally constructed notion of autonomy allowed him to access women's as well as men's feelings and to portray them accurately in his writing. Lawrence, Nin writes, "had a complete realization of the feelings of women," in fact, "very often he wrote as a woman would write" (57).

In her description of Lawrence's ability to show both sides of the male-female debates, Nin stresses two comparisons between the way he writes and "how a woman would write." First, Nin stresses the texture of the writing as having a feminine characteristic; his writing, she says, "sometimes looks crinkled up with

sensitiveness, almost bristling with it—like a woman's" (59). For Nin, this texture is linked to an attitudinal and relational "feminine" principle. Second, Nin
shows that his characters are realistic in that they reflect her own and other readers' anterior experience of the ways gender roles have been enacted in social relations. Nin meant that Lawrence's female characters "worked" for her. They
seemed realistic and believable as mimetic of women. She does not argue that
all women act in the way Lawrence portrays them, nor does she imply that there
is something essential in their femaleness to which he has access:

> In small descriptions of clothes he does not see the woman's costume flatly, vi-
> sually, as men do, but he is sensitive to the quality of materials, to the flow and
> suppleness, and intricacies of coloring. A hat has an angle, a certain mood, a
> class; so has the handling of an umbrella, so has the manner in which the dress
> is worn. (58)

Nin's emphasis in this passage is on the way Lawrence avoids objectivizing
women's experience, or seeing "flatly" in a way that would reduce the material
details of women's experience by robbing it, and them, of subjectivity.

Rather than looking at women as outsiders, Nin says, Lawrence enters into
a relationship with them and relates to their moods as he "follows the current
of small activities" such as taking care of children or arranging a table setting
(58). As an example of Lawrence's domestic sensibility, Nin cites *The
Rainbow*'s Anna Brangwen. This is a prewar characterization that has met
with little feminist objection. Nin also mentions the later works, which have
drawn much criticism. For instance, unlike Kate Millett, Nin sees *Lady
Chatterley's Lover* as an example of Lawrence's ability to portray the woman's
point of view: "every moment of the relationship reveals the woman's feelings
as well as the man's, and the woman's with the most delicate and subtle acute-
ness" (58).[29]

Nin would struggle most of her adult life to resolve what she saw as a conflict in the way she had to play out gender roles. She felt she had to choose between, on one hand, being a woman and thus a helpmate to man, and, on the
other hand, being a creative artist and thus in competition with man. Whether
she realized it or not in 1932, her depiction of the feminine attitude that she
appreciates in Lawrence provides at least a partial resolution of the gender
question in a way that would eventually lead beyond polarization of seeming
opposites such as "male" and "female" even as she learned to make other important distinctions, such as between self and other. In learning to separate
herself from her most significant other (her father), she sometimes, especially
early in her career, leaned toward the extreme separations at the heart of essentialism. Nin's emphasis of the physical texture of Lawrence's writing, however, and her attempts to link the "bulginess" of his written language to a fem-

inine principle point less to a truly essentialist position than to her efforts to define herself apart from her father's hold on her. Against his rigidities and emotional cruelties she posited another way of being, a mode she believed Lawrence understood and portrayed. That Lawrence was a man gave her hope that there were men who shared her sensibilities, from whose behavior she could separate even as she derived inspiration from their insights.

One contribution of psychoanalysis that can shed light on Nin's equation of language's texture with a feminine principle is an idea shared by critics as diverse as Cixous, Kristeva, and Lacan. This is the notion that women's identities are more likely than those of normative men to be grounded in a porousness of ego and fluidity of style. Lacan pointed out that both men and women could achieve feminine *jouissance*, an attitude often shared with artists, hysterics, and even mystics.[30] In a similar way, Nin links Lawrence's depictions of bodily consciousness to a concept of the feminine. As usual in her early work, Nin describes the access to an unconscious realm (which she believed women were socialized to retain) in terms of mysticism. For Nin, Lawrence "restated mysticism in modern terms" (*Lawrence* 76) by developing a creative tolerance for paradox. She, like Lacan, attributed that tolerance to many women as well as to mystics. It seemed to Nin that Lawrence understood the "seeming paradox" at the heart of mysticism, that "eternal being and eternal not-being are the same, in the origin and in the issue, as well as in time" (76).

This understanding of the way opposites are but functions of each other is related to her idea of art's transpersonal realm, wherein the personal leads to the universal and back to the individual, creating the possibility of reader response in the process. As a Modernist who understood these concepts, Lawrence, in Nin's view, reinvented mysticism. The basis for his reinvention was the texture of his language: "he made us feel," Nin writes, "the unity in this eternal paradox through our senses" (76). Eventually, Nin would use the connection between the texture or materiality of language and her notion of a feminine or mystical tolerance of paradox as a cornerstone in her theory of an artistic form. She sought a balance born of paradox, believing that a work's formal structure could inscribe necessary limits at the same time as it provided a permeable boundary between art and life.

One of the benefits of writing her book on Lawrence was that it led her to learn how to be a writer of fiction. This involved using literary form to establish boundaries that would, whether she knew it explicitly or only implicitly at the time, help her overcome the lack of structure that had hurt her in the past. Nin's statement that "to the poet the experience of a dream is no different from the experience of reality. . . . There is no boundary line" (29) shows her struggling to understand the relation between boundaries and literary expression. When Nin expresses her notion that "in Lawrence's books dreams and reality are often interwoven just as they are in our own natures" (30), she suggests that the creative writer represents in literature the connection he experiences in his own existence between language, the body, and perception. Her study of Lawrence's work allowed her to organize her thoughts about this relation. Lawrence, says Nin, attributes literary creativity to retention of the dream in waking life, an idea that becomes an important facet of Nin's later theories of feminine artistry.[31]

Using the example of Lawrence to make certain distinctions, Nin distinguishes for herself between the natural and feminine on one hand and the cultural and symbolic on the other. She also ties the natural and feminine principles to an ability to tolerate fluid boundaries. In this way she begins to create a "feminine" realm for herself that is closer to her own desire than to her father's or culture's desire for her. Nin acknowledges that Lawrence's tolerance sometimes breaks down, especially when the traumatic memory coincides with the absence of protective boundaries for bodily integrity. Lawrence's almost desperate attempts to formulate a "proper" relationship between the genders, especially in his postwar writing, reflect both the anxiety born of any attempt to subdue desire and to perfect relations between asymmetrical elements such as male and female and the palpability of that anxiety.

For Nin, Lawrence's writing style showed a fluidity she thought proper to the feminine mystical principle that she believed was opposed to a more rigid identity style. His rigidities showed her he found it necessary to defend himself against such openness. She believed, for example, that Lawrence's own sense of disunity became operative to an acute level as a result of the war, which she cites as a cause of a chaos implicit in his writing.[32] His creative intensity, she writes, was born of his willingness to confront this chaos and to enter into a sense of war's physical horror: "What drives him to despair is his very conviction of the sacredness of the body—and war is a monstrous holocaust of innumerable bodies" (29). For Nin, Lawrence's ability to feel the pain of war stemmed from his focus on the body as well as his permeable identificatory boundary that allowed him the kind of access to the chaos of the unconscious that Nin saw as the feminine.

Nin's emphasis on both what she called the texture of Lawrence's writing and his understanding of subjective realms of experience would lead her to an attempt to capture, in her own first book-length work of fiction, a similar effect. In addition, she would act on the belief she states in *D. H. Lawrence* that women could use their creative power and identificatory fluidity to "create their own images and their own patterns, in all professions, occupations, and arts" (50). Creating one's own pattern was an especially important idea for Nin, for on it would depend her ability to mourn her past trauma in fiction and to create herself anew in her own rather than in her father's image. This was a goal in keeping with her interest in Modernist self-making. It was also one that psychoanalysis had begun to inspire. Her next step was to prepare a manuscript on which she had been working for publication as a formal work of fiction—but one whose fluid boundaries would reflect her own struggle to establish necessary limits in her life.

FROM CRITICISM TO FICTION, 1932–1936

The absence of such limits was sorely apparent to everyone close to Anaïs during the mid-1930s, a period when her experiments in modern living led her to unusual extremes and coincided with an intensified interest in psychoanalytic therapy. Her affair with Henry Miller was in full swing. She and Hugh had met Miller in 1931 through Richard Osborn, a young lawyer who worked for Hugo at the bank. When Miller appeared for lunch one day at her home, Louveciennes, Nin seized on him as being "the true modernist she had been seeking" (Bair 123–24). His role as her lover and sexual mentor allowed her to enact the boundary-pushing she believed was at the heart of the literary modernism she wanted to pursue. Within little more than a year, her sexual experimentations had became frenzied. She had long been lying to Hugh and flying between several lovers, including Hugh, Henry, Allendy, and Artaud (who, despite his homosexuality, was useful to her for making Henry jealous and as a prototype for a character in her fiction). The most dramatic event of 1933 was her affair with her father.

After a twenty-year absence from his daughter's life except through letters, Joaquín Nin appeared at Louveciennes in mid-May 1933.[33] Nin's fictional version of their meeting appears in the novella "Winter of Artifice," written only a few years later. The "whole" story went into her diary and was eventually published in 1992 as part of the unexpurgated volume *Incest: From "A Journal of Love."* Nin's account of the nine-day incestuous affair that took place in June 1933 at "a modest hotel in Valescure, a village near St. Raphaël" (Bair 170) appears in that volume. Throughout the next few months, she would meet her father at least two more times for similar activity. It was later in the same year that Nin, who had ended her sessions with René Allendy, sent Miller to Otto Rank, whose books they had both been reading. Soon afterward, she began analysis with him herself, and in March 1934, she told him about her affair with her father that had begun and ended the previous year.[34]

Nin's published expurgated diary writings from this period obscure the mood swings and emotional violence that appear in both Bair's biography and the unexpurgated passages of both *Incest* and *Fire* (Volume 2 of *"A Journal of Love"* [1995]). These would continue through some of the most difficult years of Nin's life, during which she became pregnant with a child she insisted was Henry's and aborted at six months' gestation in 1934, exhausted herself with numerous affairs, and faced publishers' rejection of her writing. She was at least writing fiction, as she had long wanted to do. She believed that she would learn to detach from the pain of her past only by writing a novel (Bair 212, 214; *Fire* 390). The manuscript underway was "Alraune," which she would eventually divide to become *House of Incest* (1936) and *Winter of Artifice* (1939).[35] It is the first of these that truly constituted her entry into the world of writing serious literature.

NARRATIVE RECOVERY IN *HOUSE OF INCEST*

Nin's first book of fiction embodies the themes of mourning, remembering, and moving through the residual effects of previously unresolved material in her psyche in a way that highlights the psychoanalytic process of transference and reconstruction as well as the relation between bodily trauma and language that Nin saw in Lawrence's novels. Coinciding with Nin's awakened sexuality and her recognition that literature has therapeutic potential, *House of Incest* represents her narrative entrance to the psychoanalytic moment in which one can begin to mourn. To a large degree, the work of mourning involves recognizing narcissistic attachments and beginning to make distinctions that, when carried over into behavior, can result in a healthier relationship with oneself and the world.[36]

Nin's first book-length work of published fiction is her application in her own creative work of the theories she developed in her study of Lawrence. In particular, it shows her using psychoanalytic insights and processes in combination with an emergent emphasis on self-making. Both the theme and the form of her prose poem show her readiness to find a voice with which to begin what was to become her lifelong goal of creating, out of her writing, a livable life.[37]

According to Bair, "this novel is the primary source of everything fictional that followed" (157).[38] It also contains material Nin channeled from her diary, where she wrote of her resistance to writing about her father and of her desire to find a fictional form in which to attain some release from the suffering related to her relationship with him. In its treatment of unresolved sexual attachments between kin and between two women, whose identities become enmeshed through the narrator's fantasies of identificatory fusion, the prose poem speaks to the effects of both psychological and actual incest, portraying subjects trapped by their inability to move beyond destructive family myths and patterns. Nin's account of her incestuous relationship with her father as related in *Incest: From "A Journal of Love"* strengthens this interpretation of *House of Incest.* More important, it highlights the traumatic effects of literal and psychological betrayal and sheds new light on the book's themes of struggle and hope, of psychological imprisonment and potential freedom, of mourning and creativity.

An entry from *Fire* (1995), which contains unexpurgated portions of the diary Nin kept from 1934 through 1937, shows Nin's linking of the word "incest" with her father, her satisfaction in giving a name to her source of trauma, and a wider connection of the "earth-shattering" effects of early trauma around the issue of the paternal to a metaphor Jane Caputi reveals as both common and apt: that of literal bombing. Nin writes in February 1937, just after the book's distribution, that her father was "tearing his hair over the title *House of Incest*. More so because he cannot read what it contains," since he did not know English. She continues: "I love to throw bombs" (*Fire* 406). Her "bomb" was, of course, the word itself, "incest," a word whose meaning she had been conditioned by the culture of disavowal to deny, but which she would shout out over and over in her fiction.

FINDING A VOICE:
THE FEMINIST AND PSYCHOANALYTIC GOALS

In the psychoanalytic clinic, a person's inability to speak is often related to something from the past that is unsayable. From the title of *House of Incest* onward, however, Nin gives voice to this "unsayable" in her writing. She does so through a process that is, according to the narrator in the book's first image, known to "Those who write," as well as, she implies, by those who play the quena, a flute-like instrument originally made by an Indian lover out of the bones of his dead mistress. The difference between this flutist and Nin's narrator, we are told, is that the narrator does not "wait for [her] love to die" before making the instrument—out of human bones—with which to impart story or song.

The book begins, "The morning I got up to begin this book I coughed. Something was strangling me." This "something" is the narrator's heart, which she pulls out of her throat in order, it would seem, to tell its story. Here, Nin gives poetic body to the concept of grief as a lump in the throat. She opens the work by dislodging this grief, showing a willingness to pull it out. Similarly, in analysis, a narrative thread will be pulled from behind an analysand's discourse.[39] Nin's narrator tells the story of embodied trauma and its relation to psychological structure. In the telling, we can hear Nin's own story—that of patriarchy's wounded daughter striving for relief from the hysterical suffering born of that position.

Nin devoted her life, first, to finding a voice and, later, to encouraging others to do so, especially young women and artists of both genders. During a lecture she gave in 1973, Nin said that it was only writing that had taught her to speak: "Because when I was twenty I was mute. I know you don't believe that, but I didn't talk at all. . . . When I was thirty I listened always to other people, and I never said a word. . . . So I taught myself to talk, and I owe to writing the fact that we can talk together now" (*A Woman Speaks* 80).

The beginning of *House of Incest* represents, in the clearing of the narrator's throat, an entrance to the psychoanalytic process of acknowledging one's transferential desire in order to mourn what has been lost, as well as to "affirm, empathize with and, in certain respects, take leave of the other as other," as LaCapra puts it (*Representing the Holocaust* 213). Nin's case demonstrates with certainty one of the "certain respects," in which one must for one's own benefit take leave of another. The struggling with issues of fusion and separation in *House of Incest* indicates the narrator's traumatization by a lack of ego boundaries, and the author's similar traumatization. Nin's affair with her father during the writing of *House of Incest* shows her most unfortunate response to boundary issues as well as, paradoxically, an effort to work through and move away from identification with him.[40] An extreme enactment to say the least, Nin's seduction of her father in the summer of 1933 was part of the process of facing and taking hold of a past trauma in order to take leave of it.[41] Her early fiction shows her struggle—at best probably only partially successful—to move out of her role as seduced and seducing daughter. Overall, *House of Incest* thematizes the labyrinthine voyage Nin saw in Lawrence's writing and then began for herself. Its destination was emotional freedom. Its theme is that this freedom is attainable, but only for those who persevere as in psychoanalysis through many forms of embodied memory in order to free oneself from one's own attachments to the past.

DELVING INTO THE PAST:
ART AND THE PSYCHOANALYTIC OPENING

Throughout *House of Incest,* scenes of womb imagery compete and alternate with the narrator's desire to differentiate herself from a symbiotic state. This conflict parallels Nin's own efforts to work through psychoanalytic processes to distinguish herself from her father's image. In Lacanian terms, she must distinguish between the imaginary father and the role she has unconsciously granted him as a master signifier. After making that distinction, she can choose a new relation to his image. Nin's prose poem is but a first step in this process, for she would spend much of her life pursuing this goal.

First, before she can learn to take leave of the past, she must delve into a realm of suppressed memory. She does this in part through her narrator who, after the prefatory chapter of *House,* enters the narrative proper with a "first vision" that links womb imagery to a process of later submersion. The narrator's first observation is that she is surrounded by "water veiled" (*House* 15). The images throughout the first section are womblike. The narrator's emphasis, however, is less on a primary sense of union with a (m)other than it is on a process of submersion itself. This was the process by which Nin, having already recorded in her diary and reported to Otto Rank the incestuous relationship with her father, was beginning to delve within herself to look at the past.

In the next sentence, she emphasizes both a sense of separation from the past and the way events have been interpreted through the process of memory and reconstruction of the initial experience. When the narrator remembers her "first birth," she distinguishes her origins from subsequent "births" she will experience as she reconstructs the past. Whether Nin intended her narrator to represent a person recovering from actual incest or a person simply suffering from a psychological habit of seeking a symbiotic womblike state, the narrator's grasping for something that lies beyond conscious memory reflects the theories Nin had put forth in her first book. Lawrence, according to Nin, was fearfully sensitive to the body's vision and was able to capture in language something beyond the immediate surface. Similarly, the speaker of *House* intensely feels a textured memory and strives to give it body. Her description of that birth is itself overlaid with longing as the narrator feels herself afloat without an adequate anchor in a watery realm, listening with all her might for "distant sounds, sounds beyond the reach of human ears" (*House* 15). She looks as well as listens beyond her immediate surroundings, burdened with uneasy memories of something lost that she cannot quite pinpoint but that she feels drawn to seek.

The title of Nin's prose poem makes a reading of her narrator as incest victim as at least plausible. From this perspective, the real and palpable realm that in Lacanian thought lies beyond everyone's consciousness is exacerbated by a process Jane Caputi has highlighted as typical in cases of incest. In excluding traumatic memory from the surface of consciousness, Caputi writes, both incest victim and her or his victimizer are "aided by psychological responses of denial, numbing, and splitting" (Caputi 118). However, the narrator now stands on a threshold ready to begin a process of remembering, mourning, and reconstructing the past.

Nin's use of Lawrence's dream imagery as a way to access an unconscious connection among perception, memory, and bodily sensation anticipated her own use of dream in this work. For example, the lack of boundaries that throughout Nin's work points to psychological disruption and an absence of protective law is evident in this realm of "wall-less rooms" (*House* 15) and "colors running into one another without frontiers" (16). Other passages combine a Surrealist appreciation of unconscious fluidity with a welcoming of protective blindness, as the narrator floats unhampered by physical obstructions through a riverlike labyrinth.

In this section, Nin's prose reads like the speech of an analysand beginning to surrender into free association. Images of peace, comfort, and effortless movement abound, such as those characteristic of guided visualization, dreaming, and (we might imagine) the womb. Subsequent paragraphs in this section portray the narrator's entrance into the voiceless realm of a dream, where, instead of a comforting sense of fluidity or womblike security, she confronts horrific and terrifying images of crimes "accomplished in silence, in the silence of slidings and brushings" (16). An ostensibly comforting image, "a blanket of water," is predicated by a disruption of expectation, "lying over all things stifling the voice" (16). Laden with images of potential bedtime comfort, the blanket becomes an item of suppression as if to suggest the "cult of secrecy" that Caputi has written about in terms of actual incest victims. That is, Nin condenses an image suggesting an incest survivor's actual memory with psychological principles by which the unconscious can present an image and its disruption.

This disruption, rather than an actual memory, is what is wanted in psychoanalysis so that the analysand can realign herself to even those images from the past that are most traumatic. In Nin's case, even as she and her narrator refuse to keep them buried, Nin uses narrative structure to acknowledge remembered images as symbolic and subject to the fictionalizing tendencies of memory itself. In this sense, she develops an analytic goal more in keeping with Lacanian thought in its emphasis on the fictions of the psyche than on a more literal interpretation of suppressed memory typical of ego psychology. In the last paragraph of the section, the narrator relates that she "awoke at dawn, thrown up on a rock, the skeleton of a ship choked in its own sails" (17). An image to which the author would return again and again in both her dreams and her fiction, the grounded ship connotes the stifling effects of an early trauma that causes one not to "flow." The choking image echoes the narrator's choking on her heart in the book's prefatory chapter and reflects the moment in the psychoanalytic treatment when an analyst can progress toward the goal of helping a victim to confront trauma by speaking only with the victim's willingness to "pull out her heart." That willingness is the decision to delve into the painful memories of the past, to face, embrace, and take leave of them in order to move forward toward a healthier life, to free the ship and put it back into the current.

FRAGMENTATION AND FUSION:
THE PSYCHE'S RESPONSE TO TRAUMA

The next section opens with narrator surrounded by night. Like trauma victims who lose contact with parts of their lives through denial and partial amnesia, we lose a day between the psychoanalytic awakening of the last section's closing and the opening of this one. Incest victims, writes Caputi, often

"seek refuge in numbing, denial and massive repression, keeping their worst secret even from themselves because confronting incest in their own lives and
families is truly 'thinking about the unthinkable'" (Caputi 132). Fortunately,
the lapse of memory represented by the losing of a day in this part of the prose
poem is temporary, and the narrator, like Nin, eventually moves toward confrontation.

This section's initial images reflect the sense of fragmentation that Caputi
cites as characteristic of incest survivors: "Fragmentation depictions sublimi-
nally refer to and simultaneously invite the psychic fissioning induced by a sexually victimizing culture" (Caputi 131). A photograph comes loose from its
frame, the lining of a coat splits open like an oyster, and the narrator feels as
if she is falling into a fissure between day and night. Immediately following
this we meet Sabina, clearly based on June Miller, another woman for whom
the themes of fragmentation and psychic chaos had prevailed.[42]

Ironically, as a step toward embracing her own subjectivity as opposed to
fleeing it by return-to-the-womb fantasies, the narrator seeks relief from her
pain in a love affair with Sabina, believing that the human incompleteness for
which heterosexual relations provide only temporary respite is absent from this
union. She finds out otherwise. In Sabina, the narrator recognizes herself. She
strives to achieve an end to her own sense of fragmentation by "gather[ing] together all the fragments" of Sabina and "returning them" to her as a coherent
mirror image. "I AM THE OTHER FACE OF YOU," she shouts (*House* 28). The
problem with the narrator's approach, of course, is that one cannot establish
clear identity borders through fusion with another.

By contrast, a movement toward a healthier perspective depends on one's
willingness and ability to name the trauma. She must establish her own direction and (as the Lacanian critic Mark Bracher puts it) articulate a set of
master signifiers apart from the Other's desire. In Nin's case, the Other was
her father, whose image she had internalized as the main pole of her being. In
her effort to separate from her father's image, Nin allows her narrator to see
that, in retrospect, her effort to fuse with Sabina was futile. Despite the
women's "strain . . . to achieve unity," their "roots [are] tearing at each other
to grow separately," and the narrator knows "that the two of [them] have
leaped beyond cohesion" (30). The narrator enjoys contact with Sabina's exclusively female gestures and ways, but she feels she is being drawn into dissolution, a paradoxical realm in which fragmentation gives birth to madness.
She soon decides that her relation to Sabina is a "perfidious union" (24) that
has created an infinitely regressive mirror image: "One woman within another
eternally, in a far-reaching procession, shattering my mind into fragments,
into quarter tones which no orchestral baton can ever make whole again"
(22). This image represents the absence of a secure identity such as Nin saw
in June. It also portrays the unhealthy wish to literally return to the womb,

where one would be, ostensibly, safe from disruptive forces.

While all humans may experience disruption to a degree, Nin's title resonates in this image to emphasize the way universal anxiety can be intensified into traumatic fissuring for one who has experienced incest. That person, after all, has been betrayed by the very person(s) who should provide safety. Research has shown that one of the effects of such betrayal is a psychological splitting; hence the "far-reaching procession" of subjective splits the narrator sees in Sabina, an image that "shatter[s] her] mind into fragments." The narrator is sickened by a barrage of images that appear as "reflections in cracked mirrors" (29). Hinz, in *The Mirror and the Garden,* depicts mirror symbolism in Nin's work to highlight a superficial world of imposed realism, rather than the organic and natural mode of perception Nin saw as healthy. A Lacanian reading of Nin's mirror imagery complements Hinz's by showing the illusory and fictional nature of the image of wholeness that the narrator seeks in relationship with Sabina. The narrator cannot deny the threat of separation and differentiation that she had tried to escape through relationship with a woman.

The failure of the sexual relation to reestablish harmony descends upon the narrator with the full force of early sexual wounding and its border-erasing effects. The pain she feels is as if she is "walking with a sword between [her] legs" (*House* 31). In the same passage, images of external precipitation converge with those of bodily fluids to create a sensory overload and to suggest that the narrator has lost, at least temporarily, all ability to distinguish self from other. A dog's barking, her own laughter, and her lover's pain swirl together in her mind as if to suggest a psychotic breakdown. Her sensory porousness is but the extreme of that typical among adult survivors of childhood trauma.

As the passage continues, perceived sources of threat converge in the body with real force, illustrating the sense of fragmentation and openness to the flow of traumatic memories that the analytic process in the author has set into motion. Nin demonstrates the painful effort to articulate this process when her narrator's desire to speak causes "each nerve . . . to break separately, continuously, making incisions" (32). Into her open wounds "acid ran instead of blood" (32). Nin anticipates her own later theories about the ability of art to create a transpersonal realm when she has her narrator connect the pain of acid running into raw wounds with an attempt to "melt the pain into a cauldron of words for everyone to dip into, everyone who sought words for their own pain . . . words bitter enough to burn all bitterness" (32).

Alone in her quest to confront a singular past in language by speaking up for herself, the narrator strives to give collective voice to a pain that must be spoken one voice at a time. This is less a contradiction than it is a creative counterpart to the idea, which Nin had expressed in her study of Lawrence, that singular concrete experience can lead to the universal through textured literary language. The concreteness of the experience anchors her in bodily trauma and holds a body-based language as a source of reconstruction. The paradox that the words must be "bitter enough to burn all bitterness" (32) reflects Nin's idea about opposites' functioning to lead into each other, a version of the psychoanalytic idea that is shared by mystics. For Nin, the only way out of the labyrinth is the way in. Her narrator must, in a sense, experience trial by fire. She must descend into the unconscious realm—as a metaphor for the process the author was engaged in at the time of writing *House of Incest*, a time when insights alternated with bouts of depression and sometimes nearly suicidal thoughts. As Nin worked in psychoanalysis to formulate her relation to truth, in part by acknowledging its dependence on culture and language in order to restructure a relationship to her own truth, the narrator experiences her own crisis of belief, which sends her into another state of psychic dissolution.

RELIVING THE WOUND

Again, the narrator laments the sense that she is seeking something "forever lost and which [she] cannot forget" (39). This time, she is involved in a process she realizes is a reconstructive one. Much as the texture of Lawrence's writing captured for Nin the sense that something palpable, but not rememberable, lies outside language and can be reconstructed through literature, Nin shows the narrator's desire for health as the reconstruction of an unconscious pattern. "Lean over me, at the bedside of my madness, and let me stand without crutches" (39), she begs, as if the psychological wound is expressed in a bodily inhibition.

Nin returns to the body as a basis for reconstruction because the body represents a real grounding, rather than cultural systems of power and denial based on less primary connections to the real. The connection between physical lameness and psychological wounding, for instance, appears in several references to an actual or metaphorical sexual violation. In another section, for instance, a character named Jeanne feels excruciating physical and emotional pain on her wedding night because she is in love with her brother and therefore cannot love her husband. Her mental torment takes the form of an endless ringing of bells. The connection Nin draws between Jeanne's bodily and psychic suffering finds further substance in the ending section of the chapter she appears in, where numerous additional images of bodily disintegration ("I do not exist. I am not a body") merge with an acknowledgment that the sexual love between siblings is like the love of shadows, forever split from themselves, each other, and reality (48). Another example of the connection of body and consciousness appears toward the end of the book, when the narrator experiences the passing of time as "Hours like tall ebony women with gongs between their legs" (55). This image reiterates the link between a physical violation between one's legs and its psychic counterpart in the clanging of gongs.

When, in the early section, the narrator says that she wants "absolution" from the "lies" in which she has enmeshed herself but feels that she "cannot tell the truth because I have felt the heads of men in my womb" (40), Nin uses her narrator's status as a resident of the house of incest to suggest that her own proclivity to lying is an effect of a boundary violation, however necessary those lies were to her maintaining various relationships. Simultaneously, she attributes her inability to maintain a single role to her role as creative artist. Besides its sexual connotation, having men's heads in her womb refers to Nin's belief that, whereas male artists create from their intellects, women writers create from their wombs. This is a theme that runs throughout her diaries, beginning with the first expurgated volume and continuing through much of her writing.

A related theme of Nin's theoretical explorations into the nature of sexual difference and creativity continues to link her narrator's need to find absolution for lying to a boundary wound. When the narrator says her lies are "like costumes" (*House* 40), the comparison parallels a similar idea from Nin's *Diary*.[43] It is a rationalization that may partially exonerate the teller of lies but cannot heal the pain behind their construction. The narrator sees her own lies as a way of warding off painful images. Without them, she feels herself falling into darkness and is confronted with "a face which stares at me like the glance of a cross-eyed man" (40).

Another image suggesting a remembered violation restructured as art, his eyes—like those in the Cubist paintings Nin would later use as a visual counterpart to what she was trying to achieve in writing—appear skewed. As a signifier of either actual or metaphorical incest, he is literally too close. His physical presence is an unwanted, inappropriate intrusion. His relationship to the victim is familial and his violation is at cross-purposes with his role as protector.

As if to avoid pursuing this image, the narrative jumps to an alchemical image that captures the chilling effect of her memory even as it replicates the movement in a liar's speech from one version of truth to another. Nin reconstructs that movement as creative rather than pathological: "I remember the cold on Jupiter freezing ammonia and out of ammonia crystals came the angels" (40). The "angels" that can be born out of the transformative effect of delving into chilling memory through the psychoanalytic and artistic processes are the narrator's emerging abilities to provide protection and comfort for herself through art. In addition to their role as message bearers, the angels in this passage indicate the narrator's movement through re-memory toward a reconstructed future.

Nin repeats the image of the cross-eyed man near the end of the prose poem, in a passage that also addresses her stance toward truth and toward fictionalizing her version of truth as fairy tales (67). Rather than use repetition as a compulsion, Nin uses it in the "potentially revitalizing" ways Wendy Steiner has discussed in relation to Modern artists. For Nin, repeating the image at the end of *House* constitutes a subsequent step in the analytic process, by which the analysand may return to an image in order to recognize its position in her trajectory and to reconstruct its significance in a way more in keeping with her own desire.

STASIS AND STAGNATION AS SYMBOLIC RESISTANCE

Incest, the failure of human family "law" and of the father-protector function, perpetuates the wounded daughter's inability to incorporate appropriate boundaries.[44] Nin explores the theme of the psychological stagnation that can result from a lack of boundaries represented by the narrator's clinging to a fantasy of womblike safety and symbiotic union. The sibling incest of the next chapter and the stasis of the section that follows provide variations of the theme of psychic symbiosis and its corrective in the narrator's and author's increased ability to make distinctions. By contrast, the house's inhabitants have cut themselves off from all flow and remained trapped in a "mineral fixity, the fixity of the fear of death and the fear of life" (60). Not fluid, they are rigid to the extreme. Each is stuck in a separate experience, unrelated to the others. For them, as for the narrator when she participates in their stagnation, language itself has lost its fluidity and thus all creative potential: "The words we did not shout, . . . the curse we swallowed, the phrase we shortened, the love we killed, turned into magnetic iron ore, into . . . blood calcinated, . . . the mineral glow of . . . exhausted suns in the forest of dead trees and dead desires" (60).

This passage reflects the symbolic castration that occurs through language, which is intensified to the extreme for victims of paternal abuse.[45] The narrator encounters such a situation when she discovers Lot sitting "with his hand upon his daughter's breast while the city burned behind them" (52). Both father and daughter in this image are immobile as the city cracks open and falls into the sea. In a passage replete with images reminiscent of the nuclearism cited by Caputi as accompanying accounts of incest since the mid–twentieth century (and which *House of Incest* predates),[46] Nin portrays the earth-shattering effects of incest upon the consciousness of those whose lives are blasted to numbness by this "horror of obscenity" (55).

But Nin depicts an attitude of hope. The momentum of the work strives for freedom from the "dead letter office" of a permanently incestuous realm. After witnessing this scene between Lot and his daughter, the narrator looks "upon a clock to find the truth" (55), a construction that reflects her effort to reenter a realm of temporality as opposed to the stasis of an eternal wounding.

Part of the process is to put into movement, though speech, the static attachments that have become a trap. In the next paragraph, the narrator comes across a forest of mutilated trees that look like the tortured and fragmented bodies of massacred slaves (55). The narrator feels the forest's bitter, rebellious trembling and anguished cries of loss, reflecting a "failure of transmutation" (56). Both the dead figures and the grief in this passage imply the narrator's and the author's outcry against a violation. The trees' wailing and its counterpart in the narrative show that real mourning is taking place, the kind of mourning that can, potentially, lead to recovery. It is at this point in the narrative that real progress is made in the narrator's journey out of the house of incest: after entering still another forest (this one of white plaster eggs representing the potential of finding "hope without breaking"), the narrator sees a felled tree sprouting a "green live branch that laugh[s] at the sculptor" (56). This image embodies the wounded daughter's ability to come back to life, despite the violation experienced at the hands of the knife-wielding perpetrator of suffering. Nin's message of struggle and hope, of psychological imprisonment and potential freedom, of mourning and creativity, prevails throughout the passage.

The images of the next chapter are full of leave-taking as the narrator witnesses Jeanne's becoming stuck for several years at the juncture "between the moment she had lost her brother and the moment she had looked at the facade of the house of incest" (61). At this point the narrator decides to leave Jeanne and to find her own way out. Having sought to account for all the windows of the house by asking its inhabitants to hang clothes or other items out of the windows near them and to find the room where her brother is hiding from her in this way, Jeanne has discovered "one window without light like a dead eye" (60) and knows her brother is in that place of stasis and dead letters. She finds him sleeping among paintings of her and engages him in a reciprocal worshiping of each other's likenesses (61).

A LEAVE-TAKING

At the opening of the following chapter, the narrator leaves this place to "walk . . . into my own book, seeking peace" (62). The idea of entering her own book highlights the process the author is engaged in—creating her own story apart from patriarchal identification, a story in which she creates herself as a character in order to do the hard work of mourning required for healing. Aware of the painful necessities of this journey, Nin's narrator attributes her pain to "this seeing too much," which causes her to "carry white sponges of knowledge on strings of nerves" (62). Highlighting the way that language and awareness are inscribed on identity, this passage accounts for the material basis of psychological pain that she feels in the body through re-memorization: "As I move within my book I am cut by pointed glass and broken bottles in which there is still the odor of sperm and perfume" (62). From within this reconstructed space, the narrator converges with the author to realize how much the denigration of human relationships appearing throughout *House of Incest* functions through attachment to the dead letters of the past. The possibility of freedom lies in its inhabitants' retaining awareness of something beyond the walls of their isolation.[47]

The narrator thus reenters the house of incest—by way of her book—in order to discover what lies beyond its walls. Inside, she enters the room of a paralyzed man who does not do the painful work of mourning and reconstructing the past in terms of the present and who remains uncreative and stuck: "He had collected a box of paint which he never painted with, a thousand books with pages uncut" (67). He tells her his problem, in many of the same words the narrator used to relate her own dilemma, asserting that his inability to tell the truth rests on his multiple perspectives on the overtones and undertones of that truth (67–68). Rather than work with the multiplicitous nature of truth, he does not write at all, rejecting the limitations of language and reflecting the hysteric's refusal to speak. Nin, in turn, refuses this refusal. As the paralytic sits motionless, surrounded by pieces of blank paper, a new character, the "modern Christ," begins telling the narrator, Sabina, and Jeanne the ordeal of his crucifixion "by his own nerves, for all our neurotic sins" (68). "Born without skin," he also suffers from a lack of boundaries that would provide a stay against pain. Even people's voices cause his whole body to ripple with pain when they speak. The paralytic voices his envy of the modern Christ's ability to feel. Between these extremes, the narrator wishes, "If only we could all escape from this house of incest, where we only love ourselves in the other" (70). Feeling alone provides no salvation.

Although the narrator says they cannot make the journey out of the darkness of this house, fearing that the tunnel that would be their escape route might close in around them and trap them in further suffocation, they know there is daylight "beyond the house of incest," even though, as yet, none of them can walk toward it (70). Suddenly they notice a dancer at the center of the room, armless as a result of her being punished for clinging (71) and dancing as if "isolated and separated from music and from [the others] and from the room and from life" (70).[48] Yet she dances "all for herself. She danced her fears" (71), showing the possibility of embracing (however paradoxical it might be to embrace without arms) one's own wounding.

In the process, the dancer's arms are restored to her, without narrative explanation but with the implication that "dancing one's fears"—as metaphor for the creative process of mourning enacted in this text—has a healing potential. Like the wounded daughter who can reach the point of where she can take leave of a wounding other, the dancer opens her newly restored hands and, in a gesture of "abandon and giving[,] she relinquished and forgave" (71). Far from a submission to her violation, this gesture represents the narrative process of "taking leave" made possible through the willingness to mourn—rather than to repress, deny, and suppress—the past. The narrator, watching, realizes that she has been trapped by her inability to "bear the passing of things" and the dancer's movement chokes her "with anguish" (72). But the book ends with motion: "And she danced; she danced with the music and with the rhythm of earth's circles; she turned with the earth turning, like a disk, turning all faces to light and to darkness evenly, dancing towards daylight" (72). Although it is not the narrator who is doing the dancing, this ending demonstrates the narrator's acknowledgment that such movement is possible. Previously unable to summon the courage to enter the tunnel leading outside, the narrator and her companions within the house of incest can, by story's end, at least see their way out.

CONCLUSION

Writing *D. H. Lawrence: An Unprofessional Study* gave Nin the theoretical basis for teaching herself how to write the fiction whose formal boundaries she would use to begin healing. In Lawrence, Nin recognized a kindred spirit, one whose sensibility and writing style inspired her to express her own ideas in artistic form. Nin would make the idea of the texture of his writing, in particular, a cornerstone of her own later theories about interrelations among gender, creativity, and artistic response to trauma. *House of Incest* constitutes a narrative opening to the process of analytic inquiry and a corresponding action-taking in Nin's own life, as she embarked on a journey to confront her traumatic past in order to deal with its effects and allow herself to live more creatively, freer from the affective pain that tormented her. Her own difficulty in facing the past is thematized in her prose poem. Along with its representation of cyclic patterns of sleeping and waking, dream and reality, night and day, death and life, *House of Incest* parallels in form and content the delving into and drawing back from painful past that is characteristic of an analysand's guided confrontation of unconscious traumatic memory.

We do not know whether Nin was sexually abused by her father as a child. Nin's work implies that the nature of the abuse was secondary. Her later "continuous novel," for example, indicates that she believed it is one's interpretation of the past—rather than any particular event in itself—that continues to wound. What we do know is that Nin's lifelong writings show the effects of severe traumatization around the issue of the paternal, and she suffered throughout her life from these effects. Her prose poem's title and its thematic unity around the issue of incest make especially viable a reading that takes particular account of the effects of an early psychosexual violation and of a process of confronting, mourning, and reconstructing the past through art and analysis. With her first book of fiction, Nin was suggesting to herself that one does not have to remain captive to a neurotic unconscious structure. She also demonstrated that an artistic embodiment of language could be used to help a wounded daughter find a voice with which to create new structures away from patriarchal violation and desire.

2 Breaking Silence
Transference and Mourning in *Winter of Artifice*

Art. Where is the art that keeps us from insanity?

—Anaïs Nin, *Fire*

THROUGH A SELF-PUBLISHING VENTURE Nin entered into with Henry Miller and Lawrence Durrell, her second book of fiction, *Winter of Artifice,* was published in 1939, the year she last saw her father.[1] The first edition of *Winter* was a critical and financial failure (Bair 287), and successive editions brought little improvement financially.[2] The process of revising and reprinting them, however, brought Nin much experience and growth as she used the process of streamlining and revising to come to terms with all that had happened to her in the last decade. As part of her learning to distinguish her own desire from that of her father's, Nin continued in *Winter of Artifice* the self-making she had begun with her first two books.

Her accomplishment was a physical as well as an artistic one: in New York in May 1942, she reprinted the book herself, by hand, at the printing press she bought and ran with the help of Gonzalo Moré, for whom she named Gemor Press. *Winter* would undergo further revisions for its 1948 publication by Dutton, and again in 1961 when it was published by Swallow. All versions show the author's process of seeking, *in writing,* an adequate father transference in order to work through early trauma.[3] The 1961 version replicates that process in its tri-part structure as it moves from "Stella," a novella that depicts a woman trying unsuccessfully to separate from her father's hold on her, to "Winter of Artifice," the story of a woman who is successful in doing so, to "The Voice," which thematizes Nin's dissociating herself from identification with her male analysts. In addition to helping Nin distance herself from her father and his substitutes, part of *Winter's* value lies in its status as autobiographical women's literature that, more than either of her previous books, established Nin in an ambivalent relationship with literary feminism.[4] Even the early and structurally less developed 1942 edition brought some qualified praise on this basis, when William Carlos Williams's review in *New Directions* emphasized Nin's search for "an authentic female approach to the arts" (Williams 72).

Winter of Artifice's confusing publication history mirrors the identificatory confusions Nin was experiencing in her mid-thirties.[5] It also shows Nin's desire to inscribe identity borders. She had entered therapy in 1932 to deal with father themes (see Bair 135, 139) and to address her conflict about being an artist. Over the next few years, however, she increasingly came to believe that psychoanalysis, like diary writing, offered solace without providing the formal limitations she needed to heal her psychic wound.[6] Diary writing, she decided, was "a lazy act" that allowed her to write without artistic discipline about everything *except* the real issues.[7] Because she knew that it was the more disciplined writing of fiction—rather than the free associative style of her therapy sessions or unrestrained habits of diary writing—that would allow her to enact a sense of mastery over a plaguing sense of dissolution, Nin insisted to herself that she persevere toward her goal to become a good fiction writer.

She was ambivalent about giving up the diary, however, for it made her feel "whole" even when she was in pain (*Fire* 283). Rather than giving up the diary entirely, she hoped to find a way to make it "flower" into fiction (*Fire* 372). And that is in a sense what she did, even as she struggled for years to attain a formal but fluid literary structure that she would eventually theorize as possible and put into practice in the series of five books she called her "continuous novel." In the meantime, she worked on the manuscript that became her third book, *Winter of Artifice*, and whose many changes over several years illustrate the fluctuating nature of her identity and goals.

It is a paradox that Nin's attempt to inscribe boundaries in literature is inextricable from her sabotaging that goal in ways largely and unconsciously determined by early wounding. As one who had early on developed the habit of testing limits, Nin continued to do so in the analytic clinic. *Winter of Artifice* reflects some of the ways Nin's affairs with two male analysts she chose as sexualized father figures complicated her issues of paternal wounding and made it more difficult to draw boundaries in fiction or analysis.[8] Bair emphasizes *Nin's* role in the failure of the analysis.[9] But readers should not overlook the argument that the key issue for which she had entered analysis, a sense of psychic unraveling around the issue of paternal betrayal and a corresponding confusion about the relation of her sexuality to her identity, made it necessary for her to test boundaries.

Lacan's account of human development, in which the "no" of the father's name represents an interrupting element to a child's sense of symbiosis with its mother or other primary caretaker and allows a child to develop identity borders as a function of language, makes understandable Nin's habit of pushing at boundaries. Born into an environment of parental discord and paternal violence that was later reinforced by her father's abandonment, Nin developed weak identity borders and later strove to inscribe them herself. When her difficulties in writing formal literature highlighted her need for structure, she sought analysis to help her become a writer, not even fully understanding the way her promiscuity, an increasing sense of psychic dissolution, and her writer's block all stemmed from her lack of an internal differentiating signifier. Nin's "seduction" of her analysts may be seen as symptomatic of her suffering, then, and not as the cause of it.[10]

On one hand, Nin's transferential failure can be attributed to her therapists' lack of respect for professional boundaries and the reinforcing of early trauma that such a breach might entail. The clinic, after all, is the place where one *should* be able to test border issues without finding those borders as flimsily constructed as those of an early love object. Unfortunately for Nin, neither René Allendy nor Otto Rank held the line between countertransferential fantasy and action that, according to ego psychology, might have provided a substitutive cohesion on whose basis Nin could redefine a relation to the paternal.

On the other hand, transference is not a matter of identification with a parental substitute per se. In Nin's case, for instance, even an identification with a "father," who would not betray her in the way she felt her own father had, might still have failed to expose the unconscious patterns that her ego dramas obscured.[11] When Rank and Allendy accepted Nin's version of them as others whose desire for her would establish her worth, they fell into one of several "various pitfalls in transference, not the least of which is the analyst's satisfaction at being recognized" (Ragland, *Philosophy* 123).[12] Rather than interrupt the patterns by which others became the mirror in which she could reconstitute a self-cohesion, Nin's analyses with Allendy and Rank corroborated a sense of self-worth created through their recognition.[13] The degree to which Nin's analytic aims were inhibited by her failure to achieve an adequate transference in analysis with either man is especially evident in the unexpurgated diary volumes published as *Incest* (1992) and *Fire* (1995). *Fire* also reveals that Nin was quite conscious of how she had sought a father figure in both Allendy and Rank and that, in her relationships with other men in her life, she continued to look for someone to fulfill the father's role.[14]

Nin reveals that she knew why her analyses had failed when she writes the following story in her diary: during a breakfast conversation, Miller told her that she had a "'face that launched a thousand ships.'" Nin replied, "'No . . . . [it is] the face that baffled a thousand analysts'" (*Fire* 32). What Nin's face "launched," of course, was her analysts' desire.[15] In recognizing this, she began to unravel her own seductive persona, which she believed her male analysts took too seriously. The way their falling for her had increased her sense of psychic dissolution appears in the many passages of *Fire* where she refers repeatedly to images of shock, to separation, to men's lack of strength, and to the absence of order (*Fire* 215, 270, 276, 282).[16]

She also pinpoints the source of her intensified sense of isolation. In an entry from February 1935, for instance, Nin writes that she feels lost, in spite of Miller's love: "I felt again the same reproach I made to Allendy: I came for help, and I got no help, no peace anywhere. The only one who *knew*, or could know, me was [Rank], and he too got all mixed up because he loved me" (*Fire* 32). Nin's next line, "There is no truth, no reality," indicates how strongly she believed the psychoanalysis had failed her. She felt betrayed by Rank, especially. She had looked to him (appropriately) for help in resolving her need for a father—a need intensified and acted out to the extreme in her account of having seduced her father the year before.[17] But this help had been a mixed blessing, at best: "That morning I could only think of the shock, of my dependence on [Rank's] wisdom, and of his failing me. Selfishly. He said I failed him. He had staked his all on me" (*Fire* 32).

It is clear that Nin wanted to move beyond these associations, however, when she writes that she has "wept enough, now" and that she is ready to say "no" to suffering (*Fire* 32). This refusal motivates her to create in fiction, as opposed to in her diary, the father transference she could not find in analysis.[18] At the same time, she began to theorize in her diary about the role of writing in helping her to achieve a necessary distance from the imaginary father. Nin's attempts to draw a separation between fiction and the diary without relinquishing the latter appears in an entry from September 1935. She reports in *Fire* that she has developed a "Father book" that is not part of her diary. On the other hand, it is *like* the diary in that it allows her to write with an immediacy similar to that of diary writing (*Fire* 138).[19] Her ambivalence about the diary and her determination to write fiction intensify when she writes, ironically, in the diary that she has written a scene in the "Father book" in which the diaries catch fire.

In the novella "Winter of Artifice," Lilith's defining her diary as a monument she had erected to her father and her desire to "smash this monument" so that she can be accepted "in her own right" (*Winter* 67) reveals the autobiographical link between diary writing and fiction in terms of Nin's and her characters' attachment to a father, an attachment from which the author wanted to distance herself by writing fiction. At the same time, the self-reflexive nature of

Nin's fiction transgresses the boundaries between autobiography and fiction even as she worked to inscribe formal boundaries within her own psyche. A passage from Volume 2 of the expurgated *Diary* shows Nin continuing to grapple with this issue, as she tries to draw a fluid boundary and to relinquish her earlier dualities, such as "between . . . diary and . . . fiction" (2: 343).[20] Read in conjunction with corresponding diary passages, *Winter of Artifice* is a small step toward that goal.

ANALYSIS AND THE SEARCH FOR FATHER IN THE
EXPURGATED DIARY AND *WINTER OF ARTIFICE*

Whereas the unexpurgated volumes of Nin's diary make especially clear the relationship between her overt sexuality and her quest for father transference, the originally published series of diary volumes, *The Diary of Anaïs Nin*, also provides clear evidence that she had sought in analysis a way back to the father in order to heal the source of her pain. The disparities between the two versions of the diary point to some of the themes that Nin would emphasize in her later writing, including a creative embracing of uncertainty, a refusal to be pinned down to cultural conventions, and a conscious choice about when and how to present oneself.[21] Because of the way several versions of Nin's life dovetail, an understanding of *Winter of Artifice* is enhanced as much by the account Nin provides in the first volume of the *Diary,* published in 1966, as it is by the "unexpurgated" volumes, published in the 1990s.

In "Stella," Nin provides an interesting parallel to the process whereby the publication history of her own diary, although she could not have known it at the time, would mirror the way a reader could retrospectively read between the lines of Nin's *Diary* in light of the unexpurgated volumes. More important, Nin comments *within fictional form* upon the process whereby she herself translated into fiction the events of her life whose significance she did not yet understand. The following passage appears in "Stella":

> One can look back upon a certain scene of life and see only a part of the truth. The characters . . . appear with entire aspects missing . . . . Later, a deeper insight, a deeper experience will add the missing aspects to the past scene . . . so that with time, and with time and awareness only, the scene and the person become complete, fully heard and fully seen. (*Winter* 33)

Reading Nin's accounts in the *Diary* and in *Winter of Artifice* in light of *Fire* is similar to finding the "missing aspects" in the scenes Nin describes in the writing she published during her lifetime. Even for readers unfamiliar with the unexpurgated versions, however, Nin's expurgated *Diary* makes clear that she had sought analysis to heal from paternal wounding. Father themes abound, for instance, in her account of her first meeting with Allendy at the suggestion of "a friend" (who was actually her cousin Eduardo). Soon after arriving at Allendy's office for their first meeting (she writes in the *Diary*), she spills out her story about her father's harshness, his rejection of her for being a girl, his absences from the home during her childhood, her mother's jealousy of his associations with other women, and her devastation at his abandonment of her family in 1913 (1: 78). In a subsequent visit, Nin elaborates to Allendy on her relationship to her father, telling how she still loves him incomprehensibly.

Similarly, in *Winter*, Stella wonders, "Does the love of the father never die?" (*Winter* 44). Later in the *Diary's* account of the analysis, Nin describes the unorganized artist's lifestyle she has been sharing with Miller and reflects on Allendy's suggestion that in adopting a way of living opposite from her father's meticulous neatness, she is rejecting her father's values. When she wonders whether she is indeed trying to escape from her father's image (1: 101), she shows that she still has not realized the extent of her subjugation to that image. An interesting note in terms of Nin's later emphasis on women's need to speak up for themselves: she writes that Allendy notices, during their first meeting, how she speaks in two kinds of voices, one sounding like a timid child and the other mature, deep, and rich (1: 91). Nin believes the confident voice belongs to the persona she has adopted to cover her lack of self-confidence.

The mask motif is central to *Winter of Artifice*. In "Stella," the narrative itself functions as a mask that Nin wears to distance herself from her father's persona. On another level, the character Stella is also a mask. She is one of the several alter egos through whom Nin works out a way to create a selfhood apart from her father's desire for her. In addition, the story thematizes mask-wearing by presenting a title character as an actress who recognizes the fictional nature of all human roles, even as she feels wounded by the split between the masks she knows she is wearing and an authentic self she senses but cannot enact.

In "Winter of Artifice," the second novella, the narrator is able to connect her father's masklike facial expression to the distancing tendencies that "terrorized her as a child" and that led her to internalize the injunction that "Nothing but perfection would do" (*Winter* 70). Lacan's emphasis on the human ego as a fiction analogous to a work of art finds parallel in the way "Winter of Artifice" also thematizes the role of fiction in exposing Nin's diary itself as a mask. The narrator, like Nin, is a diarist. As in the account of the diary's beginnings often told by "the adult Anaïs Nin" (Bair 29; see also 529 n. 5), the narrator has kept a diary since the voyage to New York when she was eleven, "a monologue, or dialogue . . . inspired by the . . . pain of leaving him" (*Winter* 60). Much as Stella in the previous novella withdraws behind a mask, the girl narrator has shut "herself up within the walls of her diary," talking to it "as if it were a living person" and hoping the account of New York she wrote in it "would entice [her father] to come" (*Winter* 61, 63–64). The ways Nin used various enticements or masks to win fatherly approval emerged as a dominant theme in her analysis with Allendy.

Unfortunately, by Nin's accounts, these very enticements worked only too well. Again, the unexpurgated story merely makes explicit what was implicit in the *Diary*. For instance, the expurgated *Diary* relates how Nin, wanting Allendy to become a substitute father and to protect her from the emotional rejection she suffered in relation to her actual father, invites him to a piano concert given by her brother Joaquín. She knows her father will make a scene, and she hopes that Allendy's presence will help her alleviate the childhood anxiety she experienced when her parents fought (1: 99). As expected, her father behaves badly, and Nin feels strengthened by her therapist's presence. As the evening continues, Nin is aware of the impression her elegant appearance is making on Allendy as well as on others in her brother's audience. Yet, like Stella in the novella, she feels she is wearing a false self beneath a mask of self-confidence.

Eventually, Nin would reconcile her tendency to sexualize her need of a father with her desire to remake herself in her own image. One step she took toward this goal was to begin distancing herself from Allendy's power over her. It is ironic that, to reverse the roles of dependency and enact a sense of control, she "sympathized" with him (seduced him, as it turns out in the unexpurgated version) and in that sense did not heal her need to sexualize. A positive effect of her gaining independence from Allendy is that she would channel her ideas about mask-wearing into a theory about how she could use writing to create her own persona apart from paternal imagery. "How glad I am to be a writer, making my own portrait," she proclaims in the *Diary* (1: 138).

Nin's difficulty in making the necessary distinctions shows up in her ambivalence toward an independent role, however. Although she protests in the *Diary* about her right to author her own life, her text is full of uncertainty about whether she should appear as a character from a script she has written for herself or whether she should fulfill a role in another's set of expectations or myths.[22] For example, she acknowledges that her practice of wearing elaborate costumes has been "an armor" (1: 118), and she writes that she was most happy at times in her life when she went about without make-up, fancy clothes, or fabricated roles. Nevertheless, her writing reveals her fear of being fully responsible for her own "story" when she expresses concern that "psychoanalysis [might] . . . divest [her] of all decoration, . . . adornment, [and] flavor." If this happens, she asks, "then what will be left?" (1: 119).

Despite her ambivalence, Nin makes clear throughout both expurgated and unexpurgated versions of her diary her need to define herself for herself, apart from her identification with Allendy as a substitute father. In an entry dated May 25, 1932, Nin writes that she is irritated at Allendy's "quick categorizing of [her] dreams and feelings" (1: 108). She writes that, when he is silent during analysis, she makes her own interpretations. He sees this as a way for her to find him lacking. Hitting a sensitive spot, he says he thinks she plays roles that separate her from her intrinsic nature, and that her role as femme fatale is in reaction to her mother's being dominated by her father. In a passage that suggests Allendy stressed adaptation over transformation, Nin writes that this session ended with her sobbing with gratitude for Allendy's promise to help "reconcile [her] to [her] own image" (1: 110).

A few pages later, Nin once again embraces the notion that the ego is a mask and that social interaction is a masquerade: "How difficult it is to be 'sincere,'" she writes, "when each moment I must choose between five or six souls. Sincere according to which one, reconciled to which one?—as I once asked Dr. Allendy" (1: 118). Whereas Fitch has cited this passage as showing the "splitting" of the self that is characteristic of sexual abuse victims, Nin's description also shows a correspondence to the idea of a splitting that occurs as a basic fact of human consciousness. Accepting this kind of splitting, according to Lacanian thought, can provide a basis for a more healthy position than a pretense that one is whole. Without minimizing Nin's real problems around the issue of splitting, we can see her depiction of the multiplicitous self as an artistic portrayal such as that inherent in some of the Modernist art she later uses as a model for and theme of her own writing.

Nin's grappling with boundary issues is paramount during this period. At the same time that she rebels against Allendy's interpretations, as a way to distance herself from him, she also seeks an "unlimited, unrestrictive world" in her writing and in the "café life" she has adopted through Miller (1: 103).[23] This passage reveals an important link between Nin's analytic goals and the self-reconstruction she was doing through writing. Her seeing this as a separation into limitlessness, however, shows that she still seeks the very lack of boundaries that has caused her pain.[24]

Nin's attempt to redefine herself coincides with her continuing effort to work out a theory of gender difference in her diary and in her fiction. *Winter of Artifice* portrays gender difference in terms very much as it appears in Lacanian theory, as the degree to which one has identified with the totalizing properties of the ego. As Nin theorizes about her characters' weaknesses, she also places their lack of boundaries within a tradition of feminine porousness that she had formulated in her study of Lawrence. As Lawrence drew on character traits that Nin, like Lacan, associated with artists, mystics, and feminine modes of approaching life, her characters in *Winter* illustrate Nin's belief that the extreme fluidity and border-erasure that caused pain could be transformed into a source of creativity and insight. In this regard, Nin's theories find a parallel in Lacan, in the way feminine *jouissance* differs from the masculine.

A related and problematic element of Nin's relation toward internal boundaries involves her attempt to relinquish an unconscious masochism by bringing

it to the surface of consciousness. In "Stella," written several years after the experiences recounted in the unexpurgated *Fire* and the second volume of the
Diary, Nin confronts this tendency to "seek pain" (*Fire* 212).[25] The diary volumes indicate, however, that she had already begun to know her disease involved an element of masochism and resistance to closure. As narrator of the
novellas, Nin acknowledges what Stella does not yet know: Stella, like Nin herself, has incorporated the gaze of the father to the point that there is little differentiation between her self and others. As a result, she lives always trying to
fill up the gap between her father and herself by playing roles with which to seduce him and attract his constant gaze. Stella turns every man into her father,
much as Nin acknowledged she had done with Allendy and Rank (*Fire* 32).
"Every human being who fell under her spell became not the lover, but the day
and night nurse to this sickness, this unfillable longing" (*Winter* 23). Words
hurt Stella physically. Language's palpable effect, themes Nin explored in *D. H.
Lawrence* and *House of Incest*, appears in *Winter* as an aspect of Stella's
masochism when she feels her doubt of her lover as if it were a thing. "The
word penetrated Stella's being as if someone had uttered for the first time the
name of her enemy . . . . Doubt" (*Winter* 24). Later, the word "masochism" itself functions in a similar way, as Stella lies in her bedroom searching for relief
from anguish:

> Some word was trying to come to the surface of her being . . . as if she were
> going to name her greatest enemy. . . .
>   ma soch ism
> Soch! Och! It was the och which stood out, not ma or ism but the och! which
> was like some primitive exclamation of pain.
>   Am, am I, . . . whispered Stella, am I a masochist? (*Winter* 28)

Stella's question marks progress in her and her author's efforts to overcome a
binding pattern. By naming her enemy as an unconscious position of
masochism, Stella makes—by Nin's bequest and on her behalf—a move reminiscent of the dancer's gestures at the end of *House of Incest*.

The *Diary* shows Nin confronting her masochism further when she begins
to wonder whether she is not more like her mother than like her father (1:
103), a theme she would later explore in more depth with two women analysts. Here, though she barely brushes the surface of her mother's legacy of
masochism, she opens the subject by relating a story about her mother's
courage in facing her own father's cancer. Her love, Nin writes, "was brave and
virile" (1: 104). Only much later, during her therapy with Martha Jaeger,
would Nin be able to see her mother's way of loving as sacrificing, and, as the
model for Nin's own way of relating to others, a form of self-abnegation. Once
she distinguished between this role and her mother's bravery, she would be to

some degree more able, consciously, to choose the traits to identify with, rejecting self-effacement and advocating women's embracing an active strength.

Her movement toward a positive definition of a feminine role coincides with her continuing to hone a theory of creativity and gender. When June Miller tells her she has a "'mixture of utter femininity and masculinity'" (1: 138), for instance, Nin reports her negative response: "'That is wrong, June. As soon as a woman has creativity, imagination, or plays an active role in life, people say: masculinity'" (1: 138). Depicting her own status as an artist as being compatible with a feminine role, Nin reinvents the notion of motherhood that she inherited from her parents and culture. She would develop this idea in fuller detail during her next analysis.

In the meantime, she acts out her rejection of the father's desire as the defining principle of her being by rebelling against Allendy. Although she acknowledges that Allendy has taught her she does not have to remain enslaved to "a childhood curse" (1: 129), and that she need not be eternally dependent on the attentions of various substitute fathers, Nin writes that she is tired of bowing to him, as if with a daughter's respect (1: 144). When Nin reports that she made Allendy sit in the analysand's chair and that she pretended to analyze him (1: 165), she demonstrates her striving for mastery over the father, if only in order to reduce her need to do so.

Eventually, with her unattractive portrait of Allendy in the *Diary*, she "kills" her image of him into print, in an attempt to kill her father's hold on her. Unfortunately, her father's reappearance in her real life, at just this point, interfered with her psychological separation from the paternal signifier. After Nin agrees to receive her father at Louveciennes, she writes that he is coming when she no longer needs a father. This premature declaration appears verbatim in "Winter of Artifice." Nin's analysis ends when she decides that Allendy is dying metaphorically because he cannot truly live. This depiction is not truly different in character from that presented in the unexpurgated passages published later, which reveal that Nin took Allendy as a lover whom she then denigrated in her diary. What is implicit and subtextual in the first series has been made explicit in the unexpurgated diary publications, but the transferential dynamic holds in both. She likewise reports that her transference to Allendy is ended, leaving unsaid in the expurgated version the true nature of their parting.[26]

OTTO RANK AS FATHER, ANALYST, AND LOVER

The *Diary's* account of Nin's first meeting with Dr. Otto Rank in November 1933 also enhances a reading of *Winter of Artifice*. She writes that she approached Rank several months after her affair with her father, feeling

confused and lost and still in need of a father (1: 269). But before approaching his door, she waits outside, deciding which image to present. "Which self
should I bring him?" she writes (1: 270), in a passage reminiscent of her description of the multiplicitous self during her previous analysis. Since Rank has
made a specialty of studying the artist, she decides not to tell him she feels
"like a shattered mirror" (270).[27] She decides instead to present herself as "'one
of the artists [he is] writing about'" (270). She tells him that "'Dr. Allendy's
formulas did not fit [her] life'" (1: 271) and that she feels there must be more
in her relation to her father than the desire for victory over herself (271). In
Rank, Nin believes she has found another father figure, one not irresponsible
and childish like her actual father but someone to whom she can look for guidance. Identifying with him, because he too has been orphaned by a kind of father (Freud), she sees Rank as someone who has lost "not only . . . a father but
a master, a world" (1: 277–78).[28] At this point, Nin sees Rank as someone who
can help her become self-creative, unlike Allendy, who she thinks tried to put
her into rigid categories that did not allow for individuality.

Nin's attempts to relinquish her diary found support in Rank's view that the
diary is "'the story of [her] faithfulness to [her father's] image'" of her (1: 277).
Objecting to her compulsion to record everything in the diary, he urges her to
give it up so that she might create fiction. For a time, Nin believes Rank can
"help the writer [in her] to be born" (1: 305). This feeling alternates with rebellion against his formulation of gender difference, just as she had rebelled
against June Miller's depiction of creativity as masculine. Rank similarly tells
Nin that when man is cured of neurosis he becomes an artist, but that when
woman is cured she becomes woman. At one point, she describes the most joyous moment of her analysis with Rank as the one when she tells him she would
get more pleasure from his finishing *his* novel than from her completing her
own. In a response that may seem strange until one has read the re-sexualized
account in the unexpurgated version, Rank applauds this, saying that, for the
time being, she needs to become a woman. For some time, Nin's need to overcome her writer's block and to establish an effective father transference in order to overcome the effects of an early trauma begin to meet ostensible fulfillment under Rank's direction. Until she acted on her sexual feelings for Rank
(see Bair 203, 204–8), she continued to make some progress both in writing
"more fiction than she [wrote] in the diary" (Bair writes that this is "probably
the only time in her life" when this was true [192]) and in gaining emotional
distance from her father.

Nin's identification with Rank reaches its peak when she accepts an offer to
become an analyst under his supervision.[29] In a sense, the role of analyst provides the ultimate transference in allowing her to *be* him, or at least to be what
he is.[30] In the *Diary*, she cites her reasons: she studies psychoanalysis to satisfy
both her "desire to help others" (1: 324) and her hope to be financially inde-

pendent so that she need not compromise her writing in order to publish it. Of course, as she makes clear in *Fire,* Nin fuses with Rank not only in terms of identifying with him professionally but also in a sexual relationship from which she must eventually disengage in order to accept her position as authentic parent or author of her literary works and her own self-myth. Her conflict is evident: even as she identifies with Rank she must reject his authority, both by winning him as a lover (whom she can master by seducing and then abandoning him as she sought to do with her father) and by "killing" Rank's image into print as she did Allendy's (the analyst in "The Voice" appears as a condensation of Allendy and Rank). Even as she prepares to join him, as lay analyst in New York, she depicts his seminars on psychoanalysis at the *Cité Universitaire* as being boring and his lectures as being full of dry, uninspired, obvious points. She describes his humor as "inner pranks of the mind. . . . *Il pense sa vie,*" she writes. "He has no enjoyment of the flower" (1: 327).

When she abandons Rank and her patients in New York after only a few months, she has effectively completed at least one stage of the separation process, although the account in *Fire* provides a record of her deep attachment to Rank and her ambivalence about hurting him despite her need to do so. By contrast the expurgated diary, edited for publication over thirty years after the events it portrays, documents the separation as based mainly on intellectual and artistic differences. One piece of evidence—in the ending of Volume 1 of *The Diary of Anaïs Nin*—that she is vacillating in her resolve to complete the break with Rank appears in her praise of his methods: she has just suffered the stillbirth of a six-month-old fetus, and—in a comparison laden with both self-pity and a dramatic irony only fully recognizable after one realizes she had aborted that fetus—she writes that her own self-birth might have ended similarly but for psychoanalysis. Yet near the opening of the next volume, Nin reflects, even as she makes her way toward Rank in New York, that he already constitutes another loss.

THE BIRTH OF A THEORY: MOTHERHOOD AS FEMININE CREATIVITY

Nin records what Bair has called "a curious thing" that happened soon after she arrived in New York (Bair 207): Rank tells her that the diary (which he asked her to give up at the beginning of their analysis) is "invaluable as a study of a woman's point of view . . . a document by a woman who thinks like a woman, not like a man" (2: 24). Thus, Nin writes, what he took away from her as a symptom he gives back to her as a work of art. She seizes this praise and from it begins to sculpt a complete theory about the difference gender makes in writing, especially stressing her kind of writing as a form of symbolic motherhood.

Burdened as it is with the irony of Nin's recent stillbirth or abortion, her comparison of both psychoanalysis and writing to birth is among the most significant developments in her thinking about the relationship between art and gender. The metaphor also reflects much of the emphasis on feminine writing that W. C. Williams recognized in his review of *Winter,* a recognition to which Nin objected at the time but which she then came to claim as a specialty. It is quite likely that Nin's denial of this emphasis in her own work is related to the separation process from her father: not yet ready to make a complete distinction between her actual father and her unconscious interpretations of that relation, she denies a related distinction in her thinking between feminine and masculine ways of creating. Yet, as she made progress in the separation process, she also came to embrace gender as an arena in which difference could be played out.

The diary of the period during which she practiced lay analysis in New York for Otto Rank also reflects Nin's emphasis on language, gender difference, and the masquerade of the ego. In her patients, she writes, she sees the ego as a "caricature people mistake for the self, . . . the fraud, the actor" (2: 20). She refines her belief in a feminine discourse as different from the abstract and impersonal nature of a "man's language" used to disguise the self (2: 25).[31] This line of thought continues back in Paris, where she returns in "June, 1935" to "write a novel" (2: 41) and to escape further involvement with Rank after becoming increasingly restless with him.[32]

Back home in Louveciennes in mid-1935, she writes that she has reunited with Miller, who has also returned from New York and is working on *Black Spring,* dedicated to her. In comparing their writing styles, Nin realizes that she has "more to say" than Henry but thinks she will "never say it as well" (2: 61–62). Still, she works on the novellas that will join "Winter of Artifice" in the collection by that name and sees herself approaching a "feminine way of perception" (2: 45). She writes meanwhile that she does not miss Rank, and that she has finally conquered the need for a father. Yet, in January 1936, she is "'still in conflict with [her] feminine self'" (2: 69). She sees this conflict as stemming from an opposition between a desire to live "in a man-ruled world, to live in harmony with men" (2: 62) and an urge to create her own world, which she "can't find anyone to share" (2: 62). After a trip to Morocco, during which she suffers an anxiety attack about her right to speak as a woman amidst the veiled and repressed females there, she returns to France, this time to try to realize a vision of herself as an active and strong, yet feminine, writer.

During the prewar escalations in Europe at this time, Nin writes about gender difference in terms of the disparity between creation and destruction. In July 1936, she writes that the "world of man [is] in flames and blood" (2: 98) but the "world of woman [is] alive as it is in this book, as it shall be forever, woman giving life, and man destroying life" (2: 98). Later, she will recognize the limitations of dichotomous opposition, but at this point at least, this formulation enables her to assert the voice that has often been repressed. By March 1937, Nin writes that she is "becoming more and more aware" that she is "writing as a woman" (2: 184) and that this kind of writing "happens in the real womb, not in the womb fabricated by man as a substitute" (2: 184). Nin sees herself becoming "completely divorced from man's world of ideas" (2: 1) as she concentrates on "*being* the womb" (2: 1).³³ She believes her writing is an act of love, the unifying element between all people and all art and an element she distinguishes from "man's abstractions" (2: 233) and to which she refers throughout the diaries as the intellectual systems with which man separates himself from others.

At the other extreme is the porousness of identificatory boundaries, which Nin comes to recognize as both her weakness and her strength. In March 1937, as she is gaining confidence in her "woman's way" of writing, she says her "madness is that of perpetual identification with others" (2: 188). "People mingle within me," she writes, and later, "It is as if by a fluid quality, . . . I [become] like water and . . . lose myself in others" (2: 188, 285). She recognizes that such identification stems from her relation to her father, whose influence she has already begun to negate. Yet she embraces her fluidity, apart from its role in causing her to suffer, and decides that it does not have to create "an abyss . . . , but a new world. Not madness but a deep truth" (2: 285–86). *Winter of Artifice* shows Nin embracing a self-defined truth as she shapes her theories concerning gender roles and human identity into a coherent view of an active feminine artistry.

"STELLA"

The initial story in *Winter of Artifice* is, according to Nancy Scholar's estimation, the "most successful of the three pieces in this volume, . . . [because of] an emotional intensity" in "Stella"'s first section. It represents Nin's attempt to reconcile her "private needs" and "public persona" (Scholar 91).³⁴ Oliver Evans has judged it "the most Lawrentian of all Nin's narratives" and one of Nin's "most thoroughly realized performances" (Evans 97, 98). Nin's friend Louise Rainer provided a real-life model for its main character, but Stella is ultimately one of Nin's own masks. The narrator and narrative both function to call attention to Nin's belief that people develop personas more or less rigidly to defend against psychological pain. When the story opens, Stella has almost no protective boundaries. By the end of the novella, she has hidden herself behind a mask so rigid that little opportunity exists for a healthy perspective. In this way, Nin problematizes the extremes of hysteria and obsession as identity styles that are not conducive to healing and implies that a solution lies somewhere in the middle.

Just as Nin herself was searching for a literary form that could provide structure while simultaneously allowing for fluidity, she portrays a potentially healthy identity structure as depending on a balance between border-erasure and border-rigidity. She extends this portrayal to include her ideas about gender, associating Stella's hysterical porousness with a feminine way of responding to pain, as opposed to the nearly obsessional fixity with which she associates Stella's lovers. A similar characterization appears in the second and third novellas in *Winter*. Nin's emphasis on balance as she depicts its lack in Stella and other characters in the collection anticipates the way gender polarization gives way in her mature writing to a sense that gender is a matter of costuming with which a creative artist may take creative liberties.

For Stella, mask-wearing is neither creative nor liberating. The story opens as the protagonist actress watches herself on a screen and experiences a violent antipathy toward the image she sees there. She is shocked by the contrast between the fearful, quavering "child woman" she feels herself to be and the graceful image being projected. As in the closing scene of *House of Incest*, the projected image Stella is now watching dances "a dance of receptivity and response" (*Winter* 8) that seems alien to her. Unused to anything but criticism from her rejecting father and unwilling to restructure her internal stance of perpetually wounded daughter, Stella thinks about the way she recoils from even an audience's admiration. The audience's praise seems to reinforce her sense of splitting between self and image. Like the narrator of *House of Incest*, Stella suffers from too acute an awareness of such splits. More like Nin than the narrator of *House*, however, Stella seeks suture in a series of heterosexual relationships (see, for example, *Diary* 2: 328–29).

Nin foreshadows the failure of these relationships with the description of one of the love scenes on the screen, in which an artificial snowflake stayed on Stella's face longer than it was supposed to. The effect of the unmelted—and thus obviously false—snowflake is to undermine the "exalted scene" through which the audience, if not for that reminder, might have shared in "the dream of osmosis, the dream of every lover, to find a substance that will . . . dissolve, and yield and incorporate and become indissoluble" (*Winter* 12). Stella's relationship with a man named Bruno highlights Nin's awareness of the inability of human partnership to provide complete fusion with another person, the way many lovers imagine their union should. This theme appears when Bruno does "not see Stella but the dream of Stella" (14), or his idea of what she is. The "acute sense of distance [that is] immediately established" between them, "such as Bruno had never known before to exist between men and women" (15), is characteristic of the abyss between the genders that Nin was increasingly likely to see as the basis for gender difference.[35]

The aesthetic distance between the story's narrator and its main character mirrors the abyss between Stella's self-image and the screen projection. Nin emphasizes the difference between the narrator and Stella when she indicates that Stella did not know about the past scene being ruined by a flake of artificial snow: "If Stella had known it she would have been crushed. The lightest of her defects, weighing no more than a snowflake, . . . weighed down upon her soul with the oppressive weight of all perfectionism" (12). The difference between Nin and Stella is one of acknowledgment: whereas Nin strives to construct a creatively fictionalized self with which to express her own desire and move beyond identification with paternal wounding, her character Stella stays sick and blind.[36]

Bruno's characterization as Stella's opposite may likewise be understood in light of Nin's emerging gender aesthetic. The major difference between Bruno and Stella is that he has no trouble drawing and maintaining fixed boundary lines whereas Stella, characterized by mental and affective fluidity, cannot tolerate such limitations. Unable to make a cut-and-dried distinction between dream and reality, Stella wants to maintain "the illusion that each [is] the center of the other's existence" (16). Nin depicts Stella's "willingness to sacrifice external achievements or success" as "typically feminine" (16), but the extremity of certain feminine traits leaves her fighting a perpetual battle: "she became possessed again with this frenzy against barriers, against limitations, against forbidden regions" (22). Stella identifies with a punitive internal father, with whom she seeks fusion in an attempt to control his power *over* her by *being* him. Similarly, she wants also to "be [Bruno's] secret dream, his secret passion" (22). Though she herself needed constant reminding, Nin as narrator affirms that such fusion is impossible and that health depends on knowing so.

Nin connects Stella's pain to her identification with her father, who is also an actor. When Stella is summoned by Laura, her father's second wife, with a note that Laura is leaving him, Stella recounts the breakup of his first marriage, with her mother. Now Stella begins to identify with Laura whom she sees as "small and childlike" (35), an image reminiscent of the one in the story's opening passage as Stella's internal portrait of herself. Stella notices that Laura has "played this role for ten years" (35) and, seeing the "mark of a wound" (36) in Laura's eyes, Stella begins to identify with her, recognizing herself in the gaze of the other woman. Having come initially to forestall the separation, Stella now sees "instantly that her pleading is doomed" (36). She returns to her father, "carrying the word 'irrevocable'" (38) to him. Nin's portraying the word itself as a thing of weight and substance underscores her emphasis on the somatic nature of language. By carrying a tangible word to her father, Stella begins to come to terms with the real separation suffered in his name.

Stella does not complete the process of mourning and moving on, however. She is able to formulate the statement to herself, "'You killed my love, too'" (41), but because she is not able to *say* this to him, she does not attain freedom from the unconscious pattern. The result is that Stella finds it is still through her body that she must express her pain. Back in her "ivory satin bed" at home, her "eloquent body," which can usually "speak out all the feelings in the language of the dance" (44), now lies limp. Her voice "vanishes to a whisper" (44) and she feels her hands will never express anything beyond the clasp of prayer as she cowers before each potential abuser.

Nin provides keen self-analysis when she presents Stella's emergent promiscuity as a false freedom. After a brief and unsuccessful affair with a new lover, Philip, Stella barricades herself within a static "asphyxiation of the feelings" (54). The novella closes with Stella's adopting a new role, signing receipts for the flowers she receives from appreciative members of the audience. They are "flowers for the dead. . . . With only a little wire, and a round frame, they would do as well" (54).

Thus Nin frames her story by drawing attention to the aesthetic distance proper to all narratives, including the trajectory of one's own self-myth. She becomes a character in her own stories, enacting the child's prerogative to rearrange playthings so as to maintain control. Though Stella's story ends in stagnation, her plight is but one of those possible for Nin, whose continuing presence in the second novella in the collection, eventually named for the work as a whole, reflects her quest—however unsuccessful at this point—to restructure a relationship to the one who had wounded her as a child.

"WINTER OF ARTIFICE"

"Winter of Artifice" is among Nin's least effective stories because its function as mask is too transparent to provide much structure. The novella has a plot and a conflict, but Nin is so self-identified in relating to readers her conclusions about the conflicts that she leaves little room for imaginative response.[37] The greatest value of the title story lies in its status as a kind of case history, as an example of its author's attempts to move beyond identification with a false father and to attain distance from the actual father by analyzing him in fiction. Even on this basis the novella has been found lacking.[38] Despite its weaknesses, however, Nin's efforts to portray herself and her own story within a fictional narrative frame in "Winter of Artifice" is a significant part of her journey toward freedom. When read as part of the larger story of Nin's narrative recovery, its insights may reverberate with some literary power.

"Winter of Artifice" opens as an unnamed narrator awaits her father's arrival, which she thinks will close her "circle of empty waiting" (*Winter* 55).[39] As she waits, the narrator regards a glass ship mounted decoratively in a fish bowl. For her, it represents the ship on which she traveled to New York with her mother and brothers, leaving her father behind in Europe, after he abandoned the family. In a passage that reveals a breakdown of appropriate boundaries, the narrator reflects that ever since her father left she has carried an image of him that "had become fluid" enough to run through her very veins. She wonders now why she still loves ships and their promise of sailing "away from this world" (55). When she soon meets her actual father, she leans against the bowl and accidentally pushes it from its stand to break against the floor. Later, she recognizes the image she has held of him is a fiction, one that she eventually realizes she must smash as she did the fishbowl. Even so, his attentions delight her, and his words ring with relevance. In her diary, Nin reports being similarly impressed with her father upon their reunion (*Incest* 207, 237, 243).

When the narrator does portray a degree of self-sufficiency, her father is jealous and calls her "'an Amazon'" (*Winter* 79). She interprets his statement to mean that he is relinquishing the role of father, for "an Amazon did not need a father. . . . An Amazon was a law and a world all to herself" (81). His analogy provokes her to realize she has been subject to his desire, and she rewrites the metaphor, deciding that she is indeed like an Amazon woman, with one breast "cut off as in the myth, so as to be able to use the bow and arrow " and the "other breast far too tender, too vulnerable" (81). The distinction she makes between his use of the term "Amazon" and hers is a crucial step in moving out of "slavery to a pattern" (117). Rewriting a negative reference into one that helps her understand herself empowers the narrator to use her own powers of interpretation rather than to rely on those of her father. A few days later, she has an epiphany when she is riding with him in a car and, looking down at his foot, mistakes it for her own. This fantasy terrifies her, and in as clear a proclamation of her own issues as Nin can make, the narrator sees that "She must disentangle their two selves" (92).

Unlike Nin's concept of a prototypical feminine creator that she developed partly to distance herself from her father as its masculine opposite, the protagonist's father disavows the existence of anything beyond the ego and becomes fixated upon his role itself. His daughter interprets his fussy self-pamperings, the naps he takes with religious regularity, and his "mania for washing and disinfecting himself" as his effort "to cleanse . . . his soul of his lies, his callousness, his deceptions" (111). Naming these faults as her protagonist's enemy, the author gains distance from the same habits of her own father. Whereas Stella is not able to say the necessary sundering words to her father, this novella's narrator is, and does. When she confronts her father with the view that he has been false with her, however, he erects "a huge defense" (116) and thinks she is merely taking her mother's side. She realizes that his denial of splits has led him to compartmentalize himself so rigidly that integration is impossible.

As opposed to Stella, who retreats into defensive rigidity, the narrator of this story breaks the mold. She senses her image of him crashing to the floor, as foreshadowed by the broken fish bowl. When she realizes that she can never reach him and that she no longer wants to "pursue this search and poison all joys with the necessity of its fulfillment" (118), it is as if she is "coming out of the ether of the past" (119). The story ends with the narrator's memory of her stillborn child, which she had awakened to see the "last time she had come out of the ether" (119). Now, she believes, the "little girl in her was dead too. The woman was saved. And with the little girl died the need of a father" (119).[40]

With its ending image of a stillborn child that she strives to expel, "Winter of Artifice" becomes an act of rebirth. It represents Nin's attempt to rewrite the script of her delivery, giving birth not to a stillborn child but to a woman still being born. Having aborted the child that she believed would be damned by the same paternal failure she had experienced in her life, the author strives in fiction to enact change in both her narrator and herself. The ending lines of a similar passage in the second volume of the *Diary*, however, indicate that the process of understanding would be long in coming: "The great emotion with which I wrote the last pages, and the last lines, was so strong that it was only much later that I understood their meaning" (2: 62).

"THE VOICE"

Represented as an embodied voice, a psychoanalyst in the next story tries to help his patients to "throw . . . out what [is] dead" (*Winter* 124), similar to the way the narrator in "Winter of Artifice" pushes out dead identifications like a stillborn child. "'What refuses to live in you will become like cells through which the blood does not pass'" (124), the analyst narrator tells another of Nin's fictional counterparts, Djuna. In relating the seemingly incessant stories that emerge through his analysand's free associations, the character known as The Voice is also one of Nin's fictional personas. In this story, Nin draws upon her experiences as both analysand and lay analyst, presenting an account of psychotherapy with much insight but little objectivity. The ending, in particular, denies narrative closure by portraying Djuna's descent into dreamlike images rather than allowing a resolution of her conflicts.

Nin pursues the birth theme through several additional characters. Two in particular are Lillian, a woman confused in her gender identity, and a "cripple" named Mischa who suffers from an "impotent" leg and hand. Lillian feels inadequate because she is unable to have children but reports that she wants only lesbian relations anyway. Dismissing the possibility that she could enjoy sex with a man, Lillian attempts to find fulfillment by experimenting with and fantasizing about various alternatives, such as masturbating with a violin bow and dreaming about injecting mercury into her veins (128). She also objectifies the analyst. She reports that ever since she came to him she has "a feeling so warm and sweet and life-giving which belongs to [her alone]." She says that she knows he gave it to her, but now that it is inside her, he "can't take it away" (130).

Mischa achieves a similar sense of life-giving energy in his analytic session. The narrator portrays his lameness as "the facade of [an] image," behind which lies "a terrain of broken, cutting fragments" (132). Like the narrator of "Winter of Artifice," Mischa has been living "with a dead fragment of [him]self" (133). But when analysis forces him to confront the psychic "immobility" (133) that his dead limbs represent, the defensive strategies he has erected begin "dissolving" and "loosening" (134), and he goes from the session as if delivered of the resistance to death and to life that prevents his living freely. In the street, he has a "warmth in him like a fire that would never go out" (134), similar to the living warmth Lillian feels in her, the opposite of a dead fetus.

The theme of birth versus stillbirth appears yet again in the next scene as Djuna witnesses the suicide of a pregnant woman. Djuna feels "the shock in her body" when the woman hits ground after falling twenty-four floors. She is "dead, of course, . . . and with a five-month child inside her" (136), an image that resonates with the impact of Nin's emotional response to having aborted her own child at six months' gestation, a fact known to her reading public only long after her death but encoded in her texts with palpable resonance.[41] Djuna's horrified reaction contrasts with that of the analyst who, at this point in the narrative, has made Djuna his main countertransferential object and tells her his wish to be "'desired, possessed, tortured too'" (137) like his analysands. For him, the suicide is but one of many otherwise metaphorical deaths. "'They all have more to say than I have time to hear,'" he tells her. The scene ends with his statement: "'I could sit here until I die and even then there will be women throwing themselves out of the window'" (138).

With this narrative gesture, Nin points to the necessity of healing oneself rather than seeking a curative truth in analysis. Having made this point, she turns the narrative lens upon a set of characters that appear as thinly veiled portraits of herself and her brother Thorvald, from whom she was estranged for most of their adult lives (see Bair 527 n. 19, 546 n. 18). As Lilith waits at a boat dock to greet the brother she has not seen for twenty years, Lilith remembers him as a "boy in a plaster cast of hardness, of dissimulation. Intent on defending himself against all invasion by others, against feeling, against softness, against himself" (138). Like Bruno in "Stella" and the narrator's father in "Winter," Eric appears as an obsessional counterpart to an hysteric female. Eric and Lilith are like "brother and sister stranded" in a "ship they had boarded together at birth [which has] never moved" (140). Lilith tells the analyst that neither she nor her brother has ever freed himself of the father's desire. Instead of gaining mastery through their child's play, they are orphaned within it: "The world of our childhood closed with his departure" (143).

According to the analyst, Lilith has reacted to "'outer change'" by forming "'an inner static groove'" (144). "'Because the father failed you,'" the analyst tells her, "'You cannot depend on others. You prefer to be depended on'" (145). Like Nin herself, Lilith takes on others "'with a desire to carry them'" (145), as if to counteract poor fathering with mothering. Whereas Nin strives to change this desire through analysis and writing, her character Lilith continues to enact it. One sign of her resistance is her decision to "touch something" within the analyst "which will affect . . . him" (146), that is, to make him dependent on her. Several pages later, Nin connects Lilith's sexuality to her search for "an absolute uncapturable" (158) in all aspects of her waking consciousness. Lilith is always in flight,[42] looking into strangers' eyes for clues to life's mysteries, and always so tightly strung that she cannot relax.[43] We can see that her neurosis stems not simply from her perverse conversion of sexual unfulfillment into chronic hypersensitivity but also from the breakdown of boundaries like that which Nin believed she recognized in Lawrence and which she portrayed in *House of Incest*. Because the analyst in this novella has "reached into the roots of her being" (159), Lilith experiences transference love for him, believing that he will meet her needs where others have failed.

After Djuna tells her that she is chasing a mirage, Lilith turns her desire toward a woman, "wishing perhaps to be a man for a moment," in order to take on the body of Djuna, "but as a woman knowing there is no other way of possessing a woman but as a man" (160).[44] Lilith's effort to retain a primal connection with Djuna leads to the kind of fragmentation that Nin portrayed in *House of Incest*. The narrator of "The Voice" comments on Djuna and Lilith's union: "You are caught. The rhythm is broken, you dangle, you are mutilated" (162). Faced with the illusory quality of any sexual relation, Lilith returns to the analyst to explore her existence as it has been molded by her name, which stands for "'the woman who cannot be truly married to any man'" (162). When the analyst reminds her that it was her father's failure that causes her to depend on him the analyst, the analyst fades in her vision and becomes a mirage.

But she cannot escape his voice, which she hears as she stops to buy a bracelet for herself. The repetition of the analyst's words "You see? You see?" parallels a passage from the second volume of Nin's *Diary*, in which Nin portrays Rank's enthusiasm for her every act through a kind of double lens of both suspicion and reflection (2: 39). In the *Diary*, Nin comments that Rank's interpretation of her every move—from writing a page of *House of Incest* to buying a bracelet on Fifth Avenue—reduced her to being an actress. Rank, she writes, would "pounce" upon every detail she could tell him, mining its significance until she "felt like an actress who had not known how moving her voice and gestures had been, their tremendous repercussion" (2: 39). She would be drawn into the part and, "to please him," would trace back over her narrative steps looking for additional details that he might "feast . . . upon as if it were one of the most colorful tapestries he had ever seen" (2: 39). Similarly, in "The Voice," Lilith feels "like a creator who [has] prepared in

some dim laboratory . . . a life like a legend . . . [to be] read . . . out of an enormous book" (*Winter* 168; this wording appears nearly exactly in *Diary* 2: 39).
Unable to escape from her father's voice as an oppressive superego indicating that she is never good enough or pretty enough, Lilith quits analysis because she senses an "illusory quality of all man's interpretations" (*Winter* 169).
Whereas Nin leaves Lilith in her rebellion, Nin continues her own quest to
interpret her life for herself in the enormous book of interwoven diaries and
fictions that she, unlike Lilith, can enter and exit at will. She uses this prerogative to shift her point of view and to end "The Voice" with six pages of italicized stream-of-consciousness material from a dream of Djuna's in which Nin,
once again, reconstructs a stillbirth into a rebirth.

In the dream passage, images of primordial fragmentation revolve with the
fantasy of an *"ecstasy without death,"* in which *"life began only behind the cur-
tain of closed eyelashes"* (*Winter* 172). Reminiscent of the closed eyes of Nin's
own dead child (*Diary* 1: 346), the image portrays Nin's desire to expel dead
fragments in order that they might be reborn, to liberate the dreamer parent
as well as the dreamed-of dead child, a theme that motivates and becomes the
dominant structure of Nin's next book. The end of Djuna's dream contains
condensations of several of Nin's lifelong themes. First, a boat is stranded out
of water, representing the way Nin's relation to her father stranded her at an
early age in a series of dead-end attachments. As the boat is *"chokingly struggling to pass along the streets"* (*Winter* 173), it symbolizes the dead baby that
Nin the diarist describes expelling from her body. Here, she writes, *"I was
pushing it against the resistance of earth"* (173) and *"the boat labored painfully"*
(174). In the next paragraph, words distance the dreamer from the boat, which
now represents the dream itself:

> *I was not altogether asleep. The night was . . . black. . . . But while there was still a
> slit of daylight there were words floating around her. They were sharp, they cut like
> knives into the feelings, they separated, they scalded. . . . The moment the words cut
> into the dream, . . . the pulse ceased to beat.* (174)

Similarly, in her account of her stillbirth experience in the first volume of her
Diary, Nin describes the doctor's and nurses' words sharply and painfully entering her consciousness (1: 340–46). In the next passage of Djuna's dream,
Nin revisits the choice she made, during that traumatic event, to live despite
the extent of her loss and the depth of her pain. At the same time, she shows
how difficult that choice continues to be: *"I was certain that I had already
known the feeling of standing at this window looking down at the two avenues like
opened legs. . . . My route constantly split in two, the whole structure of my life
constantly splitting open into two sections. I could never make a choice"* (*Winter*
174–75).

As a story about the potentialities and limitations of analysis as well as the value of fiction in reconstructing one's own relation to life, "The Voice" concludes *Winter of Artifice* with the kind of nonclosure that is typical of Nin's works: *"The life on the stage . . . dovetailed with the daylight, and out of this marriage sparked the great birds of divinity, the eternal moments"* (*Winter* 175). The ending shows how Nin resisted completing the process of mourning and thus failed, in a sense, to live up to a narrative promise of completion. At this point she was unable to let go completely of her father and unable to make a firm choice about the direction her writing career should take. Still, "The Voice" marks a departure in two important ways. One is from identification with the image of an authority figure (father *or* analyst) who, Nin had presumed, knew the answers to her boundary questions. For the most part after this point, Nin would rely mainly on writing and on female analysts for help in her recovery from trauma. The second departure was to mourn her abortion. Most of the hard work of mourning she learned must be done alone, and this included facing up to her own responsibility for the parts of the past over which she had a choice.

CONCLUSION

Winter of Artifice shows Nin employing the formal constraints of fiction in conjunction with psychoanalysis in order to work out both the trauma of her past and the difficulties she experienced during her mid-thirties. Although it is not as solid a work of literature as her earlier or her later fiction, *Winter* is important as a record of Nin's attempt to make sense of—and to move on from—her relationship with her father and his substitutes, as well as her abortion in 1934. All versions show the author's process of seeking, in writing, an adequate father transference in order to work through early trauma. *Winter of Artifice* provides both a transference and a transition to the more polished style of her next book of fiction, the collection of short stories entitled *Under a Glass Bell,* whose ending story, "Birth," mirrors the account of the stillbirth Nin provides near the end of her second expurgated diary volume.[45] *Winter's* motif of death and rebirth also parallels the publication history of her work during this period. Her third fictional book, which she was to publish herself in 1944, would signify the birth of Nin's career as writer when it drew the first serious critical response her writing would receive by a New York critic, in this case Edmund Wilson.

3

Exile and (Re-)Birth in
Under a Glass Bell

Wilfulness, exaggeration, overstatement: these are characteristic styles of being an exile, methods for compelling the world to accept your vision—which you make more unacceptable because you are in fact unwilling to have it accepted. It is yours, after all. Composure and serenity are the last things associated with the work of exiles.

—Edward Said

EDMUND WILSON'S FAVORABLE REVIEW of *Under a Glass Bell*, in the *New Yorker*, April 1, 1944, compared Nin's writing to Virginia Woolf's and praised Nin's artistic style, which Wilson valued above that of most of the literary surrealists.[1] According to Bair, Nin could hardly believe the brief good fortune brought by the review (294), especially since she had put the collection together from old material she had revised. Although Wilson's review was not overwhelmingly positive, it truly brought new life to Nin's career.[2] It came at a time when she was destitute both emotionally and financially, living out the war in a kind of voluntary exile from her home in France. She had not yet identified herself as American, and her emotional state paralleled in many ways her sense of dislocation upon arriving in New York at the age of eleven. She was also ill, having exhausted herself hand-setting and printing the collection of stories at her own Gemor Press in early 1944.

This time Nin had done most of the hard work of running the press herself, receiving little help from her partner and lover, Gonzalo Moré. Along with his wife, Helba Huara, Moré was more of a burden than an inspiration. Nin's relationship with Miller had ended the previous year after dwindling since 1939,[3] but she still suffered from a debilitating compulsion to spend more energy in mothering other artists than in working on her own material. Her tendency to devote herself to people like Henry Miller and Gonzalo Moré had by this time motivated her entry into another round of analysis.

Realizing that she had not been able in the past to resist "wanting to impress and seduce male analysts" (Bair 284), Nin believed the Jungian therapist Martha Jaeger, as a woman, could nurture her creativity and help her to shift focus from her relationship with her father to her identification with her mother. Nin would become stuck in mother-identification for over two decades, unable to distinguish between her own real desires and the ideal woman she strived to be. Nevertheless, it was an appropriate step to make in her effort to come to terms with the real dynamics at work behind her suffering. Her admitting her own seductive tendencies shows she was willing to go beyond the self-mythologizing proper to the narratives of the ego and to confront the figure who, according to Ellie Ragland, "symbolizes the loss that becomes the unconscious" (*Philosophy* 288). It is significant that Nin writes in the *Diary*, after her first visit to Jaeger, "The father is absent from this drama" (3: 240).

The shift to a mother figure also sheds light into the nature of Nin's increasing use of mothering, during this stage of her career, to theorize the kind of creativity she characterized as feminine. Incorporating Jaeger's insight that creation does not have to oppose femininity, that literary creativity can be an active not an aggressive act (3: 259), Nin continued to explore her roles in her diary and her fiction, specifically in relation to the polarization of masculine and feminine represented in Volume 2 of her *Diary*. An important distinction she makes at this point places her further outside the ostensible gender essentialism that her earlier formulations had implied. In her writing of the early to mid-1940s she separates her idea of woman's need of relation from her own need of a father's love. In a related insight, Nin sees that she has associated artistry with a danger to her womanhood and to her relationships with men (3: 256). She acknowledges that she considered creation threatening to her love life and to all relationships with others (3: 256), and that she feared that her asserting her artistry would cause others to feel inferior and to love her less as a result (3: 259).

She writes that by speaking with Jaeger, in conjunction with writing in her diary, she is learning that it is possible "to give without injuring one's self, [and to be] compassionate without masochism" (3: 248). Her self-compassion, as well as the mothering metaphor, reflects her sense of loss over the abortion she had in 1934 and her effort to move beyond a restrictive ego ideal that she associated with nurturing others at the cost of her own art. Nin's efforts to achieve integration of two "selves"—the creative and the maternal—were also related to a need to reconcile the two forms of writing that she still considered in opposition—diary and fiction. The *Diary* shows her working toward resolving both sets of dichotomies and establishing a dialogue between her interest in practical women's issues and her effort to theorize gender differences: "I wish I could write END to the diary and begin the outside story . . . the theme of the development of woman" (3: 215).

Her ability to place equal value on her inner and outer worlds manifests in the "tighter, more economical style" that Nin sees in her later diary entries (3: 97). Near the opening of the third volume, Nin reports that in 1941, as she looks back over old diaries she brought with her from France, she finds in them an increasing maturity and a lessening of neurotic pain. The early volumes reflect a state that she compares to opium smoking, where the slightest incident or glance had exaggerated effects (3: 97), but the later diaries show evidence of a clearer vision and a higher level of integration between art and life, between diary and fiction. Her *Diary* shows, too, that she was indeed beginning to pay more attention to the practical problems of women during this period. While making observations about her friend "Moira," for instance, Nin draws the conclusion that the story of women's expansion is painfully difficult, especially because many men seem to curtail their partner's development (3: 234). Moira has chosen a passive man, one who will not hold her back artistically or intellectually (3: 234). But his weakness destroys Moira, much as Nin describes how Moré's inabilities diminished her own enthusiasm for life.[4]

Another passage from this part of her *Diary* links her thought on this practical women's studies issue to her earlier metaphor of mothering as creativity: "This is a phase in the evolution of woman," she writes (3: 234). Woman "wants to divert her strength from biological motherhood into other forms of creation." The next sentence, especially, shows that her efforts at theory, like most of her fiction, are based in a personal conflict and that she is using writing as a way to work it out: "But [woman] needs man's blessing and man's help" (3: 234).[5]

Nin often had the help of several men; but the third volume of her *Diary* and its corresponding passages from *Ladders to Fire* show the toll her partnership with Gonzalo was taking on her. As she and Gonzalo work to print *Under a Glass Bell*, Nin discusses its theme in the *Diary* and makes clear the interrelation between its characters and herself. She argues that, whereas most people have sympathy for others who are malnourished or injured, most do not understand that an anxiety attack, such as one that strikes her as she crosses a street, is more devastating to her than a specific catastrophe. Her next line provides the link between her personal experience and her characters': "Anxiety is a woman screaming without a voice, out of a nightmare" (3: 276).[6] Yet it is clear that Nin has moved toward health when she writes on the last page of this volume that "for the first time" (3: 314) she can experience joy, can bear to hear a door close without feeling abandoned, and can listen to music without falling apart. "The telling of stories is the only balm" (3: 314) for life's pain, she writes, and she can tell hers from several perspectives.

The *Diary* volume ends with her giving herself permission to "close the door and window upon the world for a moment, turn to the diary for all its musical notations, and begin another novel" (3: 314). She was still associating diary writing with dependence on her father's image, and it was becoming increasingly clear that she needed to work out a good part of her own analysis in fiction. The more unified style and increased artistic control of *Under a Glass Bell*, like the changes she saw in the diary, reflect the relative degree of success she had achieved in establishing borders within literary form, especially in terms of content that had been written earlier and then reworked.[7]

As she reshaped, revised, ordered, and printed the stories for the collection, Nin had to face her own reactions to both internal and external material. As a result, despite the repetition of themes in the new work and in the earlier prose poem and novellas, we may recognize in this collection at least three changes over her former work: (1) a greater sense of distance between the author and the material than she had achieved in her earlier work, (2) a more skillful alteration between the sensual, fluid style of the prose poem and a more objective point of view, and (3) the beginnings of a link in the fiction between the individual struggles that represent the author's own psychological processes and a social, political commentary by which Nin portrays a wider sphere of struggle as an extension of the individual realm.

The third of these is especially important to the purpose of this present study, for *Under a Glass Bell* shows its author moving from the subjective absorption of the earlier work to her theorizing a link between individual and collective responsibility. The notion that war can be understood as an extension of individual violence toward the self (toward repressed painful memories, for instance) is a theme that begins in this collection and continues throughout Nin's mature work. Benjamin Franklin V and Duane Schneider present Nin's comments from the original preface to *Glass Bell* in order to show that "although . . . some characters in her fiction . . . never confront the pain of reality so long as they can maintain their unhealthy dream state" (Franklin and Schneider 42), the work itself represents Nin's "awakening" to the necessity of confronting, rather than leaving "buried and ignored" (43), the fears inherent in a post–World War II worldview. They also link Nin's awareness of this necessity to "a general awakening in the Western world," in a way that underscores a crucial link in Nin's work between personal and social holocaust (42–43). *Under a Glass Bell* responds to these threats in both theme and structure.

In addition, *Glass Bell* portrays Nin advancing her process of writing-as-analysis and strengthening the link between her narrative and analytic aims by confronting what Lacan described as a universal human exile from imaginary unity. Many stories in the collection move individually from unconscious and painful states of alienation, through a "labyrinth" of despair and discovery, to a creative acceptance of the "birth" into a realm of culture and language from which all humans are subsequently exiled.[8] The work as a whole mirrors this movement.[9]

In its 1944 and subsequent editions, *Glass Bell* moves—and takes as its subject the movement—from a state of exile into which one has been thrown to a state of cultural alienation that becomes the basis for creative acceptance. From the first story, "Houseboat," to the ending story, "Birth," the stories in *Glass Bell* show Nin at a strong stage in her writing career, striving to give voice to unspoken pain from the past while reshaping, in language, one exile into another. One trauma in particular had continued to haunt her. By placing the earlier-written story, "Birth," as the last in the collection, Nin begins to come to terms with an exile that had begun to wield more power over her than even perhaps her earlier losses of father and country. As she dealt with father-loss and mother-identification, she used the process of revising *Under a Glass Bell* to come to terms with her self-imposed prohibition against biological motherhood and the permanent banishment of the child she had aborted in 1934. The effects of these losses would echo throughout the rest of her life.[10]

"HOUSEBOAT" AS NOT-HOME

"Houseboat" is among the best stories in the collection, in terms of both her artistic control and her treatment of the exile theme. Like much of Nin's fiction, it adopts a stream-of-consciousness point of view that oscillates with an editorial voice-over. "Houseboat" moves, dreamlike, from one thought or theme to another without warning, which makes the traditional critic's job difficult. Issues and themes weave in and out of the text, coming first to the surface, then sliding under another thought to resurface later. The reader, however, need only "flow" with the momentum established by Nin to grasp the text's essential unity around the interrelated issues of exile and psychoanalytic self-discovery. Under this thematic umbrella come both the author's process of redefining herself in relation to a signifier for law and boundaries and the necessity to become an artist in order to achieve an acceptance of limitation and the ability to reshape oneself in relation to it beyond patriarchal desire. Nin's feminist and artistic goals coincide as she shows again that, for her, the way out is also the way in. Social conscience comes out of her journey into the personal labyrinth.

Written from a first-person point of view, the first story in *Glass Bell* grew out of the author's actual experience with two houseboats in Paris: the *Nanankepichu,* of which Nin rented a part in July 1936 as a trysting place for her and Gonzalo Moré and which she kept until she was evicted for nonpayment of rent (Bair 229, 241), and *La Belle Aurore,* which she rented from February through August 1938 (Bair 245, 247).[11] The name Gonzalo gave to the first boat, "a Peruvian Indian word . . . [meaning]] 'not really at home'" (Bair 228), reflects Nin's desire for the privacy to conduct an affair as well as the theme of her alienation. Nin incorporates this meaning of not being at home into the story "Houseboat," where she moves toward acceptance of several kinds of alienation as part of a healthful attitude toward the flux of life. Nin was, after all, exiled emotionally from her home, her husband, her lovers, and, most important, her own conflicting roles as she rewrote the stories that comprise *Under a Glass Bell* and rearranged them into publishable order.

Glass Bell's first story involves a distinction between exiles that the Lacanian critic Jonathan Scott Lee sees as central to the therapeutic process: recognizing that all humans are barred from having control over their unconscious minds and, at the same time, recognizing that, although each individual must deal with his or her singular circumstances, one need not take the state of exile personally.[12] In a related distinction, "Houseboat" problematizes the tension between a productive acceptance of limitation and a passive submission to the status of victim. The narrator is unconsciously drawn by a current of forgetfulness and conventional repression. But the narrative strives against that current to establish a distance from itself, much as the narrator seeks in analysis to achieve distance from internalized oppression in order to heal. The story mirrors this analysis.

The current that seeks to pull the narrator into the role of passive victim and keep her subjugated to a sense of universal exile appears at the beginning of the story, where a group of homeless mariners mill about aimlessly, unaware of any relation between their discourse and their social position. The mariners cast language and differentiation into the "flow of blood" to avoid the shock and violence of a confrontation with the effects of their social position. By contrast, the narrator's status as viewer puts her at some distance, so that she can begin to call into question the degree her own desire for flow without pain is a "refusal to obey" convention and, on the other hand, the degree to which it is a refusal to mourn the past in order to establish the truth of her life. The opening paragraph addresses the issue of a driving "hunger and desire" that motivates its protagonist and narrator away from an imaginary attachment to a way of life that represents the author's need for "flow" in her life.[13]

The tramps whom the narrator notices at river level have "fallen out of the crowd life" and have "refused to obey" a number of conventions, including "houses and clothes." Although they are alone, they are "not unique" in the way that they "re-enacted the ritual of abandon" (*Glass Bell* 11). This passage shows Nin's acknowledging that abandonment itself can be ritualized and con-ventionalized, an important recognition for her as she learned to disengage from the victim status. It also shows that a refusal of convention may itself be-come a trap, especially if one is simply "falling" out of the conventional rather than choosing a path of resistance to the current of forgetfulness that charac-terizes repression on a social level. The following images link language to such rituals: "They threw the newspapers into the river and this was their prayer: to be carried, . . . down, without feeling the hard bone of pain in man, lodged in his skeleton. . . . No shocks, no violence, no awakening" (12). By portraying the homeless mariners' prayer for flow without pain, in opposition to feeling, and by equating the absence of "shocks" and "violence" with absence of aware-ness ("no awakening"), Nin thematizes the roles of language and of real pain in the body: no pain, no gain. Her message is that one must accept the condi-tions of life and be willing to feel the "hard bone of pain in man" in order to take part in a process of transformation.

"Houseboat" shows its author's struggle to establish boundaries that would help her mourn the border-erasure of early trauma. But Nin—like her narra-tor—must resist a current so strong that it seems to keep pulling everything into the undifferentiated and undifferentiating realm for which the tramps pray.[14] The story is replete with passages about anger: "Everything was slipping into anger again" (12). Yet even the anger that for many analysands provides a provocation to change, through confrontation with the past, is subsumed within the static depths of the river. This subsuming mirrors the desire on the part of the early wounded to deny, repress, and bury memories around which they have anchored their identities: "A fit of anger and only the surface erupted, leaving the deep flowing body of the dream intact" (13).

A later image in the story corroborates the theme of resisting stasis and go-ing with the flow in order to heal. The image is one that triggers the narrator's memory of her childhood: a child has been abandoned by the riverside, told by his mother to wait for her return. The narrator learns from a street cleaner that the mother will never return. The child, dressed in his little black school apron and dangling his thin legs over the edge of the dock, has been left for the orphanage. The street cleaner combs the child's hair and tells the narrator that he, too, was abandoned as a child. When the child hears this he runs away; the street cleaner says he will be caught. Nin's implication is that there is no escape for the child who has been abandoned, except perhaps through adult re-memory and reshaping of the experience, motivated by the kind of compassion shown by the street cleaner. Realizing that the child has been abandoned leads the narrator to feel as if the child's life, and possibly her own, is a "voyage of despair." However, the willingness to experience anxiety, hinted at here, constitutes a movement away from trauma.[15]

Later, the narrator revisits her own abandonment when she awakens from a nightmare to find her hair wet from sweat, as the child's was wet from the river. As if this nightmare is too much to deal with consciously, she enters a passage of dreamlike underwater images that might have come from *House of Incest:* "Fish, plant, woman, equally aware, with eyes forever open, confounded and confused in communion, in an ecstasy without repose" (18) take part in the "white hysteria of the poet and the red-foamed hysteria of woman" (19). This distinction between hysterias is important; it anticipates and thematizes the author's movement toward a theory of gender and creativity that will help her articulate her own desire apart from patriarchal discourse. It also enacts a process of differentiation through which she can resist the border-erasure born of earlier trauma. However, to do so, Nin, like the story's narrator, must resist a constant current drawing her into stasis and repression.

The work's momentum—and Nin's—is toward an active state in which the smells of "rancid wine" are replaced by images of something "greener, washed by cleaner waters" (20). Toward the end of "Houseboat," the prose itself moves out of a kind of stasis and takes an anchor in a reality of movement, dialogue, activity. A sense of renewal permeates the last scenes of the story as the narrator, refreshed after her nightmare by the movement of her houseboat into cleaner waters, goes ashore for "candles, wine, ink, writing paper, nails for the broken shutters" (20)—tools with which to re-create the trajectory of her life in relation to the past. She knows that part of her trajectory involves delving into the "deep undercurrents," the river's "deeper undertows of dark activity," where she rejoiced with the river "at teeming obscure mysteries of river-bottom lives" (20).[16]

Nin demonstrates her own partial opening to the effects of early paternal traumatization in the way "Houseboat" shows a relation between "father" and "law." A Lacanian reading provides a viable explanation of Nin's associating the two concepts with each other: in Lacan's account of identity development, the "no" of the father's name functions as a necessary interruption to a sense of symbiotic oneness. Without the intervention of the paternal function, one would never enter the symbolic order of culture and language. One whose paternal interventions are especially traumatic can have trouble establishing an identity, becoming aware of one's own existence as an entity separate from the environment and other people, and understanding the concept of law as a system for upholding proper boundaries and respecting limits.

"Houseboat" shows Nin using writing to provide a healthier paternal intervention than she experienced in childhood. An example of a passage in which this need becomes evident is the narrator's comment that the windows on the houseboat facing the quays are shut while those facing the river are open. The narrator, adrift on the river in the houseboat, is unable to see the edge of the river or, by extension, to acknowledge or establish psychic borders. She is, however, able to hear the sound of oars coming from the direction of shore and decides that what she is hearing is the rowing of "the phantom lover . . . who haunts all women . . . who stands behind every man, with a finger and head shaking—'not him, he is not the one'" (15–16).[17] The image captures the psychic pain born of an inability to establish intimacy, another defect pointing to a weak paternal relation that keeps her in the futile search for one to fulfill the role of father. Nin's attempt to fill that role in literature is clear when, as the story oscillates between static symbiosis and structured movement, Nin interrupts her own text to propel the narrator toward healing. Rustling curtains in one passage and swaying pictures on the walls in another indicate that things are at least beginning to move.

In another passage, the narrator interrupts the river's and the narrative's continuity, without explanation, to say that "someone" has left a revolver on the table, thinking that the narrator might use it. As an image of violence and law (or lawlessness), the revolver signifies a point of departure from the symbiosis of the static dreamworld toward which the narrative has been leading. It acts also as agent, through which the narrator may draw a connection between individual subjectivity and the social. The sight of the gun reminds the narrator of some crime she has perhaps committed, or of some repressed memory of catastrophe. As Nin's earlier work shows, the memory of some original "great catastrophe," to which all subsequent subjective experience refers (the proverbial Fall from Grace inherent in many accounts of human experience), may be overlaid with violent affect for those whose entry was accompanied by trauma such as abuse. Another effect of such trauma, a tendency to blame oneself, appears here as well: as the narrator points the gun into the river, she is afraid she "might kill the Unknown Woman of the Seine again—the woman who had drowned herself here years ago and who was so beautiful that at the Morgue they had taken a plaster cast of her face" (14).[18] This confusing passage shares with the *Diary* and later pieces Nin's refusing an anonymous womanhood. The passage serves, in addition, to link the personal and the potential to the social and the actual by problematizing unconscious attachment to dead images from the past.

Several interesting developments in the text at this point show Nin's fear of artistic failure. A failed-artist motif appears in several places in *Glass Bell*. In this case, an old deaf man plays the violin, or "plays at" playing, unaware that no music comes from his instrument, only "tiny plaintive cries" (14).[19] The next paragraph establishes a linguistic and social connection between the failure of artistic expression and the next development, the theme of law as both defining and inhibiting. A one-sentence paragraph also portrays a connection between law and those who are outside it, yet whose status as exiles is nonetheless established *by* law: "At the top of the stairs two policemen were chatting with the prostitutes" (14).

Again, Nin plays with paradox, this time in terms of social deviance and its relation to law, to draw a flexible boundary for herself between art and life and to establish structure without binding herself too tightly to convention. That she must become an artist in order to reestablish proper order in her life means that she, like many artists, must walk a thin line between deviance and compliance with social law. She must remake herself in her own image and supply her own law signifier even as she learns how to fit into a social role that does not quell her artistry. At the end of the story, Nin returns to the idea of a law subject to compromise when she receives a police chief's suggestion "on the sly" that, though the "law remained adamant," she creatively circumvent an official order to remove her houseboat from public view (22).

Still another interruption to the flow of images performs two functions when the narrator awakes from sleep to the sound of a woman shrieking. Like the previous interruptions, the shrieks have an effect analogous to that of a differentiating signifier. They also propel the narrator to a greater sense of others' real existence and efficacy. This time it is not the mythological Unknown Woman of the Seine but a real woman, one whose particularity represents both Nin's own quest for singular identity and Nin's conflict between the role she sees as conventionally feminine and the desire to be an artist. This image also imparts a sense of responsibility. The narrator participates in the drowning woman's rescue, as the author uses fiction for her own rescue.

Immediately afterward, Nin hears news of the impending war and the tramps' "description of tomorrow's world. An aurora borealis and all men out of prison" (16). The beginnings of social commentary, the passage draws a link between personal healing and social conscience. The narrator's participation in the rescue of the drowning woman and the narrator's emergence from a timeless dreamlike state to one of greater awareness reflects Nin's acknowledging political, temporal realities. In addition the passage establishes historical reality as involving perspective and interpretation through the portrayal of the outcasts' description of the coming revolution in Europe as a natural light show.[20] The "show" results in all men being let out of prison, either in a metaphorical sense of revolution toward universal liberty or (more likely) in the practical sense that prisoners could be drafted to war. The oldest of the outcasts, however, is in "the prison of his drunkenness" from which there is "no escape" (17). Another editorializing passage, this comment brings home the point that Nin seems to be trying to convince herself of through the process of writing: that the refusal to face the past or the present leaves one futureless. This tramp "did not know about tomorrow" (16).

Now, at least, the narrator is connected to others; she receives letters from friends, which appear to have been wept upon because the narrator's mailbox leaks and has let in the rain. The image is a significant one, for its "letters" are only ostensibly wept upon and thus represent an image whose exposure *as* image conveys that whatever one habitually or automatically perceives as tragic may in fact have an alternative meaning. Also, the letters have reached their destination, as opposed to the "dead letters" of the past, which can signify the sick attachment to unhealthy aspects of the past as enacted to the extreme by the characters of *House of Incest.*

The next section of the story is the natural outcome of a distinction she and Nin can make between victimization and acceptance. "One morning what I found in the letter box was an order from the river police to move on" (21). Psychoanalytically interpreted, this "letter" (*l'être* or "being" in French, Nin's first language, the one from which she was exiled) signifies an analysand's motivation to "move on" from the sick moorings in the past. The motivation is initiated through the river police, as law, because it is through law as boundary that she can accept the limitations upon being-as-existence (*l'être*). She can articulate her own desire, by moving away from a fixed equation of paternal law with actual father or with paternal abuse.

As the narrator and her river companions discuss the orders they have all received, their small group represents the wider social community into which an analysand may enter more effectively as she moves away from the self-absorption of neurosis. That the narrator rejects some of her neighbors' suggestions for rebellion against the orders and tries to have the orders changed officially also distinguishes between community and blind complicity. To the relief of readers emerging from the dense imagery and poetic density of many parts of the story, the narrator's movement away from past "dead letters" coincides with the author's partial movement toward more clarity in her prose style: "What could happen?" she asks, matter-of-factly. "At the worst," she decides, the police would have to tow them all away "like a row of prisoners" (21).

But one of her companions, the one-eyed cyclist, is overwhelmed with fear at this prospect, believing that his boat would not survive being pulled by the heavier barges (21–22). In that visual perception of depth is usually dependent on the use of two eyes, the "one-eyed cyclist" appears as a metonymy for one whose lack of depth constitutes rebellion on the level of ideology, rather than on the level of analysis. His fear of disintegration shows the author's acknowledgment that, although she has made a gesture toward political awareness, she does not consider ideology to be politically efficacious. Rather, as she later asserted, it is through each person's individual confrontation of the warring factions of oneself—through analysis—that one can begin to effect political change (*A Woman Speaks* 56). The one-eyed cyclist's rebellion alone cannot lend him or his barge the strength to challenge unjust social conditions. He leaves the next morning "at dawn like a thief" to be "towed along by a friend who ran one of the tourist steamers" (*Glass Bell* 22). The adjectival "tourist" conveys a sense of expedient convention that operates on a surface level, without depth.

The fishermen's prayers, the narrator thinks, have been heard above those of her neighbors and herself. A humorous touch of the kind only possible when one has achieved a certain distance from the object of transference, this narrative gesture pokes fun at a belief in an Other outside the limits of discourse to whom humans may address their desires. It also introduces an authorial recognition that there is a similarity between such supplication and the narrator's quite sincere belief, expressed in the next paragraph, that she is somehow immune to law: "I always believed an exception would be made for me, that laws and regulations broke down for me" (22).

Here, Nin underscores her own tendency to exempt herself from social protocol by courting others' complicity. In doing so, she exposes the logic on which the narrator's expectation is based as paradoxically both flawed and substantiated by experience: "I don't know why except that I had seen it happen very often" (22). Pursuing such an exemption, the narrator receives permission to wait in the police offices for days on end. She spends the time becoming "versed in the history of the Seine" (22). Her historical literacy is a matter of knowing the numbers of "sunken barges, collided Sunday tourist steamboats, of people saved from suicide by the river police." The irony of this passage shows the author's light attempt to critique the terms of conventional understanding of history as a catalogue of disasters and conquests over accident. It also shows Nin making fun of the narrator's and her own perspectives on life as being disastrous, an interpretation made more significant by the momentum by which the narrator and narrative have progressed from dense prose and static images to a lighter style and thematic freedom.

Much as Nin seeks resolution of a conflict she feels between formal boundaries and artistic fluidity, the characters reach a solution: the police chief makes a suggestion, "on the sly," that the narrator take her houseboat to a repair yard where some repairs can be made while she awaits "permission to return" (22). Nin herself returns again and again to the image of a grounded boat and to the themes of stasis and movement, passivity and activity, ideology and analysis. The paradoxical relation between seemingly opposing elements was one Nin had long considered. She had admired, for example, what she considered a "mystical" as well as an artistic and feminine ability in D. H. Lawrence to tolerate the kind of paradox that she portrays here in the fate of the houseboat to "keep moving" toward stasis.

As a tugboat pulls her upriver to the repair yard, the narrator celebrates an uncanny feeling that she is both in motion and staying still, both freeing herself of the past and carrying it with her in the telling.[21] Nin's momentum from stasis to movement and her narrator's movement in this story from convention to exile take place in the anticipatory status of an "always already" exiled; the shape of the progress is spiral rather than linear. "Houseboat" is informed and motivated throughout by the theme of alienation from which the author-as-analysand comes and to which she returns in the end.

As the tugboat pulls the narrator toward a temporary respite from the order to move on and the captain's wife serves lunch to the well-to-do, the narrator notices "with anxiety that the barge was taking in water. It had already seeped through the floor" (23). The narrator tries to pump it out but cannot "control the water" and calls for help to the captain, who laughs. "He said: 'We'll have to slow down a bit.' And he did" (23). Similar to the way that an analysand may get in over her head if she identifies with past trauma, rather than recognizing its transformation into narrative, the narrator has, perhaps, taken on too much. She has passed the point of no return, however. The narrator's plan to receive an exemption from the orders to move on is unsuccessful; "no law was made to permit" her return. While still at the repair yard, the narrator must accept that "the more pieces of tin and woods the boss nailed to the roof, the more rain came in." In a narrative gesture toward the return of the repressed, the one-eyed man comes back briefly also. He is immediately expelled, but another neighbor—who is aligned with law in a formal sense because "his brother was a deputy" (25)—is permitted to stay. The narrator is not aligned with law. The author must continue to realign herself *in terms of* law at the same time that she must resist, at times by enacting and working through it, a tendency to identify *with* the paternal signifier. "So passed the barge into exile" (25).

"Houseboat" represents an important stage in Nin's narrative recovery. It shows her willingness to continue to confront the pain of the past, without dissolving into that pain or maintaining a victim's status, while it also portrays a voyage analogous to that of an analysand in psychotherapy. As a story with formal boundaries, "Houseboat" also characterizes Nin's grappling with the paradox that fiction could provide both a stay against confusion and a permeable membrane between art and life. One of her messages to herself is that to define oneself as an artist rather than to be defined by social custom means, paradoxically, that one must accept the conditions of life and be willing to feel the "hard bone of pain in man" in order to take part in a process of transformation. This acceptance, however, need not be based on paternal or social law but rather on her own ability to instill a sense of order and law on her own terms even as she walks a thin line between inner and outer realms of experience. Another narrow border that "Houseboat" draws is between society's concepts of what she should be and the selfhood she would develop in the process of Modernist and feminist self-making. The next story continues Nin's portrayal of her progress toward reconciling these elements as it parallels her movement from individual self-absorption to social consciousness.

THE POLITICS OF OTHERING IN "THE MOUSE"

In its treatment of women's connection around the issue of a failed abortion and its resistance to established class boundaries, *Glass Bell*'s second story speaks multitudes about Nin's emerging social consciousness and her attempts to place the experience of her own abortion in terms of that emerging consciousness.[22]

It also shows Nin's concentration on the social inequities of women and on the bond between women even when they come from different backgrounds. By acknowledging difference, Nin avoids appropriating otherness as she deals again with the idea that the personal is often representative of the universal. "Mouse" portrays a character—a servant on the narrator's houseboat—who is, on one hand, the personification of timidity, and on the other, a wounded daughter with whom the narrator feels a connection.

As women, both she and the Mouse are wounded daughters, living in a kind of moral exile as a result of their potential or actual pregnancies. Mouse has conceived a child outside of wedlock and the law. Although she apparently cares for the man and plans to marry him someday when they have enough money, she attributes her pregnancy to fear. After all, she protests, it was the narrator's fault for being away from the houseboat one night and leaving the Mouse by herself so that she had to grant her boyfriend sex in order to entice him to stay with her on the boat. When the Mouse steals from her employer to finance the abortion she now needs, Nin depicts the Mouse as criminalized by economic, rather than moral, distinctions—as if to call into question the basis of such categories as "moral" and "immoral," "lawful" and "unlawful." By portraying these distinctions as somewhat arbitrary, Nin stakes a rationalizing position that substantiates her own tendency toward the border-eraser that is characteristic of those who have been wounded as children.

A tension between rationalization and confrontation reflects a cultural splitting around the issue of abortion. It also shows Nin's efforts to find the terms with which to accept a degree of responsibility for the ending of her own pregnancy in 1934, while confronting the social inequities by which women are made to bear the brunt of patriarchal law. "The Mouse" thematizes the relation between law and the real of the body in terms of Mouse's pregnancy and her body "language." The narrator, who has tried to put the Mouse at ease by assuring her that the servant will be treated according to the narrator's standards of fairness rather than by a separate standard for servants, discovers that "No gentleness could cross the border of the Mouse's fear, which was ingrained in the very skin of her thin legs" (*Glass Bell* 27). In other passages, the portrayal of psychological states as "borders" or "frontiers"—at which language stops—indicates how far the Mouse has been conditioned to speak conventionally while pushing past limiting signifiers in silence: "I could not cross the frontier of the Mouse's fear" (29), the narrator says, though she has assured the Mouse that she will not hold her responsible for accidents such as breaking china. The narrator somewhat naively bases her efforts to establish trust on the assumption that the two women are equal in their subjection to the possibility of pregnancy, the "accident" that occurs as a result of their being women. While their femaleness is not a sufficient cause for pregnancy, it is a necessary one, one that distinguishes between how they are held responsible for the effects of their sexuality and how their partners are not. Nin shows this social reality is exacerbated when class and gender coincide to increase one's degree of exile. Her narrator, somewhat indignant that the Mouse does not share her desire to bridge the gap between them, stands in contrast to the author as she attempts to reveal how class lines mirror those between genders. Nin problematizes the nature of boundaries themselves. That Nin's treatment of class and gender boundaries in "Mouse" anticipates her questioning of artistic and genre borders is borne out in her later work, where the feminine becomes less polarized than in her early work and comes to represent the ability to find structural form beyond fixed lines.

Both wounded daughters of a system in which a woman is held culpable for the effects of sexuality, but in which the penalty for such culpability is greater or lesser depending on class, the Mouse and the narrator must confront the terms of their respective exiles. The issue of class becomes paramount when the Mouse becomes ill after using ammonia to try to induce an abortion. The narrator calls a doctor. He, "a *grand blessé de guerre*" (30), is annoyed that he should have to cross the gangplank from land to houseboat and, by extension, to cross a line between his high social status and that of the vagabonds who live on the water: "I can't be taking care of people who live on houseboats" (30). He examines the Mouse but informs her that he will not come back. When she becomes feverish during the night and the narrator tries to summon another for help, the doctors' class consciousness heightens their reluctance to become involved with an abortion: "As soon as they heard what it was about they refused to come. Especially for a servant. That happened too often. They must learn, they said, not to get in trouble" (32).

The narrator does not deny that the terms of women's exile from patriarchal culture are harsher than are those of men's as a result of their sexual vulnerability.[23] Despite her empathy for the Mouse's situation, the narrator keeps her distance. Her ability to analyze how unevenly culture prescribes their exiles is one element that sets her apart from the Mouse. As Nin contests an elitist class bias in social definitions of women and resists social limitations by which a person of one economic class is viewed as inferior to one from another, she and the narrator also dissociate themselves from the Mouse's helplessness and failure to achieve solace through art. The Mouse, for instance, goes about the houseboat singing seven bars of one song over and over without completing the tune. Like an echo of the plaintive cries that emerge from the instrument of the deaf violinist in "Houseboat," Mouse's unfinished song thematizes the resistance to narrative closure that is characteristic of wounded daughters.

The Mouse's corresponding inability to find healing stems, at least in part, from economic lack: the Mouse's only book is a threadbare child's reader whose first ten pages she has read over and over again. With her seven bars of melody and ten pages of reading, the Mouse is truly trapped by the very repetition that

Nin acknowledges fighting within herself. By providing for dialogue between two asymmetric categories of narrative and narration, Nin mirrors her own distancing from artistic failure. Whereas the narrator stands back to comment that the Mouse can barely finish humming a tune, the author contends with a writer's block born of conflict and fear and transforms it into motivation to write. The contrast between the Mouse and the narrator emerges as that between a voiceless victim of patriarchy and the analysand or artist who articulates her desire despite and in relation to limitation. At the same time, Nin shows compassion for those who cannot overcome limitations to find artistic healing and avoids blaming the Mouse for her failure. The narrator reveals that the Mouse's class, gender, ignorance, and fear all together led to the event that forms, with those limitations, another bar of her social prison: "this pregnancy, accomplished in the dark, out of fear. A gesture of panic, that of a mouse falling into a trap" (34).

The narrator's frustration over the Mouse's complicity in her own subjugation is palpable even as she acts to intervene in that pattern of subjugation. The Mouse herself resists the narrator's attempts at class erasure and role reversal. As the Mouse holds onto her status as victim, the narrator perseveres in affirming their bond as women. The narrator challenges the hospital officials who badger her with unending questions and turn the Mouse away. When the narrator protests that the Mouse is losing blood and that this is no time to be asking for past addresses and places of employment, one official demands to know not only the answers but also why the Mouse has never stayed in a position longer than two years. He acts, says the narrator, as if "her not having stayed in the house longer were surprising, suspicious. As if she were the culprit." Then he turns his suspicion on the narrator: "'You performed the abortion perhaps?' asked the man turning to me" (33). Once again, the narrator's challenge exposes a connection between the economic realities of servitude and the blame-the-victim mentality of social judgment. After all, the narrator's indignation implies, it is subjection to others' plans for them that may prohibit employment stability among the servant class. Nin's narrating this challenge questions the penalizing of those who call into question the system itself.[24]

In the story's penultimate paragraph, the narrator is given an implicit warning that she will be held accountable for the illegal abortion if she persists in her challenge of patriarchal authority represented by the "man behind the desk." The story ends with both the narrator's poignant observation that the woman bleeding on the hospital bench means nothing to the hospital authorities, and the corresponding and contrastive sense that the Mouse and the trap into which she has fallen have a great deal of meaning for the narrator. Similarly, both characters are makers and bearers of meaning for Nin, whose progress toward narrative recovery includes a confrontation with and an effort to accept responsibility for her own abortion, at the same time as she stakes a position away from that of sexually wounded daughter of patriarchy.[25] "The Mouse" and *Under a Glass Bell* as a whole show Nin on an unstoppable course toward confronting both issues.

ANOTHER OTHERING:
"THE CHILD BORN OUT OF THE FOG"

Nin continues her exploration of the politics of othering in a story she added to *Glass Bell* after its first two printings. Like gender and class in "Mouse," race emerges as a basis for exclusion in "The Child Born Out of the Fog," the eleventh story in the collection and one Franklin and Schneider consider among the strongest of the additions (56). The story encompasses the themes of social ostracism and an accompanying sense of loss and exile in its portrayal of an interracial couple, Sarah and Don. Sarah is white, Don is apparently Peruvian Indian and included in Sarah's father's category of Negro. When they fall in love and have a child, Pony, they must live ever afterward with the reality that because of racism, the three of them face "a daily danger of loss" (85). One of several places in *Glass Bell* where Nin confronts loss in terms of motherhood, this story is a rare example in Nin's work of a child who remains with her parents. At one point, Pony appears to have been abandoned, but the reader soon learns that this is an illusion and that the real threat is the racism that appears in the story's title as a metaphorical fog. Nin builds this analogy to racism on the literal fog that surrounds the young couple in the park one evening as they are falling in love: "The fog isolated . . . ostracized them: two lost beings, one lost in the pain of betrayal by [another], the other in danger of death and ignominy and betrayal by all" (84).

Sarah and Don believe the racial mix they have given to their daughter has resulted in a perfect skin color. Referring to a fable that portrays race as a matter of "doneness" for a Baker-God, the parents muse that white people are like cookies baked to ashes and black people like cookies still not quite perfect. Their child, by contrast, has "come out . . . *à point*" (83). The ending reverberates with irony when Sarah and Don realize they cannot even carry their "perfect" child "safely through the streets." They must live through even short separations as if covered in a fog of anxiety. They are always afraid that when the fog lifts, such as when they come home from their errands or get off the bus, one of their loved ones will be gone, a victim of racial violence. The plight of Pony and other children like her, born as "exiles in their own land" to use a phrase from Martin Luther King, Jr., speaks to the theme of social marginalization to suggest that the dominant culture's "othering" of people of color is as deep a wound in cultural past as Nin's sense of abandonment by her father was in hers. Nin's realizing this shows her movement through her own labyrinth to an external sense of responsibility. Though autobiographical in that Don is clearly modeled after Gonzalo Moré, "The Child Born Out of the Fog" extends beyond authorial self-absorption to encompass a personal-as-political social view in its treatment of cultural and individual wounds that the author is now willing to mourn—rather than repress, deny, and suppress.

BACK TO THE HOUSE OF INCEST: "UNDER A GLASS BELL"

In "Under a Glass Bell," a section from an early version of *House of Incest* that appears as the third story in *Glass Bell*, Nin revisits the theme of stifling self-absorption. Its inclusion in the collection allows Nin to return to the themes of incestuous desire and psychological stasis as traps that preclude their captives' ability to take action. Sharing its character Jeanne and many of its themes with *House of Incest*, the story opens with a masterly description, in which Nin incorporates dream imagery with more realistic prose whose themes mirror Nin's own efforts to move beyond past attachments. The house itself is "stately" but on the verge of disappearance. It carries an air of secrets kept in its "heavily impregnated furniture" (*Glass Bell* 35). Throughout the story, the images of stasis abound: in Jeanne's detachment from her body (37), her own and her brothers' failed marriages (37), the presence of dust and absence of wind (40), a room of mirrors where "Woman [is] imprisoned in the stillness of mirrors washed only by jellied colors" (40), Jeanne's obsession with death imagery, and her re-creating her mother's neglect of her in her own maternal failures (36, 38). The broken guitar string at her feet in the story's final image (42) signifies another artistic and analytic failure. Those attached to the "dead letters" of the past are unable to achieve artistic freedom.

The story's thematic and structural basis is the border-erasure treated at length in *House of Incest*. The ironic phrases "No violence here, no tears, no great suffering, no shouting, no destruction" (36) describe the space that ends at the transparent borders of the narrative, which Nin portrays with the notion of a glass bell. According to Bair, the term "glass bell" refers to "the gardening apparatus French farmers use to keep delicate plants safe from predators or frost" (Bair 289).[26] It is an appropriate image for referring to Nin's use of fiction to provide permeable, but structuring, boundaries through which to observe an incestuous realm. As children, incest victims themselves often live within a kind of glass bell, trapped in a situation from which they have little hope of escaping but able to see the danger that lies just beyond a set of rigid and arbitrary parental rules.

By putting the trauma itself—as well as the breakdown of boundaries between identifications, language, and the real effects of trauma—under a fictional glass container for observation and protection, Nin reshapes material from *House of Incest* to attain a greater distance from it. Instead of being trapped inside a structure designed by others, she grants herself the analytic and artistic freedom to view the past from a position of safety. From her position outside the glass bell of her narrative, she can experience events doubly, from both inside and outside, in order to live more in keeping with her own goals than she could if restricted to one position or the other. Such *"dédoublement,"* as she describes it in *Fire* (397, 409), grants her the status of "creator pulling strings, . . . a me which *plots* without plotting, a driving impulse of which I am aware, which makes me instinctively live my life and create it" (*Fire* 387). She also distances herself from the illusion that a static absence of emotion would offer the freedom she seeks. Rather, it can lead only to death. While the character Jeanne remains trapped in a "room of mirrors" (*Glass Bell* 40) and becomes frustrated by the process of watching herself at such a close distance that she cannot gain perspective, the author chooses a freedom that includes suffering. She rejects a death of the emotions that would grant only an illusory safety and leave her imprisoned within a realm of eternal wounding.

Besides portraying incestuous attachments as psychologically dangerous, this story portrays socially constructed male privilege as the furniture of a suffused sexuality, protecting gender and class hierarchies and "full of debonair assertion like [that] of the ancient men of the family in their white stockings" (35). Everything in the house contributes to the sense that there is more going on behind the scenes than meets the eye and that a great deal of money and energy have been invested in its suppression to maintain the illusion of propriety. In a narrative diversion, Nin uses a play on words to deconstruct the pretensions of authoritarians, who by their natures uphold an illusion of privilege and power.

Nin's idea that the ego is itself a covering provides the basis for her refutation of the kind of male privilege that turns a blind eye toward incest: when the first-person narrator sends Jeanne romantic prints, which are delivered on her breakfast tray, Jeanne believes them to have been sent by a suitor, "the Prince," with whom she has become disenchanted because of the ordinariness of his language. Because they depict a series of courtship scenes between lovers, Jeanne thinks the Persian prints are the Prince's token of love. When she visits him, however, she realizes that the prints could not have come from him because he is, in fact, still unable to articulate his desire for her. In response, she returns to her own garden where she is "at ease" kissing her brother's shadow (40). The narrator's comical play on the homonyms "prince" and "prints" highlights the inability of language to be what it signifies and underlines the narrative self-questioning whereby Nin embraces the notion of using imaginative and playful language in the service of healing. She rejects the opposite use of language—to uphold identification with illusion of autonomy—and makes fun of the static fixity that falsely equates "the prince" with "the prints" and that allows one to believe that one *is* what one says.

That the prints come not from a suitor but from the narrator herself points to Nin's presence in the text as an alternative authority figure. Rather than deriving her authority from cultural systems of disavowal, the narrator draws on Nin's authoring to send a message to Jeanne about the nature of repressive systems. Like the human ego that Nin depicts as a facade comprised of an illusory autonomy, the appearance of normalcy reigns in this narrative realm as its title establishes its existence *as* narrative. Similarly, the writing-as-analysis process in which Nin is engaged establishes the ego as fiction, not to disempower but to allow her an artistic control over her identificatory priorities in the same way that a writer's role grants a certain degree of choice. Acknowledging narrativity is also to acknowledge limitations in the same way a writer chooses to work within the limitations of form and language. Again, Nin draws on the formal limits of fiction to buy herself freedom without relinquishing altogether her fondness for fluidity.

NEGATIVE MODELS IN "THE MOHICAN" AND NIN'S SURREALIST STORY

With the fourth and fifth stories of the collection, "The Mohican," and *"Je suis le plus malade des surréalistes,"* Nin continues to explore the themes of stasis versus temporality. She reiterates the self-reflective theme of the futility of obsession and psychological entrapment as if, again, to establish action and movement as desirable ends for herself, worth pursuing in spite of the suffering such a pursuit entails because of her tendencies toward neurosis and despair. The title character of "The Mohican" is an astrology aficionado whose interest in galactic calamities occludes his internal fissures. Like the Mouse and Jeanne, the Mohican is trapped; he is weighed down by memories, "preoccupied with the fear of what might happen if the sun burst" (*Glass Bell* 43). Like someone inside a glass bell looking out at an all too visible predator, he has "intolerably open eyes" with which to look at the "depths of his past" (43). Repeating her ego-as-covering theme, Nin portrays the Mohican as having "armature of the aristocrat." Something stands between him and "all he wanted to touch and feel" (44). He carries "people up and around always at the same mathematical distance" and provides an illusion of scientific truth while remaining unable to "interpret his own horoscope" (47).[27] He talks "like a peeper" at a distance from himself and from the events he is telling (45).

Nin's narrative begins to fail when she editorializes overmuch in "The Mohican" and *"Je suis le plus malade des surréalistes."* Instead of letting the text condemn the protagonists' self-absorption, Nin lays negative upon negative so that the characters become servants of her own distaste rather than rounded figures. A similar narrative failure would plague parts of Nin's later "continuous novel," *Cities of the Interior.* As expressions of Nin's own narrative recovery, however, these short stories and the later novels accomplish Nin's need to explore *in fiction* certain relationships with others that have affected her in her actual life. The short stories in particular show Nin's continued movement from the self-absorption of her earlier work to a political and social consciousness. For instance, the Mohican seems less a character than a theoretical representation of what Nin does not want to be (obsessed with formulaic expressions about life). Still, the story's ending with the coming of war and the Mohican's arrest by the Nazis for being a "celestial saboteur" ironizes condemnation. In doing so, it also calls into question the bases for the particularly horrifying "othering" engaged in by the Nazis.

It is not irrelevant that Nin's "surrealist" story, which depicts the narrator's failed sexual encounter with a theoretical inventor named Savonarola, opens with a comparison of his gaze to that of book-burners in the Middle Ages. The opening paragraph concludes: "Between us there was this holocaust burning, in his eyes the inquisitor's condemnation of all pleasure" (48), a statement that recalls the previous story's theme of stasis and obsession. The opening paragraph also draws a connection between this theme and many kinds of identificatory fixity, such as the murderous form of nationalism employed by the Hitler regime. Bair and others have criticized Nin for seeming oblivious to the war in Europe as she pursued her own goals from a safe distance (Bair 245, 246, 308). However, the horrific nature of the Holocaust finds palpable expression in these stories and in Nin's continuing attempts to formulate an alternative paradigm to the ego dramas she believed were at the heart of all wars. In the same way that Nin's response to the trauma of her personal life lies most powerfully between the lines of what she could bring herself to express, her reaction to the Holocaust resonates in the ways she imbedded her horror behind a protective narrative membrane.

Savonarola's crossing of boundaries established by social convention provides a thematic link between the surrealist's embracing of the absolute and a dangerous crossing of boundaries that leads to explosion. The irony of the passage contrasts Nin's own efforts to defy convention in her lifestyle and her writing with her theorizing the need for clear boundaries. Throughout the collection, she plays out her ambivalence toward the issue of respecting limits, similar to the way that in "The Mouse" and in the later story "Birth" she explores class and gender hierarchies as based on inappropriate boundaries and explores medical rigidity as a defensive reaction against female sexuality. On the other hand, in stories such as "Under a Glass Bell," Nin's emphasis seems to lean toward, rather than away from, the need for clear boundaries such as those between siblings.

These emphases are not conflictual, however. In each case, the boundaries that society has established for the purpose of maintaining existing hierarchies such as male privilege and class structure operate through an equation of phallus with power. The boundaries she establishes for the purpose of healing operate through a recognition that narratives and egos are analogous. Nin's work distinguishes between abusive limits and limits abuse. Throughout her work from the 1940s onward, she stresses that the ability to make these distinctions is paramount to the artistic perspective she believed could lead to ethical human relations. In depicting the Mohican, for instance, as one who cannot "distinguish between potentiality and fulfillment, between the dream and the actuality" (47), Nin condemns the failure to make distinctions.[28]

TRANSFORMATION AND FRAGMENTATION IN "RAGTIME"

"Ragtime" is the story in the collection cited most often by critics as the piece that illustrates Nin's aesthetic theory.[29] It is also the story that most energetically embraces nonwholeness and celebrates the creative potential of life's fragmentary elements. In "Ragtime," a ragpicker seeks bits and pieces of discarded items for their reconstructive value, preferring their partiality to wholeness because partial objects have transformative potential. Truly imaginative and fictional in a way that the preceding stories (with perhaps the exception of "Houseboat") are not, "Ragtime" (then spelled "Rag Time") was among the stories especially praised by Wilson. An unidentified female first-person narrator tells the story, viewing a ragpicker's meanderings as he progresses with his sack from within the city to its edge. With his swollen bag, he is symbolically pregnant. He is also delighted with every scrap of fabric, "twisted piece of pipe," or "basket without a handle" (*Glass Bell* 59) that he finds. He especially likes the faceless pocket watch that he presents to an unknown woman, whom he tells that "since its face is blank they will never know the time" (60).

Capturing the timelessness of a dream state or of the unconscious, the story presents a kind of freeze-frame view of life lived on the edge of convention, by people who have fallen through the cracks of a society that does not care about them and whose real-life details become transformed into artistic potentialities.[30] Their environment is full of "Plain earth trodden dead. Shacks of smoke-stained wood from demolished buildings" (59). They have "Rags for beds. Rags for chairs. Rags for tables" (59). Nevertheless, the transformational potential exists as a matter of perspective: "The brats sitting in the mud . . . trying to make an old shoe float like a boat" (59) represent not an image of poverty and hopelessness but the imaginative condensation of several Nin motifs, including that of the grounded ship. Contrary to its static signification for

Lillian in *Seduction of the Minotaur,* for instance, the ship attains mobility through the fantasies of children, whose status as "brats" also shifts to one of artistry rather than of burden and responsibility. The narrator herself is transformed when she buys from the ragpicker a "basket without a bottom" and, wondering if she is complete herself, takes off her shoe to find a blue rag glued to her sole. Suddenly, she is narrating from "a hill of corks perfumed by the smell of wine" (60). She is allowed to traverse a path to its end and finds there a blue dress that has somehow been retrieved from her teenage years. "I try to put it on and come out the other side. I cannot stay inside of it," she laments in a tone of discovery tinged with sadness: "Where are all the other things . . . I thought dead? . . . Can't one throw anything away forever?" (60).

With this last question, the ragpicker and his companions sing a "serpentine song" about the transmutation of the old into the new. It is an appropriate near-ending to a story thematically central to a book that signifies a trajectory from an old and universal exile to the newness of rebirth. The paradox that rebirth leaves one exiled in another way appears as one of the elements of transforming potential. The story ends as the narrator falls asleep and is placed inside a bag, one fragment of potentiality in the world of the ragpicker-as-artist and a representation of its author's attempt to transform a past wounding into something of value through art. Images of fragmentation and splitting are so common in Nin's fiction that their repetition eventually begins to wear on many readers. In "Ragtime," however, where shards of broken lives and fragments of lost memories receive new life in a musically rhythmic narrative, readers may find Nin at the pinnacle of her abilities, combining craft with artistic sensibility in a way that supports her narrative recovery.

OUT OF AND INTO THE LABYRINTH

Several selections from *Under a Glass Bell* portray Nin at a new stage of her career, pursuing themes of exile, rebirth, and the voyage to awareness with increased artistic control. Other stories seem merely repetitious, continuations of other stories, or for those readers who have read it first, the *Diary.* Just as this collection's "Under a Glass Bell" appears as a retelling of *House of Incest,* the next two stories in the standard edition of *Glass Bell*—"The Labyrinth" and "Through the Streets of My Own Labyrinth"—are coterminous.

Despite their repetition of theme and subject, however, both labyrinth stories contain significant passages that are valuable either as poetic condensations of larger themes or as signposts pointing to the rebirth that is to come at the end of the collection. As in much of Nin's other work, the labyrinth represents her own journey of self-exploration through her diary and her psychoanalysis. Here, the narrator reports that she was "eleven years old when [she] walked into the labyrinth of [her] diary" (*Glass Bell* 63). Repeating the story that she told from childhood about the origins of her diary-writing habit, Nin is fictionalizing here only to the extent that she fictionalized the original account (Bair 29–30). Jason, following Scholar, treats the connection between the accounts as important to a full understanding of the work's resonance. Scholar, he writes, "finds a genuine passion in Nin's meditation on her relationship to the Diary and in her development of the labyrinth metaphor . . . [and] in [Nin's] revealing both the lure and costs of autobiographical writing" (Jason 51).

Motivated to retrace her steps into the past through the diary, the narrator writes that she "did not count the turns, the chess moves, the meditated displacements, the obsessional repetitions" (*Glass Bell* 63). As a result, she eventually loses track of the steps although she retains a sense that she must experience everything a "second time" before moving forward into the future through a process that in *Fire* she calls *dédoublement* (397, 409): "If I were forced to go on, unknowing, blind, everything would be lost" (*Glass Bell* 63). Not knowing *why* she must find her origins but feeling "an anguish over something lost," the narrator travels backward in time, becoming lost upon "a stairway of words" and wondering why she has "not numbered the pages" to guide her way back (64). She becomes stuck in a spider web and sinks into "a labyrinth of silence" (65), an image reminiscent of both Nin's early shyness (*A Woman Speaks* 80) and the in-between ether-induced state of consciousness Nin experiences during the birth scene described later. Several images, such as "stillborn desires" and a cave tunnel that transforms into a "wooden, fur-lined crib, swinging" (*Glass Bell* 65–66), suggest that, as she arranges the stories in *Glass Bell,* she is making her way toward acknowledging the painful effects of her 1934 abortion. After several more lines of dreamlike images that convey a merging of environment and body, the narrator expresses her fear that she "might lose [her] voice forever" if she does not return to a verbal realm (65).

Mirroring the way Nin forced herself to write fiction, the narrator tries to retrieve lost words from memory by forcing her mouth to move. Eventually, the narrator awakes from the series of surrealist images when she hears the "sound of paper unrolling" (67). She finds herself walking upon the pages of her own diary. Each unrolling page of paper forms a street beneath her feet. She becomes lost in her past confessions of "acts unveiled only in the diary" and hears a recurring "cry of solitude" (67). A cave opens to reveal on its rim the figure of an eleven-year-old girl "carrying the diary in a little basket" (67). The image combines the retrospective sense of a past recovered through writing. Writing this past has created a future.

The next story, "Through the Streets of My Own Labyrinth" finds the same narrator revisiting scenes in Cadiz that she saw as a young girl on her way to America with her mother and described in her diary. This former child is nowhere to be found, for the "last vestiges of [her] past [are now] lost in the ancient city of Fez." Its "tortuous streets, its silences, secrecies, its labyrinths and its covered faces" remind her nevertheless of her own life. In a passage that underscores a key issue in Nin's own quest for freedom from the effects of past trauma, the narrator draws a sense of relief from the environment, finding that "the little demon" that has haunted her for twenty years has been quieted, here, in this city with "sicknesses one could touch and name and see, visible sicknesses, leprosy and syphilis" (68).

Like the wounded child shamed into silence by a dysfunctional or abusive family, who seeks a way out of that imprisoning silence later, the narrator finds something to celebrate in the open embracing of even death and decay. Even failures and madness can be displayed openly here, where "little donkeys bleeding from maltreatment" represent how the burdens of the past can be taken to the marketplace: "Pain is nothing, pain is nothing here; . . . The little donkey—my diary burdened with my past—with small faltering steps is walking to the market" (69). The two-page narrative ends without closure in form or content as Nin portrays herself as a sorry, mistreated little donkey, plodding along, wounds and all, trying to take her goods to the place where they can be displayed for public consumption. The *Diary* finally made available to the public beginning in 1966 would reveal, between the lines, the places where its author was "bleeding from maltreatment." Its "small faltering steps" are still discernable. Nowhere, despite Nin's belief in formal constraints, is the line between art and life less rigid.

STORIES OF THE GAZE: "THE ALL-SEEING," "THE EYE'S JOURNEY," AND "HEJDA"

In the next two stories, "The All-Seeing" and "The Eye's Journey," Nin introduces a narrative dynamic that is dominant also in her erotica, that of the gaze as constructing a power relation between the seer and the seen.[31] The first of these stories presents its protagonist from both positions, returning him in the end to the role of gazer. That position, while normally associated with the more powerful role, leaves him isolated in an obsessional realm. Nin's characterization of gender that is evident in the second volume of her *Diary* also finds expression here, where a classically obsessional character takes the "masculine" role of the looker, reducing a loved other to an image and rejecting all real women. He tells the narrator that she is the mirror in which he can see his own freedom. The second of the two stories continues to explore, in terms of the gaze motif, the oscillation that is so common in Nin's works between subject and object positions. In "The Eye's Journey," the protagonist ends up outside the dichotomy between subject and object positions. A later story in *Glass Bell* that also develops the gaze motif is "Hejda," whose protagonist has been repressed and censored to such an extent that she is not aware of her need to mourn. Her social exclusion on the basis of gender leaves her seeking, from behind a kind of cultural veil, recognition in the gazes of others.[32]

The first sentence of "The All-Seeing" introduces the gaze motif: "When I rang his bell . . . I knew he could see me through a little glass eye in his door [but] I could not see him" (*Glass Bell* 70). The story of a sensitive and perceptive man, Jean, whose mother destroyed his first passion years ago by scorning as unmanly his desire to study violin, "The All-Seeing" in its opening twice switches narrative points of view. It moves from the introductory image of Jean to a description of the hallway, and then, in its third sentence, to the narrator's impression of Jean's eyes: they "light up" the hallway "like the aurora borealis, . . . an immense and deep phenomenon of light like the *eye* of the universe" (70).

In this story, Nin also explores the boundaries theme so important to her work. Whereas her own response was to lean away from all fixity and to suffer from a lack of clear identificatory boundaries, Jean inscribes formal boundaries to an extreme, effectively walling out any possibility of remembering and thus mourning the past. He says that whereas other people are "sewn together . . . with a space in between the stitches for breathing" (76), he is "sewn too tightly" and feels he is suffocating. His rigidities are evident in his use of language. For though Jean seems soft and porous before he has spoken, "when he began to talk . . . one saw how chained he was to his obsessions" (73).

Keenly aware of subjective splits and aware that his dream of perfection is unattainable, Jean is lonely. He turns "every woman into a mirage," then laments "the absence of warmth and humanity" of those mirages he has created (74). Yet he is unable to accept the fluidity of life or the imperfection of a real woman and falls in love with one of Nin's symbols of the absolute, "the Unknown Woman of the Seine." Believing that "In death alone there is no betrayal and no loss" (74), Jean carries in his mind a picture of the plaster cast that the morticians, in order to preserve her beauty, had made of the Unknown Woman's face. His illusion only intensifies his loneliness, for, as the narrator implies, the love of a mirage is no love at all. This realization forms the bedrock idea in Nin's quest to define herself for herself rather than to seek others' approval and reinforcement of her projected self-myth, which she recognizes as a mirage.

It is no wonder the narrator tells Jean that he must eventually accept his own body and the conditions of a human life. As an artist, the narrator engages a paradoxical pleasure in a state of being that is based in corporal experience even as it is not identified *with* that experience. As Nin participates in the psychoanalytic goal of accepting what is limiting in human experience and reformulating a relation *to* that limitation so that it is not so debilitating, the narrator tells Jean that he must accept suffering in order to be free (76). Jean's penultimate statement is that, although he is indeed in a prison, the narrator is also in a prison of another kind, for she is a "voluntary prisoner who will not walk out *alone*" (77). He implies that she cannot be free as long as she retains compassion for those behind her. A reflection of Nin's own self-image, this portrayal speaks to one of Nin's reasons for entering analysis with Dr. Jaeger, to explore her need to care for others more than for herself and her own art. In "The All-Seeing," however, Nin justifies her need of others as a quality that distinguishes her from Jean.

"The Eye's Journey" continues to explore the relation of narrative perspective to power structures and neurosis. Its protagonist, Hans, is an avant-garde artist who lives in a netherworld of weblike light and color. Like the ragpicker of the earlier story, Hans collects "lost fragments of irretrievable worlds" (78). Unlike the ragpicker, however, Hans is rooted to an atmosphere of stagnation and stillborn images, as if a storm hovers constantly over his consciousness, threatening to explode into lightning. The image points again to an often recurring theme in Nin's work: a catastrophic event to which the rest of one's life continues to make reference. In Hans's case, a small eye appears again and again in his paintings to tell its story as his signature: "The small fixed eye in the corner of the painting was hypnotized with terror. A world about to vanish always, on the brink of absolute catastrophe" (78). The exploration into victim and victimizer roles that follows provides a related and poignant inquiry into the nature of cruelty.

Nin provides an implicit psychological explanation for Hans's sadism. When a bout of drunkenness, paranoia, and claustrophobia leads to his commitment to what is apparently a psychiatric hospital, Hans begins to muse about his regrets. His strongest misgiving is that he will miss seeing a snake at the zoo being fed with a terrorized live mouse. The snake, he believes, enjoys the mouse's fear and prolongs it by watching, "enjoying the certainty" (80). Hans identifies with the image, for he believes that he is awaiting his own devouring by another. He knows that his paintings, as well, will be consumed. Hans's art, rather than being transformative, becomes a formal defense against a catastrophe always already imploding in his life as he quests for even the kind of certainty that the snake's relation to the mouse-as-victim ensures. Rather than mourn the loss of the belief that he can be the imaginary object of Other desire, Hans, as opposed to Nin, refuses to mourn his losses and thus remains in pain.

Another story in which Nin explores the gaze motif is "Hejda." The penultimate story in the standard Swallow edition of *Glass Bell*, it was originally included as part of *This Hunger* (1945). Beginning with the statement "The unveiling of women is a delicate matter . . . [that] will not happen overnight" (*Glass Bell* 86), "Hejda" is especially interesting in the context of Nin's exploration of gender theories. In particular, the story shows Nin linking the physical and social oppression of women to a censoring of their language. This censorship operates, the story implies, through a dynamic parallel to that by which the human ego constructs stories to repress the unconscious. For Nin, creative transformation becomes possible only when one accepts the fictional nature of the self. This was a liberating idea for her, undergirding her idea that cultural change can occur through individuals who come to terms with the reality lying beyond cultural facades. Hejda, a seventeen-year-old Oriental woman, represents one who tries without ultimate success to do so.

Even after Hejda is able to shed her veils and mantles, her history of censorship and inarticulateness results in her "still convey[ing] the impression of restraint" (87). Her manner is as that of one wearing an invisible veil, behind which her eyes look outward for approval. Hejda represents one whose oppression mirrors repression, and thus she is barred from awareness of what is to be mourned, an exclusion that leaves her, from behind a kind of cultural veil, seeking the gazes of others. A potential change looms on Hejda's horizon when she meets a timid Rumanian painter, Molnar, whose timidity and air of secrecy indicate to her that he also lives an interior life. Love's transformative potential remains unrealized when Molnar tries to suppress her further, making her hide her breasts and leading her to feel ashamed of her feminine body. Hejda feels oppressed and compressed, but at the same time begins to find an outlet in caring for Molnar and for his art. Although she also paints, "Her small canvases look childlike standing beside his" large paintings. Believing she can attain a kind of maternal freedom by doing so, Hejda slowly begins to put more energy into promoting his art than into creating her own (91). This detail once again represents one of the most intense conflicts Nin experienced, that between her nurturing of others' artistry and her being an artist herself.

Hejda eventually achieves freedom from Molnar's constraints. He leaves her after an illness prevents her from promoting his work and they both fall into poverty. Hejda's newfound freedom anticipates Nin's eventual ability to "speak" as an artist. Nin's birth into this freedom, however, depends on her avoiding the trap she portrays Hejda falling into: Hejda begins to take the value of her unleashed language as being identical to her own value. She also becomes competitive, enacting one of Nin's great fears about creativity. Hejda engages in rivalry with other women as well as with the past, a competition that leads her back into the limitations of that past. With this ending, Nin imbues her story with a warning about the dangers of the ego's keeping fantasy and desire repressed. In addition, while she seeks to define her own role as a female artist working at odds with patriarchy, she emphasizes the possible dangers to be encountered by a women's emancipation movement that fails to recognize the linguistic nature of cultural repression long reinforced through historical construction. For Nin, women's freedom, like all cultural change including attitudes toward war and violence, must start with a personal journey.

"BIRTH" INTO ART AND EXILE

In its treatment of psychological and emotional exile, *Under a Glass Bell* moves structurally and thematically toward its last story, "Birth." Among the best in Nin's repertoire, this story signifies the first instance, according to Bair, in which Nin successfully used the diary as a basis for fiction. "While readers of the birth story praised the harsh reality of her real-life suffering," however, critics of the story as it was published in 1937 "ignored her genuine ability to re-create the event in fiction" (Bair 234). Nin's account of the story in the un-expurgated *Fire* indicates that she wrote the story separately from the rest of the diary and inserted much of it later (*Fire* 394–95). This accounts for Wendy Dubow's objection, before the publication of *Fire*, that the stillbirth story that appears in the *Diary* exists as a "set piece" whose emotional efficacy is lost through its encapsulation in its own section and the lack of reference to the loss in any other place in the volume ("Elusive Text" 33).

In the short story, this formal constraint is a strength rather than a weakness. For many readers, "Birth" contains an emotional intensity that carries its author and its readers beyond the consideration of the theme that Scholar finds most significant: "a woman's struggle to give birth to her own identity" (Scholar 101) without man's help (Jason 50). In "Birth," writes Erica Jong, Nin "delivered herself as an artist" as well as repudiated "with one act . . . her mother, her father, Henry, Hugo, Rank and all the men who want to possess her" ("Donna Juana's Triumph" 3). Her struggle culminated in the writing and printing of *Under a Glass Bell* by her own hands and almost single-handedly while continuing to mourn the loss of Rank, of her home in France, and of the world's peace. The most significant loss Nin mourned with *Under a Glass Bell* was the baby and the parts of herself that she had aborted. The part of her that "did not want to push out the child" (*Glass Bell* 96) lost its battle to the part that did.

Read without knowledge that the stillbirth the story describes was actually an abortion, "Birth" stands on its own as the account of a first-person narrator whose efforts to deliver a six-month-old fetus she has already been told is dead are hindered by her own grief and resistance to giving up the part of herself the child represents. She also resists the demands of an authoritative and time-pressed doctor whose admiration of her womanly charms turns to hostility when her body's rhythms do not conform to his schedule. "He wants to interfere with his instruments," the mother thinks, "while I struggle with nature, with myself, with my child and with the meaning I put into it all, with my desire to give and to hold, to keep and to lose, to live and to die" (99). When, after several hours of pain and exhaustion, the narrator begins drumming on her belly in a kind of intuitive, primitive ritual, the doctor and nurses stand amazed and watch while she delivers the child's dead body. They protest when she demands that they show her the baby, but she insists. When they hold it up, she sees that "it is a little girl . . . perfectly made, and all glistening with the waters of the womb" (101). This is the ending image, at least in this version of the story. A mother's grief over the stillborn child resonates with the final view of a small, glistening girl baby who will never reach her potential.[33]

When read within the larger context of its emergence not only in Volume 1 of the *Diary* (1966) but also in its unexpurgated retelling in *Incest: From "A Journal of Love"* (1992), "Birth" carries an increased emotional impact for many readers, including, for some, a sense of betrayal by Nin's withholding the fact that the "stillbirth" was really an abortion.[34] For others, the accounts in expurgated and unexpurgated versions of the diary work together to signify that Nin's loss, whether stillbirth or abortion, was a devastating loss. In addition, the disparity between the two versions of the stillbirth experience functions as a performative element of one of Nin's dominant themes—that the ego is itself a fiction whose construction is analogous to and, in this case, overlapping of the process of writing or storytelling. Nin's own relation to literary form is implicated in the gaps between her fictional and diary versions of this story. As hard as she tried to draw a clear line between art and life, the line she drew would eventually give way. Later, she would embrace diary writing as the only literary form capable of capturing life's essence. In the meantime, especially in "Birth" and the fiction to follow, Nin achieved a way to mourn her losses within the safe realm of fiction.

CONCLUSION

The stories collected in *Under a Glass Bell* represent a stage in Nin's narrative recovery in which she sought to reconcile a number of disparate elements in her life, mourning her emotional and physical exile through both writing and analysis as she recorded and self-published her responses to cultural and personal upheaval. In achieving a clearer prose style than in her earlier fiction, Nin demonstrates she had achieved a healthy distance from the self-absorption portrayed in *Winter of Artifice*. As its stories move from alienation, through despair, to acceptance of the terms under which one is inevitably exiled, *Under a Glass Bell* also embodies a connection that Nin was beginning to build between individual and collective responsibility.

In *Glass Bell*, Nin asserts her need to use art in keeping with her feminist and psychoanalytic goals as she redefined herself in relation to a limiting signifier for protective boundaries and law. Her short-lived but efficacious analysis with Martha Jaeger had led Nin into exploring the related issues of her mother and the metaphorical motherhood she sought. She would not easily resolve these issues. In addition to the biological children whose lives she curtailed through abortion, her "children" were her own art and other artists, siblings often in conflict. Nin's efforts to further characterize creativity in terms of gender would grow out of her efforts to come to terms with her internal contention around this issue, as would several repetitive but ultimately dynamic characterizations in her next fictional work, a five-volume "continuous novel" published from 1946 to 1961. Above all, *Under a Glass Bell* shows Nin mourning the past by beginning to confront her own responsibility for the ways she had continued to suffer.

4

Repetition and Resistance in *Ladders to Fire*, *Children of the Albatross*, and *The Four-Chambered Heart*

The chronological order of [Nin's] work . . . suggests a developmental pattern which reinforces the theme and structure of the individual works. From her first creative work in 1936 to the most recently published novel, 1964, there is a steady progression from subjectivity to objectivity both on the part of the narrator in the novel and in Nin's own handling of her materials. That such a plan was more intentional than accidental is indicated by her "Preface" to the first edition of Under a Glass Bell.

—Evelyn J. Hinz

A NEARLY TWENTY-YEAR CAREER as novelist followed Nin's publication of *Under a Glass Bell* in 1944. During the first half of this period, Nin's resistance to the analytic process of letting go left her repeating herself in a series of novels whose greatest weaknesses as literature are also their greatest strengths. In particular, Nin's use of repetition provides insights into a number of psychological principles: the psychoanalytic notion of transference, the physical entwining of language with memory, and the nature of resistance itself. Nin's novelist stage began with a self-published work entitled *This Hunger* (1945) and culminated in her last novel, *Collages* (1964). Between these works, Nin would write her "continuous novel," *Cities of the Interior*.[1]

In this chapter I show how the first and third novels in this series reflect

Nin's conflict between artistry and her interpretation of womanhood as a kind of metaphorical mothering. Ultimately, the continuous novel offered a partial resolution of the conflict as she worked toward coming to terms with her desire *on her own terms*. In the process of writing out her pain, Nin finally freed herself to a significant extent from some of the suffering that had plagued her for much of her life. She also grew as an artist. The first installment in the "continuous novel," *Ladders to Fire* (1946), and the second installment, *Children of the Albatross* (1947), combine Nin's keen psychological insights with pages of prose that, according to critics, is often obscure, abstract, confusing, or embarrassingly self-identifying.[2] Between the second and third novels, however, something changes. The result is that by the end of the third novel, *The Four-Chambered Heart* (1950), Nin's fiction reflects a transformation in her own movement out of analytic impasse toward the self-acceptance and embracing of individual desire that characterizes her later years.

This transformation is reflected in Nin's personal life as well as in her relationship with her nonfictional writing. In 1947, Nin met Rupert Pole, the man who would become her primary partner for the rest of her life. By that time Nin's dependence on the diary, which she had tried intermittently for years to give up because it represented to her an attachment to her father and to pain, had lessened. Nin would change her mind, of course, about the diary's link to neurosis. She believed at the end of her life that the *Diary* was her greatest artistic achievement, one whose fluid genre boundaries and style could become part of a new body of literature sorely needed in American letters.[3]

Still, from the late 1940s, the "diary" she kept was different in kind from its predecessor. Rather than pages and pages per day of coherent prose, her diary became a scrapbook of letters, notes, itineraries, appointments, and reviews (Bair 328). Either Nin had successfully written herself out of dependence on diary writing by writing fiction or, at the very least, she had successfully channeled her writing-as-therapy needs into fiction, which at the time she considered more in keeping with artistic goals of discipline and form.

"THIS IS NOT THE PLACE; HE IS NOT THE ONE": SOMETHING OF ONE IN *LADDERS TO FIRE*

After the publication of *Ladders* in the United States, Nin's reputation grew among college students and other young people, many of them artists who found "something in her writing that mature critics either could not see or did not value" (Bair 318). Years later, when *Ladders* was published in France, it received a number of negative reviews there as well, predictably by male critics who found Nin's female characters lacking and their psychological quests annoying. "With a certain degree of intuitive accuracy," writes Bair, Nin asserted that male critics were threatened by her emphasis on the unconscious and on women's search for a way to create their own patterns (Bair 465).

The theme of women's self-authorship is evident in a comforting bit of feedback she had received earlier from Tom Paine, an editor at Avon Books who had bought for publication the paperback rights to her novel *A Spy in the House of Love*. When Nin asked him, in 1959, why her work was receiving so much less favorable attention than that of her friend Lawrence Durrell, Paine told her that, whereas Durrell's novels provide brief glimpses of the human unconscious, softened by pages of more conventional prose, hers exposed the unconscious in a way that was too pure and direct for comfort. Paine also told her that she was ahead of her time and that it was her being a woman that was a problem for male critics (Bair 431).

As this anecdote suggests, gender is among the important motifs in *Ladders to Fire* (1946), a motif interwoven with the psychoanalytic insights expressed in the novel and its function as part of the process of writing-as-analysis in which Nin was engaged. From its opening sentence, "Lillian was always in a state of fermentation" (7) to its closing image of Djuna being whisked away to the "dream of a Party that she could never attend" (152), *Ladders to Fire* provides a literary enactment of its author's need to continue the confrontation with the past that is required by the psychoanalytic process. Mourning past traumas in order to take leave of them—and reconstructing their significance in a way more congruent with her own desire than as established by a patriarchal system of signification—continued as her goals. The difference between *Ladders* and Nin's early works is the difference between description and embodiment. Her prose poem, for instance, and several stories in *Glass Bell* link form and content by replicating the fluid, organic form of the unconscious in prose seeking to describe that unconscious. By contrast, the first volume of *Cities of the Interior* takes a step toward integrating the relation of form to content in the work's structure as well as toward providing a wider context of analysis, in which the thematic treatment of the unconscious can be understood.

Ladders to Fire advances several themes: the role of language in upholding images of the self, the role of gender in relation to and as self-image, and the role of art as medium through which one can access and accept the chaos at the core of consciousness in order to transform anxiety into creativity. The first, eighty-one-page section of *Ladders*, a part entitled "This Hunger," develops the first two of these themes.[4] The second section, "The Bread and the Wafer," emphasizes the transformational properties of language. As a whole, the book shows a connection between these elements and Nin's theories about the relations of Modern art to anxiety, war, and identity in the twentieth century, particularly in terms of the fragmentation and the psychological splitting that characterizes many of her protagonists. Even as her main emphasis is on the personal, Nin strengthens *Under a Glass Bell*'s theme of social responsibility in *Ladders to Fire* by linking individual accountability with compassion for others.

In "This Hunger" both of Nin's alter egos, Lillian and Djuna, suffer from an inner attachment to a turmoil they can feel but cannot name. Lillian suffers from the "nameless anxiety" that Nin describes in the fourth volume of the *Diary* (4: 166), an overwhelming despair that hits her at unexpected moments—even when no external cause or blanket excuse for her suffering, such as war or specific personal tragedy, is evident. Lillian is "always in full movement, in the center of a whirlpool of people, letters, and telephones" (*Ladders* 7). She seems "always poised on the pinnacle of a drama, a problem, a conflict" (7). In keeping with the patterns of one who has a stake in denying the past, she has a habit of skipping the reflective moments that life might afford her to explore the effects of early trauma.[5]

Lillian's psychic violence also anticipates the bodily catharsis that will come only at the end of the fifth novel of the series, when Lillian finally comes to terms with the way her unconscious has superimposed images of past abuse at her father's hands with an eroticized longing for intimacy. At that point, both Lillian and her author attain an emotional release of deep frustrations that have become part of their identities and have structured their relation to their own and others' bodies. It is at this point that Nin will effectively have written herself out of identification with and attachment to paternal wounding as a master signifier (for further discussion of this point, see chapter 5). In *Ladders,* though, Lillian appears as the embodiment of a "great fury," a "freakish windstorm" (42), who, along with Djuna, seeks the source of her inner chaos and strives without success for both sexual orgasm and substitutive relief in her work. A professional pianist, Lillian channels her passion into music, using it to "tell . . . how she wanted to be stormed with equal strength and fervor" (79). But she is unable to achieve the bodily catharsis through sexuality or through music, remaining subject to the intensity of "unspent forces" (79).[6]

Djuna, too, is isolated in a solitary suffering, born of intense emotionality, an "extraordinary intensity of vision, of awareness" (18), and relieved only by her friendship with Lillian, with whom she shares ideas without having to put them into words. Both women strive for a form of heightened living characterized as "explosion" (18). Similar images of chaos and annihilation link the women in an identification with each other that mirrors the border-erasing effects of Nin's own response to trauma. For instance, a photographic metaphor links emotional sensitivity with early trauma and foreshadows the ending Nin would write for the five-volume "continuous novel" fifteen years after the publication of *Ladders:* Lillian and Djuna share a "vulnerability and sentience" that make them "tremble . . . like the eye of the finest camera lens," which will snap shut at bright light or the world's "crudity and grossness" causing "instantaneous annihilation of the image" (18). In *Seduction of the Minotaur,* Lillian comes to recognize "the double exposure created by memory" (80). As a result, she chooses instead to look through the lens of her "own eyes, and . . . with her own vision, . . . return home" (89). The annihilation in *Ladders* becomes a recreative restoration in *Seduction*.

In a passage similar to Nin's description of the hot winds blowing in the south of France during her affair with her father, Djuna likens her inability to reach sexual climax to the winds she experienced on a Spanish island where she lived for a while as a child, winds that "reached no climax, no explosion" and kept the body on edge, wishing for release (*Ladders* 45). Typical of Nin's own hysterical tendency to hold on to the cause of her suffering, Djuna's and Lillian's frigidity stems from an associative link between their repressed desire and, through their metonymous relation to Nin, paternal betrayal. Links among language, artistic creativity, and gender identity are furthered when Djuna and Lillian visit a bar and Djuna forgets her gendered position and looks at other women "with the eyes of an artist and the eyes of a man" (41), a passage that hints at Nin's difficulty in reconciling her own status as a woman with the role of artist. In her attempt to reconcile this conflict, Nin portrays gender as a matter of whose eyes one looks through.

One example of gender as linguistically overdetermined occurs when Lillian and Djuna argue over the meaning of words or phrases such as "maternal" or "femme fatale."[7] Lillian responds as if the universe has come unhinged when Djuna describes her as having a "real maternal capacity." Djuna herself prefers adults to children and prefers being a mistress to being a wife (42). Lillian is married and has children, but she resists being pinned down to a definition of the maternal. Djuna, who meant no harm, jokingly offers to write a personalized pocket dictionary for Lillian, which would stabilize the meaning of language by listing all the non-injurious connotations of phrases that others use. Her emphasis is on Lillian's tendency to overreact and to personalize everyone's words. The dictionary, she tells her friend, will contain "all the interpretations of what is said," in nonthreatening terms. It will contain the "right" definition of each word, "that is, the one that is not meant to injure, not meant to humiliate or accuse or doubt" (43). Whenever Lillian feels insulted, before she panics or gets hysterical, she can look in the dictionary to make sure she has understood correctly.

Of course, the task would be impossible because, as Lacanian analysts emphasize, there is no fixed meaning to words. Their meanings depend at least in part on interpretation, as notions of gender depend to some degree on perspective. Lillian is unconsciously programmed to hear the meaning Djuna insists is not there, however. She is filled with a sense of pervasive shame over even minor infractions like missing buttons on her clothing or runs in her stockings. Her external flaws reveal her identity as a costume and signify that she cannot hold her self together, another image of identity as a construct worn like a costume to provide unity over a shattered psyche (44).

Nin's view of gender is difficult to define when Lillian tries to "be" Djuna, to adopt her mannerisms in order to find the "lost femininity . . . imprisoned in the deepest wells of her being" (46). On one hand, Nin distinguishes between a "true" femininity and one that is culturally constructed. On the other hand, an earlier passage (14) portrays more ambiguity about the issue, suggesting that gender involves both costuming and an individual desire for the excluded parts of one's being to become reconciled in order to be at peace. Lillian's attempt to "be" Djuna leads her not to a "true" sense of self or of femininity but to a memory that points to the fictional status of engendered identity. In the process, Lillian moves out of a view of men and women as polarized opposites and toward compassion for those—women or men—whose costuming covers suffering.

Immediately after trying to adopt Djuna's way of being in order to access her own femininity, Lillian tells Djuna about the first time she was hurt by a boy. She relates going home from the hurtful scene and donning her brother's suit: "Naturally as I put on the suit I felt I was putting on a costume of strength. It made me feel sure, as the boy was, confident, impudent" (47). She also believed, she tells Djuna, that boys did not suffer; it was "being a girl that was responsible for the suffering" (47). In the next lines, Nin's character reflects a distinction the author has made in her diary between men's objectivity and women's emotionality. Lillian writes that she was able to learn to be like a man, like her husband, by taking action and by affecting an objectivity based on reason. As an adult, Lillian would come to realize that it is not only women but men too, her husband in particular, who could feel a "great choking anguish" (47) even though they learned different defenses. Rather than to feel like a woman made to wait at home while men make war, she says, she prefers to be like Joan of Arc who could ride beside men with her own suit of armor.[8]

In this story-within-a-story, Nin portrays gender as being a matter of constructed defense systems. The male in Lillian's depiction is one who has learned a mode of social behavior that wards off the suffering to which a female may be subject, if she accepts a mode of behavior suggested to her by a society that values such typically "feminine" characteristics as softness and accessibility. In trying to *become* a man, however, Lillian leaps "into a void" (49)—as she reveals through an anecdote of an event that happened when she was about sixteen. Having arranged to meet a boy she liked, at a point halfway between their respective towns, she became anxious, worrying that perhaps her boyfriend would not come and that she would be devastated by the rejection. Instead of waiting to see, she decided to get the rejection over with. Driven by fear to pedal her bicycle too fast, she found evidence of her self-fulfilling prophecy of abandonment in the boy's absence. The point, of course, is that she brought the rejection upon herself, an idea that culminates in Nin's con-clusion to the *Cities of the Interior* series. The adult Lillian laughs as she remembers how she left the scene before the boy had a chance to arrive and how she afterward enacted a similar scene in all of her relationships with men: "Later it was not the drama of two bicycles, of a road, of two separated towns; later it was a darkened room, and a man and woman pursuing pleasure and fusion" (49). The image of "the woman who dressed as a man and pedaled too fast" (50)—in order to subvert suffering by being its cause—is an image of one who has never learned an injunction to dif-ference but who tries to adapt a normative psychic structure. Nin shows that, in order to achieve peace, one cannot simply don a different psychological pat-tern as one would an outfit but must come to terms with the underlying cause of that pattern, a goal emphasized by Lacanian analysis. Lillian achieves this goal four-and-a-half novels later as she leaves Mexico to return to her husband and children as a woman freed from emotional ties to the past.

Just after the bicycle story, Nin introduces a character named Jay who is modeled on Henry Miller. Behind his facade Lillian sees a "lost man" (50). Through Jay, Lillian explores the metaphor of masculinity as a costume as well as a newly introduced theme to *Ladders*. As in *Glass Bell*, Nin uses fiction to develop a link between personal responsibility and compassion. Jay wilts be-fore commitment and responsibility, fleeing when there are difficulties but staying around for any pleasure Lillian and her friends can offer. He is a painter but carries within him "no thread of connection" (57), so that Lillian feels she is sewing not only his buttons onto shirts but one piece of his frag-mented life to another (57). His torn shirt sleeve represents to her that he can-not hold her, unlike her husband, whom she remembers as the epitome of manhood (59). She sees in Jay evidence that, as she realized as a child wearing her brother's suit, the walking wounded include men. Some men, like Jay, defy the "normal image of the man covering the woman" (59) by being more child than man.

Here, "covering" depicts the protectiveness inherent in the normative ex-pectations associated with husbanding and points to the breach in the fabric of Nin's childhood. She believed that her father, like Henry Miller later, "lack[ed] all protective instinct" (*Fire* 380). In the earlier questioning of the maternal as well as here, where Lillian must act as a mother to Jay, Nin explores gender in terms of issues of responsibility, eventually turning the exploration to consider a mother's relation to the baby in her womb and thus to indicate, once again, that fiction functions for Nin as a form of analysis through which she can work through her own sense of guilt, shame, and responsibility.[9]

Another anecdote points to the difference between Lillian's and Jay's ac-countability to others. Jay demands care and support from Lillian but insists that when she comes to see him, she be "ready to discard this mantle of responsibilities" (*Ladders* 61). His favorite story illustrates his penchant for the absurd and the playful, which Lillian opposes to her own serious attitude toward relationships: as a youth, Jay tells her, he was asked to make some rather complicated arrangements for a neighbor to exchange an old piano for a new one. One moving company had to remove the old piano before the second company could bring in the new one. Jay promised his neighbor he would take care of it since the neighbor could not be present and was anxious about the switch. Having promptly forgotten to keep his promise, Jay came home one day from visiting his mother in the hospital to find both pianos sitting outside in the rain. Rather than feeling bad about his broken promise, he laughed, continuing his gaiety in the retelling to Lillian.

Jay finds enjoyment in the disrupted expectation signified by the "'surrealistic sight'" (63) of two pianos sitting in the rain in the middle of a New York City sidewalk. By contrast, Lillian, though laughing at first at his story, feels a stab of pain. A pianist herself, she empathizes with the owner, who must have returned home expecting to find his new piano in place and finding, instead, a total ruin. The image carries the weight of her own expectations of care and responsibility from a man. Neither Lillian nor the narrator comments upon the possibility that Jay's having been at the hospital with his mother might indicate he was traumatized by her illness and that this was the reason he forgot his obligation. He "simply laughed it off, and walked out unconcernedly, never remembering" (63). His nonchalance is similar, perhaps, to the armor against anxiety that Lillian has already decided is proper to men. But Jay is more a child than a man, she feels, and it is for this reason that she decides not to leave him. She tells herself that "no woman ever judged the life stirring within her womb" (63).

As a mother, albeit an absent one as she spends long stretches of time away from husband and children to explore her life's meaning and to conduct affairs, Lillian is willing to extend to Jay the same acceptance she would to a child. Henke interprets Lillian's non-judgmental attitude toward Jay as a way to ward off judgment "by the [internalized] patriarchal figure who dominates her life" ("Lillian Beye" 135). As metonymy for Nin, Lillian also speaks to Nin's repeated efforts to justify herself in terms of the child she aborted in 1934 after deciding it was better off dead than to live in a world without responsible fathers (*Diary* 1: 338–39). The scene from the *Diary* is repeated almost verbatim later in *Ladders* when Lillian, having discovered she is pregnant with Jay's child (he insists on an abortion) addresses the fetus in her womb and ostensibly provokes a "miscarriage" at six-months' gestation (*Ladders* 77–78). In some similarity to Jay, who habitually sees himself as a victim, "holding others responsible for his behavior" (65), Lillian shows herself still taking refuge in a fictionalized version that exonerates her of culpability for the child's death. Her child conveniently miscarries, after all. Paralleling Jay's irresponsibility in leaving the piano out in the rain "to be ruined" (64), Henry Miller's lack of potential as a father left Nin, she felt, no choice but to abort.

By giving voice to her grief and anger but suffusing it in the kind of didactic philosophical tone Djuna used in childhood to ward off pain, Nin mourns publicly, in fiction, that which she could not say aloud. That her self-justification continues over many books and years indicates that her language has successfully covered up the points of rupture introduced by her characters' shame. Paradoxically, Nin's success in channeling her grief into literary form leaves both author and characters stuck, for the time being, beneath a narrative covering. Even so, at the end of "This Hunger," Lillian realizes that her guilt over leaving her family to "be the mother of creations and dreams, the mother of artists, the muse and the mistress" (Nin's words to describe her own choice) cannot "be shed like an old coat" (72) any more than she can leave by the wayside her regrets about the past.

Lillian's relationship with Jay becomes complicated by his relationship with Djuna, who asserts that he doesn't believe in her "'as a woman'" (68). Jay also bonds with another woman, Helen, whom he meets and brings home so that Lillian and Djuna can get to know her. Helen's function is little more than as catalyst for Lillian's further self-exploration, especially of her tendency to "wear the man's costume" as "warrior armòr" to protect herself against the "core of love" (77).

But Djuna is central to the story. Jay associates Djuna with the image of himself he sees in the mirror, projecting an image of himself onto his view of her. His painting, similarly, appears as a metaphor for a transitory state of illusory identity. The canvas beneath the paint is a metaphor for reality, on which he projects his desire (69). But Djuna sees through the images that Jay paints: "The greater . . . the attachment, the larger she saw the fissure through which human beings fall again into solitude" (70).

"This Hunger" ends with an image of three mirrors in a garden just outside a room where Lillian is giving a concert.[10] The mirrors have been placed there to alleviate the painful truth of nature by reflecting the artist's image and creating the impression that she is playing there as well. "Art and artifice had breathed upon the garden . . . , and all the danger of truth and revelation had been exorcised" (81). The ironic narrator points out that, though only the "mist of perfection" is visible to the audience, there are "subterranean passages" under the whole scene, "and if no one heard the premonitory rumblings before the explosion, it would all erupt in the form of war and revolution" (81).[11]

The last image is one of universal womanhood asserting its strength, but the narrative emphasis lies in the individual woman's efforts to pay heed to the rumblings that Lillian, pounding at her piano, accesses through art. As Nin would say in *The Novel of the Future* (1968), art serves as the medium through which elements of the psyche that would otherwise be repressed can be explored and organized in a life-affirming rather than destructive way. Nin links this function of art to personal responsibility, which lies "in our ability to control each wave of anger, distortion, hatred, which we send out into the world like homemade bombs" (*Future* 12).

The next section, "The Bread and the Wafer," emphasizes the transformative powers of language. This motif emerges as the artistic medium related to the element of fire. For some characters, such as the newly introduced Faustin, however, language is the element by which one can continue to build a defensive ego. In a passage replete with narrative irony, we learn that Faustin's presence at the café leads to immediate abstraction, "without any gradual ascension. It would start with the problems of form, being and becoming, physiognomics, destiny versus incident, the coming of the fungoid era, the middle brain and the tertiary moon!" (*Ladders* 88). In making fun of Faustin's talk, Nin performs a crescendo from a quite immediate and self-referential problem, that of form, to one slightly more abstract, the notions of "being and becoming." From here she moves up a list of increasingly abstract ideas to the absurdity of a "fungoid era" predicted through the study of history on a planetary scale. Although any of these topics could well be the subject of a conversation among friends who are writers, artists, and philosophers, the catalogue nature of the list draws attention to the tendency of even slightly inebriated people to get too wrapped up in their own talk, taking their own explanations a bit too seriously.

The novel's portrayal of identity similarly indicates that human beings may well use language to construct themselves as subject and to believe the rhetoric of their own egos. Nin thematizes the relation of form to content through her performative use of narrative in a way that provides a critique of Surrealism as well as a Modernist view of technological influence: when Jay hears Faustin talk, Jay's language begins to split off as if it has been run through a shredder. Earlier, he is presented as embracing chaos—telling a friend, Colette, that only drunks and insane people "make sense" for only they have "discarded the unessential for chaos" (87). His language regularly "bursts its boundaries" (86). But when confronted with the abstraction of Faustin's conversational style, Jay's "phrases would begin to break and scatter, to run wild like a machine without springs, gushing forth from the contradictory core of him which refused all crystallizations" (88). Jay's resistance to commitment and personal accountability takes form in language as the motif of identificatory border-erasure that has run through all of Nin's fiction thus far, a motif linked here (as it is again in Nin's third novel, *The Four-Chambered Heart*) to the fragmentation born of modern technology.

Nin would continue to explore the relation between literary form and twentieth-century social patterns, emphasizing—before it was fashionable among literary and cultural critics to do so—a "personal as political" philosophy.

Whereas Nin valued the innovations of the Surrealists and their privileging of the dreamworld, for instance, she also believed that it is only by confronting one's own past and coming to terms with one's own anger and pain, so one can be creative rather than destructive, that political efficacy can be achieved. Psychoanalysis provided her the way to do this. As Nin began to use fiction to assert in *Under a Glass Bell* and as she formulates in her later nonfiction, it is only by delving into the past in order to restructure a healthier relation to the present and future that one can reach an effective approach to social and personal issues. Thus *Ladders* returns quickly to the natural elements, not only to the fire motif but also to the depiction of sexuality that appears several pages after the Faustin incident.

Lillian's mistake is to try to resolve her own issues through Jay, who still suffers from the "shock" (93) of his parents' betraying him as a child. The particular incident that still rankles is their telling Jay they were going to see a famous battleship and allowing him to look forward to the event with immense expectation. In reality, he was being taken to have his tonsils out. The physical pain of the surgery was greatly intensified by his feeling of having been set up. A similar story of his mother's refusing to let him put his hand in her muff further arouses Lillian's compassion. As she tried to *become* Djuna in order to reach her own femininity, she now tries to become the muff for Jay, to be the battleship he wanted so badly as a child to see (95). As before (when the attempt to be the agent of connection between split elements failed on the basis of its illusory status), Lillian's effort to stand in for the missing elements of Jay's past is ineffectual. The transference is only substitutive, not substantial. "Lillian did not know then," the editorializing narrator remarks, "that the one who believes he can pay this early debt meets a bottomless well" (95).

In the same paragraph, Nin indicates that one who looks to others to fill a lack may wield a quest of retribution against the rest of the world. This is Nin's explanation for warfare and violence in general. Here, it provides explanation for Jay's irresponsibility, for the violence of his paintings, and for Lillian's identification with him on the basis of their shared suffering. Lillian forgives him his infidelities since they stem from his past traumas.

His paintings are more difficult to accept. They are "a kind of bomb" that Jay substitutes for avenging his past through bloodshed (97). Lillian recognizes that she shares with Jay an emotional explosivity (103). Whereas the effect of Jay's paintings on some viewers is positive and almost curative, like "an act of birth" (102), Lillian's sense of fragmentation is reinvoked by his having "exploded" onto the canvas, painting not only fragmented images but "dissolution and disintegration" itself (101). For Nin, the artistic act provides a means for transforming dissolution into life. For Jay, art is a way of keeping accounts.

In an italicized section representing Jay's thoughts as he sits on a park bench across from a pawnshop where he has tried to trade his painting for cash, he expresses his bitterness at being misunderstood by the critics and undervalued in the economic system of exchange—a theme to which Nin would return in *Seduction of the Minotaur*, as well as in the third and fourth volumes of the *Diary*. In a passage reflecting Nin's disappointment over the reception of her works, Jay decides that his painting has been devalued because "[e]veryone *'meets his enemy'*" in Jay's art (107). Like the Minotaur in Nin's mythological labyrinth in the last title of the *Cities of the Interior* series, the enemies one meets in Nin's art, in her estimation, are one's unresolved attachments to the dead letters of the past and the socially constructed concept of "woman" whose indefinability threatens those invested in notions of stability and fixedness.

A new character to the scene, Sabina, introduces the novel's title passage. Jay meets her during one of his excursions around Paris and brings her home, as he did Helen. She arrives with the "sound and imagery of fire engines." Dressed in red and silver, she gives the impression "everything will burn" (108).[12] Sabina's hysterical manner sends the message that she can rescue the artist-child at the core of a man. Her "ladders," though, lead to fire rather than away from it (108). Like Lillian at the opening of the novel, Sabina's "fiery course" is characterized by her not having any time to reflect. She leads an un-examined life and talks, like Jay, in broken sentences, exhibiting always an "ap-parent desire to be elsewhere" (109). The many stories she tells leaves others unable to distinguish whether she is the victim or the victimizer. She has no accountability to autobiographical truth. (This is an interesting detail in light of Nin's own habit of lying and of the controversies that have arisen over the *Diary*'s narrative authenticity.)[13] Perhaps most interesting of Sabina's traits is the one that causes Jay to hate her; she regards men the same way that he looks at women, as potential love objects. Jay feels that her gaze strips him of his unique status and singles out in his gestures, manners, and body language only the evidence of potential availability as a lover (111).[14]

As Nin works through autobiographical confusion around the conflict be-tween independence and relational dependence on another, the characters that represent the opposing sides of her psyche—Lillian and Sabina—are con-trasted in Jay's thoughts. Lillian makes Jay feel like a man in debt, trying to fill up an unfillable void. Sabina at least makes him feel like an equal, in that she can take care of herself and "answer treachery with treachery" (113). His ex-pecting Sabina's betrayal finds some fulfillment in a relationship she develops with Lillian. Lillian offers the newcomer a true love as opposed to the "false role of play" that a relationship with Jay entails (115).

It is ironic that Sabina courts Lillian not by telling the truth but by con-forming "to what she imagined Lillian expected of her, which was in reality not at all what Lillian wanted of her, but what she, Sabina, thought necessary to her idealized image of herself" (115). Once again, as she continues to repeat throughout the novel series as well as in her diary, Nin pinpoints her own impasse in the analytic process. She has become stuck at the point where she must separate her self-myth from her idealizations. She knows she must do so in order to move on, but she acts on a repetition compulsion until much later in the series. The reason, she indicates in *Ladders,* is the fear that telling the truth leads to a loss of love. Lillian, for instance, demands "a truthful love" yet remains terrorized that "this very truth might destroy the love" (116) she demands of others.

The equation of truth with loss is, of course, part of the subtextual territory of all of Nin's writings. The source of the equation is open to debate but its effects remain—palpable in early works like *House of Incest,* analyzed in *Winter of Artifice,* thematized in many of the stories in *Glass Bell.* Whether analogous to that equation or part of it, the theme of psychological incest as a breaking of identificatory boundaries runs through the "subterranean regions" beneath the self-described labyrinth that is Nin's text. In *Ladders,* the theme is implicit. For example, Nin often invokes the transgressing-of-limits motif as one that links the border-erasure of hysteria to the breaking of rules such as the incest taboo. (Earlier, Jay is depicted as having "no fear of incest" [107].) When in one scene Sabina and Jay square off in the center of Jay's studio, it is because they are both "law-breaking lovers" (112).

From a psychoanalytic perspective, the notion of breaking law is tied inextricably to issues of internalized paternalism. In Freudian thought, the paternal takes the form of the superego; in Lacan, the father's name provides an essential interruption to symbiotic union (the "no" of the father's name that serves as an injunction to difference) and establishes law while alienating one from its terms forever. Nin's repeating the theme of her characters' estrangement from self and other through the masquerade of ego shows her difficulty in resolving her grief over this element of human existence, at least until she is able to take some responsibility for her own interpretations and superimposition of the motif upon all perspectives.

One way that Sabina and Lillian respond to the alienating effects of language is to turn against Jay and against the rigid classification systems they associate him with. To Lillian, Sabina's evasiveness seems an erasure of linguistic certainty. Sabina seems to elude the effects of being defined by "man" or, by extension, by systems of meaning rendered masculine through their associative link with symbolic efficacy and phallic fixity. Just after deciding that they will "laugh at him, the man," however, a great loneliness overtakes both women as they remember that their focus is still on Jay (119). Turning against Jay's image in a conscious choice to "hate Jay tonight," to "hate man" (199), they become "frightened by the vagueness of their desire, the indefiniteness of their craving" (199). As in *House of Incest,* the quest for a symbiotic union through a love affair with a woman is an unsuccessful one. It fails not because it is with a woman but because any relationship must fail to provide an absolute unity such as the unity Sabina and Lillian seek in each other. Though they believe they are "sliding beyond the reach of man's hands" (*Ladders* 122) when they dance together at a nightclub and end up getting thrown out for their behavior, what they are seeking is "a slit in the dream" (122). To use Bracher's explanation of what happens in a successful analysis, these "slits" are the needed ruptures in the fabric of social relations through which they might find the missing elements of their psyches.

They cannot find these elements by trying to merge, however. When they try to make love, they see it "was not that" which would provide the sense of oneness they want (125). Nin repeats a variation of the phrase "It was not that" in the closing scene of the novel, where Djuna seeks for the "something of One" that Lacan describes as the lost unity many humans believe romantic or sexual love will reinstill.[15] Despite this realization, their both being women is cited as the reason for their relational failure (frequent shifts of narrative perspective make it difficult to tell whether the women themselves are realizing this or whether the narrator is once again editorializing). The would-be lovers get out of bed without having reached satisfaction, Lillian shouting angrily that it is really Jay whom Sabina loves. As she trembles with anger in spite of Sabina's protests, a narrative shift reinstates Jay as the focal point of the narrative.

As the scene changes, Jay theorizes about his own status as artist, comparing the birth of an artist to the birth of a baby from the womb (127). An artist, however, is too impatient to wait nine months, he insists. Nin, in the *Diary*, returns to protest the terms of her pregnancy and her molding them into her own metaphor of a "motherhood beyond biological motherhood" (*Diary* 1: 213). Jay's restlessness causes him to re-create himself through his art work, he tells Lillian, and it is the same restlessness that creates his requirement of more than one woman (*Ladders* 127). Later, as Lillian and Djuna meet again to discuss Lillian's predicament, Lillian confesses that she had expected Jay to create *her* as a work of art. Nin's description of Lillian's speaking style provides either a self-reflective critique of her own writing or a parody of several critics' judgment: Lillian speaks in phrases that are "Unformed, unfinished, dense, heavy with repetitions, with recapitulations, with a baffled, confused bitterness and anger" (132). By contrast, in a passage that again links the personal to the social, Djuna refutes this view of love, insisting that each must make of oneself a "'self-creation'" and that women in general are participating in an ever-widening circle of "'independence and self-creation'" (133). Lillian must accept her past failures and regrets and move on, Djuna says. Despite this prescient advice, Lillian walks on, as the novel nears its end, absorbed in her interpretation of Jay's neglect and of her resulting pain. Whereas Djuna represents the willingness to move to a new circle of awareness, Lillian refuses it, preferring to focus on Jay's indifference. After all, she has structured herself around such rejection.

Nin anticipates moving on to new awareness in the ending "Party Scene" of the novel. This long passage is one of the best known of Nin's literary innovations, combining Surrealist images, abstract characterization, and the techniques of Modernist art to undergird the theme that the ego is a mask that alienates the wearer. Nin consciously modeled the scene after Martha Graham's choreography, believing that Graham's dancing troupe had found a new way to depict the "disintegration of the personality" that characterized twentieth-century neurosis (*Diary* 4: 152; Bair 316).[16]

Jay and Lillian host the party on their top-floor apartment. It is a masquerade of identities, to which each guest comes "dressed in the full regalia of his myth" (*Ladders* 146). First comes the guest through whose eyes the narrator now gives an analysis of each character at the party. Soon afterward others arrive, including Faustin the Zombie, Djuna, an Irish architect, Sabina, a Chinese poet, Rango (a character based on Gonzalo Moré and featured in *The Four-Chambered Heart*), and Stella. Some of Nin's truly brilliant writing may be found here, as in the lament against the dehumanizing forces of technology-inspired art: "the steel and wood mobiles turning gently in the breeze of the future . . . the new cages of our future sorrows, so abstract they could not even contain a sob" (142).

Lillian, characteristically, wants to dance with someone who can provide a sense of unity. It is Djuna whose imaginary fusion with an idealized notion of love leads to the fatal phrase: "This is not the place" and then "He is not the one" (150). As she stands alienated from the rest of the group, Djuna becomes engulfed in an anxiety described in terms reminiscent of the novel's earlier passages regarding her inability to find closure or catharsis. She is in a "dream without exit, without explosion" (151). The novel ends as she is "abducted" by a "drunken man" (152) who brings her a chair, on which she is transported by memory to a scene from her adolescence in which she experienced an acute sense of exclusion and marginalization. In this scene, she relives an event closely based on one Nin recounts in the *Diary* when she was not invited to a party she had hoped to attend (2: 240). Nin ends the novel on this note, as if she has already decided that her continuing struggle with issues of closure and resistance will require a longer analysis.

TRANSITION: *CHILDREN OF THE ALBATROSS*

The second novel in Nin's *Cities of the Interior* series is essentially (and especially) repetitious, providing several extremely well-written, psychologically insightful passages amid a rather plotless series of events in Djuna's life and, to a lesser extent, in Sabina's and Jay's. The first section, entitled "The Sealed Room," revolves around Djuna's relationship with men more than ten years her juniors and in whom she finds a poetic vulnerability refreshingly free of some of the trappings of conventional masculine constructions.[17] Among the most interesting motifs in the development of Djuna are (unfortunately for readers of Nin's previous work) also among the most repetitious, indicating Nin's inability to move beyond attachment to these images. They are the shattering effects of the past on one's body (*Children* 8) and the resulting psychological splitting (4–5, 17), the long-lasting effects of betrayal (13), the wish for an elusive and impossible fusion with others through relationships and the resulting alienation (21, 23). Jay's character exhibits the same characteristics as in *Ladders*, primarily his fear of possession by women (*Children* 28). Gender theorists can mine some useful thematic gems here as well, such as the use of women as objects of exchange (27) and gender as a matter of costuming analogous to self-mythologizing (47, 88).

Despite the unease with which the reader aware of the autobiographical nature of this work may greet the idea of an adult woman fraternizing with seventeen-year-old men, or the odd sense of the author's self-inflation and lack of aesthetic distance, there are some wonderfully striking images. One of the young men—Lawrence—works at "a place which made decorations for shop windows" (42). In a passage describing his work, Nin portrays Lawrence playing whimsical, childlike fantasy games with the mannequins and "papier-mâché horses . . . fabulous animals" (42). Djuna compares his adolescent changes of moods to a rainbow's subtle mutations, falling like crystals or "colors on the wings of butterflies after yielding their maximum charms" (42). Nin also captures the disillusionment that comes with the end of a fantasy when, at a fair, the music stops—to make audible "the dry shots of the amateur hunters and the clay pigeons falling behind the cardboard walls" (9).

But her true potential as novelist is hindered in this book by a cut-and-dried depiction of the parents of Djuna's young lover, Paul, as severe prison keepers (readers are more likely to identify with the parents, I believe, than with Djuna here). The characters, like the argument itself, are presented in two dimensions, much like the cutout poster images Nin uses to critique commercial culture in the fourth and fifth novels of the series. Striking ironies appear throughout *Children,* but there is little irony in the point of view. As a result, the tears sliding down Djuna's face—"the unbearable melting of her heart and body" (51)—do not carry much pathos.

The smaller, ending section entitled "The Cafe," however, opens with two pages of effective imagery describing the enchantment of an internationally designed café, where Jay, Sabina, Djuna, Michael, and his lover, Donald, meet to revisit Nin's tried-and-true themes of the self. The section's featured character is Sabina, who (the narrator tells us) seeks an identity that resists the cohesive tendencies of the ego. Sabina structures her identity around others' expectations of her (74) and eludes a fixed identity for herself, letting each man

live an image of her, which "she saw . . . take form in his eyes" (74). She also
relates to others in a way that makes them lose their identities: "they became
objects of desire, objects to be consumed, fuel for the bonfire" (75). She lives
in endless fear that she will be discovered as having an identity beyond a lover's
expectations of her or that her "enemies" will expose her pretenses: "People felt
the falseness at times and sought to uncover her" (75).

In this depiction, Nin is self-reflexive. In her lifetime, and afterward, a critical enterprise grew up around the legend of Anaïs Nin as critics devoted themselves to uncovering the truth about her life, beyond her known deceptions.
Nin shows Sabina in pain, trying to live up to an impossible expectation, living in suspension between past and future. The novel ends with a series of
stream-of-consciousness images in Djuna's mind as she walks home from the
café, considering "this surrender of the self [that] began a sinking into deeper
layers of awareness deeper and deeper" (111). Anticipating the inner exploration that Djuna and the other characters still had to do, Nin had decided by
the time she ended *Children of the Albatross* that it and *Ladders to Fire* would
comprise novels in a series, readable as separate works or as parts of a larger
whole that she would call a "continuous novel" (Jason 56).

BACK TO THE HOUSEBOAT: IDEAL AND
EGO IDEAL IN *THE FOUR-CHAMBERED HEART*

The third novel, *The Four-Chambered Heart* (1950), in Nin's five-volume
series *Cities of the Interior* is a more conventional novel than either of its pre-
decessors. Djuna is once again the protagonist and Nin's alter ego. As a dancer,
Djuna—like Nin—values her role as an artist. The other main characters are
the jazz guitarist Rango, closely modeled on Gonzalo Moré, and Rango's wife,
Zora, for whom Gonzalo's wife, Helba Huara, provided the model. *Heart* explores issues of artistic transformation of the past as well as the somatic nature
of language: "Every word spoken in the past accumulated colors in the self"
(*Heart* 10), the narrator says of the way Djuna, as at the end of *Ladders to Fire*,
carries in her psyche a sense of the unattainable. As she leans toward Rango
while he plays his guitar, his chords point toward her memory of an "unattainable island of joy," represented in her girlhood by a party she witnessed
from her window but which she had not attended (*Heart* 6).

Recurring images such as this party show Nin's keeping alive the internal
alienation that has become her mark of self-recognition. *The Four-Chambered
Heart* repeats the fluid structure of "Houseboat," while pursuing the theme of
a labyrinthine search for self. Like the earlier story, *Heart* mirrors the psychoanalytic process of diving deep and surfacing, spiraling through repetitive cy-
cles of progress and regression. In the last half of the novel, Djuna makes some

important distinctions that mirror Nin's attempt to separate ego from ego ideal and to clarify her ideas about gender. In *Heart*, Nin pursues the interrelated motifs of gender and costuming, advancing the notion that men and women wear different personas, which become infused in their identities.

From the beginning, Djuna feels a conflict between obligation and freedom. This was one of the main conflicts for which Nin had sought therapy with her first woman analyst, Martha Jaeger, and which she continued to explore in her writing and in therapy with Inge Bogner. Nin's issue throughout adulthood was how to nurture others and at the same time be an artist. Her notion of the symbolic motherhood she believed D. H. Lawrence had advocated made it necessary in her mind to mother "life, hope, and creation" (*Diary* 1: 213), a formula that translated in her actions to her caring for a number of others as a way to bolster her sense of worth. In *Heart*, it is Rango's wife, Zora, that Djuna must meet and eventually care for as a condition of Rango's love and approval.

The condition is ironic since she is first attracted to the sense of the unattainable she believes she hears in his music and a sense of freedom and boundlessness in his being. Similarly, when Djuna accompanies Rango to his house, she notices it is "too gray, too shabby, too cramped for his big, powerful body" (9), a depiction reminiscent of Nin's own belief that reality itself was too dreary for an artist to bear and that the only livable life for an artist was one enhanced through one's own creation or chosen perspective on the circumstances of one's life. Rather than being truly free, Rango is bound by obligation to a wife he married when he was seventeen and with whom he has lived the past six or seven years in a sexless marriage because of his partner's constant illness.

Likewise, the author's tendency to seek freedom—in a kind of mothering beyond the biological—becomes a trap until she is able to resolve her conflict between the various configurations of her loyalty to her father and the creativity she saw as opposed to that loyalty. Djuna's realization, when Rango insists she try to help his wife, that "this appeal was made to her good self" and her rebellion against wearing this good-self costume (81) underscore a felt tension among Nin's various "selves." Like Djuna, Nin realized that living up to others' expectations causes the freer aspects of herself to atrophy. Yet both Djuna and Nin find it difficult or impossible to resist those "invitations which are like commands" (81) to the "idealized self" (82). In a remarkable two paragraphs regarding this conflict between her artistic desire and the "good self" (which Djuna believes her artist self holds up as a standard), Nin provides a classic example of the ideal ego and an analysand's efforts to define it as such in order to separate from it.[18]

The theme of father as signifier of limitation and law is also repeated in this novel, where Djuna's linking a policeman to the notion of a restrictive father invokes Nin's continued exploration of the effects of her own father's abandonment and perceived betrayal. More than ever, the fictional status of the novel form becomes a metonymy for the fictional status of the self-myth she has built around the story of her father's abandonment. That Nin told, throughout her adulthood, a story about the beginnings of her diary that Bair has shown was at least partially fictional highlights the narratives of the ideal ego that need to be disrupted to accomplish the goals of analysis. Nin's account that the diary began as a bridge between herself as a young girl and an abandoning father whose image had structured her identity served to reinforce the splits in her life.

The places in Nin's formal fiction that illuminate the split most significantly are those where a character such as Djuna discourses on the father themes in a way that exposes the author's displacing her anxiety around this issue. An example appears early in the novel, when Djuna goes in search of a houseboat where she and Rango can escape the confines of conventional morality and engage in an affair that she believes is justified on the basis that "love fills certain people and expands them beyond all laws" (13). This line and a relatively long passage that follows, in which the editorializing narrator discourses on the freedom such love affords, appear immediately after a statement that Djuna, after spending the night with Rango, arrived home a half hour before her father knocked on her door, "because he was ill and wanted care" (13). Djuna's father is a parallel to Rango's wife, who also is ill and needs care. As objectified rather than subjective others, both appear as obstacles to the sexual love characterized by Djuna and by the narrator as a truer form of reality than the dull confines of social obligation.

Others, to Djuna and Rango, represent limitation. Their limiting function finds metaphorical expression in the figure of a police officer whose presence near the water launches Djuna into an internal monologue on the nature of artistic dreaming and its relation to her love for Rango: "Oh, you can, if you wish, arrest me for reverie, vagabondage of the wildest sort, for it is the cell, the mysterious, the padded, the fecund cell in which everything is born," she imagines herself saying to the policeman (14). This passage establishes resistance to boundaries as the structuring principle of Djuna's identity. It also shows Nin's central tension between artistic creativity and obligation to others. She still associates creativity with transcendent motherhood; obligation with mothering as a law-defined function, through which a woman must serve as support for a patriarchal structure.

In her internal monologue to the policeman, Djuna decides that Djuna's father and Zora, the "victims" of "love's expansion," should be "gentle and gay about these trickeries" of love. Her imposing on them the obligation to support her fantasies makes transparent the ego's self-justification and shows a lack of resolution stemming from analytic failure. When Djuna implies she is justified in her affair with Rango, because if she were to stay home she would die of boredom, we see one of the many attempts Nin has made in both fiction and diary writing to indict the father as death signifier. That is, she attempts to acknowledge her aggressive feelings toward him and to change the way she has assigned value to *not* having those feelings. We do not yet see, however, the kind of disruption in the narrative of her identity that Bracher has argued can set the process of both individual and cultural change into motion (Bracher 65). The narrative is still reinforcing a dyadic opposition between "good" love and "bad" restriction and thus engaging illusions of certainty.

The effort to separate ego from ideal ego does punctuate *Heart* with small disruptions. Djuna tells Rango she is afraid of shallow living and prefers life on the water where she can look through the holes in the floor of the boat to see "the layer of water which lies at the bottom of every ship, like the possessive fingers of the sea and the river asserting its ownership of the boat" (*Heart* 18). Here, the boat's flooring appears as a metaphor for the narrative trajectory of one's self-myth, below which "every ship" or person has an unconscious that exerts possessive control. The holes in the floor of the ship are like disruptions in speech, which, when interrupted or punctuated by the analyst, can point an analysand in the direction of acknowledging the repressed part of his or her being. Here, it is the authorial voice that provides an interruption, when the narrator intrudes to comment upon the characters' lack of knowledge about the nature of their relationship's possible disintegration. The narrator tells us that Djuna and Rango believe they are safe from the dangers of the world when they are on the boat. They are like all lovers, according to the narrator, in that they believe all "dangers to . . . love . . . came from the outside, from the world, never suspecting the seed of death of love might lie within themselves" (19).

The narrative progresses to a metaphor for the disruption itself. The point of view also shifts at this point from the editorial to a more objective perspective of the way the characters' sense of unity has been established to block any threat to their love, much as the ego constructs a narrative to ward off any threat to its illusory cohesion: when Rango begins to undress Djuna on the boat, they hear "something fall into the water" (19). Djuna laughingly compares the sound to that of a flying fish; Rango replies that she is the flying fish whom he cannot hold on to. His saying this as part of their lovemaking establishes his putative possession of her in a relational unity. Djuna's opposing statement appears when, during their lovemaking, an oil lamp falls and breaks. The oil spreads and breaks into many small flames, which delight Djuna with their multiplicity and violence.[19] Shortly afterward, Rango breaks down the door to the watchman's room to interrupt his drunken singing, and Djuna is relieved by the disruptive quality of his act.

Later in the novel, the image of fire reappears in an indictment of Rango's multiple unfulfilled passions: "All the little flames burning in him at once, except the wise one of the holy ghost" (72). By that point, Djuna is not so taken with his violence and has already begun to question its value, much as Nin is turning herself away from violent emotions. Djuna realizes that her patience with his chaotic urges and violent temper stems from the fact that "Rango lived out for her this self she had buried in her childhood" (86).

The author's own quest for artistic identity and her connecting that to a concept of gender surface in Rango's account of his Guatemalan birth and later teenage years in Spain. The story charms Djuna. She wonders, though, why the experiences he has described have not made him an artist. Similarly, Nin's multicultural upbringing provided a rich source of experiences on which to draw for artistic inspiration, so she was perplexed that her writing often refused to flow naturally from those experiences, except in her diary. Nin's formulations of gender identity are also evident in Djuna's thought about Rango's consciousness: first, Djuna notices that "the little blue flame of music and poetry shone only at night," during lovemaking, whereas during the day, his body seems to exhibit the habits of a conqueror (38). Next, Djuna draws a connection between Rango's animal-like physicality and his consciousness. She universalizes Rango's mode of being to that of all males as a gender class: "as if man's consciousness were something he had thrown off during the night, and had to be recovered like some artificial covering for his body" (39). In the next paragraph, it is his body that must "be laid aside like a superfluous mantle" (39) so that the connection between body and awareness comes full circle. Later in the novel, Djuna muses that Rango has no need to invent because he was raised in a natural environment as opposed to her own city upbringing (75), a contrast suggesting that artistic creation is born of a lack of something provided by nature. More important in Nin's movement toward psychic freedom is that she engages a familiar opposition between the language of "man's abstractions" and the kind of language and modality she characterizes at this stage of her career as a more feminine mode.

A polarization of gender appears when Rango becomes obsessed with the issues of revolution and war, and Djuna believes he is engaging in a typically male concern: "It seemed to her that he was ready to live and die for emotional errors as women did, but that like most men he did not call them emotional errors; he called them history, philosophy, metaphysics, science" (72). Djuna, on the other hand, chooses commitment to Rango and to love, believing that it is her "feminine self" that leads her to smile inwardly at "this game of endowing personal and emotional beliefs with the dignity of impersonal names" (72). Djuna realizes, "men smile at women's enlargement of personal tragedies to a status men do not believe applicable to personal lives" (72).

As the passage continues, Nin enlarges the dichotomy in a way that mirrors the *Diary*'s division into camps corresponding roughly to the "masculine" as abstract creation of impersonal systems and cities, and the "feminine" as a kind of nurturing creativity based on personal relationships (72–73). By the time she writes *Seduction of the Minotaur* (1961), Nin critiques such reductive stereo-typing per se, showing her own movement away from the seeming binarism of her early work. Here, in the middle novel of the *Cities of the Interior* series, po-larizing the issues remains a tool in Nin's effort to define and resist the terms of her problematic notion that being a woman meant *not* being an artist.[20]

A fascinating connection Nin makes is between "man's abstractions" and so-cial mechanization. Her portrayal of the Modernist theme of mechanization along these lines condenses a microcosm of the ego's totalizing tendencies with an explanation of the process by which artistic consciousness can be rendered abstract and thus be robbed of its efficacy. This occurs when Djuna-as-narrator decides it is the city that has broken Rango's natural rhythms: "Clock time, ma-chines, auto horns, whistles, congestion caught man in their cogs, deafened, stupefied him. The city's rhythm dictated to man; the imperious order to re-main alive actually meant to become an abstraction" (39–40).

The pages that follow also provide insight into Nin's relationship with More, whom she describes in *Fire* as having "deep animal soul, the unformu-lated soul [which] seems like the knowingness of a woman" (*Fire* 396), but whose lack of motivation or ability to fulfill his goals left Nin feeling stifled.[21] Gonzalo further motivates Nin's notions about gender difference as he comes to stand in her mind for the war-making of men as opposed to the life-giving reproduction of women (*Fire* 270). Gonzalo's desire to participate in revolu-tion leads to little action, however.

His fictionalization as Rango reveals Nin's understanding that his lack of ef-ficacy results from an exaggerated resistance to clocks and to all other mecha-nization.[22] In setting up Djuna's understanding, however, Nin also indicates that, in her own quest, she wants to avoid the dangers of not only the mecha-nization and abstraction to which Rango/More has fallen prey but also the ex-cesses of circularity by which he is equally trapped by his rebellion against those forces. Later in the novel Djuna remembers how, as a child, she often became "tangled in her own high rebellions" against her parents' injunctions that she always *"be good"* (*Heart* 83). Otherwise, they threaten, she will not be loved.

Although, or perhaps because, she understands how Rango's "aborted mo-ments" weigh him down as if he carries stones in his pockets, Djuna sets her-self up as his opposite, "tenderly seek[ing] to unwind him, just as she picked up the pieces of his broken glasses to have them made again" (42). The image is reminiscent of Djuna's paradoxical human urge to help another person see his way clear of confusion or doubt, paradoxical because this "help" might equally enable his blindness or dependence on others for reinforcement of a self-concept. A later passage brings the seeing motif together with the theme of Djuna as helpmate and of Rango's natural tendency toward violence: "What Djuna believed was that like a volcano his fire and strength would erupt and bring freedom, to him and to her. . . . But fire too must have direction" (70).

Djuna sees herself as the artist who, like the ragpicker in Nin's earlier story, attempts to pull fragmented pieces of life and love together into a work of artistic value. More likely, she is the artist manqué, who has still not achieved the ability to do so without becoming weighed down herself with the stones of another's aborted desires.[23] *Heart* frequently revisits the dangers of becoming trapped in one's own resistance. Nin draws connection between this resistance and the concept of personality as a set of fictions that one constructs. As the novel progresses, Djuna begins to move away from—instead of continuing to identify with—the resisting elements of her own mythology.

Perhaps the most important theme in *The Four-Chambered Heart* is that of the "impossibilities of fusion between human beings" (44) and a corresponding possibility of fulfilling one's emotional needs in literature instead of in romantic relationships. This link appears in the novel's title passage, a quotation concerning the physical compartmentalization of a cow's four-chambered heart whose dividing membranes prevent communication between chambers. First, the image leads Djuna to imagine her past loves isolated in separate chambers so that her lovers can remain separate and thus avoid the kind of debilitating jealousy to which Rango is subject (54).

Later, the image is revisited: in a rather confusing metaphorical passage, Djuna remembers that during her childhood she was able to access her creativity through books. In their imaginative realms the distinction between inner and outer compartments of her inner spiritual heart, as an extension of the bodily heart, became erased (76). Literature provided her (as writing it provided Nin) with the continuity and oneness not attainable through romantic love.

In *Heart*, as elsewhere, the failure of romantic love to allow its participants to attain a mystic oneness appears as an issue of transference. When Djuna feels her desires are mocked by Rango, for instance, she reflects on her father's past mockery of her childhood wishes. One wish Rango scoffs at without understanding Djuna's need to avoid being displaced by another is her wanting to continue cutting his hair even after Zora comes home from the hospital and can resume doing it. Rango also labels as "'Mystic nonsense'" Djuna's idea that sexual love is like the coming together of "great rivers of inheritance transmit[ting] traits and carr[ying] dreams from port to port until fulfillment, and [giving] birth to selves never born before" (61). Djuna believes he sabotages their love out of fear of creating (67), resurrecting the dead loves of her past in order to engage in psychological necrophilism (65). When he admits he is irrevocably fatalistic and will always fail to bring his dreams to fruition, Djuna replies with one of Nin's standard protests against the kind of romanticism that is attracted to death and the kind of literature or philosophy that endorses it.[24] Earlier, *Heart* contains an indictment of the kinds of conventional writing that fail to provide "armour against moments of despair" (53). Her later protest is an affirmation of self-analysis through art. It is also a resistance to the kinds of writing she believed keep one locked in the narratives of repression.

Nin's battle with "the indestructible good self, this false and wearying good self who answered prayers" (85), as she describes it through Djuna, takes an interesting turn at the point in the novel when Rango asks Djuna to meet and eventually help care for Zora, who is always ill. The writing style changes at this point from the philosophically poetic prose that preceded it to one of Djuna's un-ironic and self-absorbed series of laments about her condition. The paradoxical nature of Djuna's perspective hinges on her complaining about traits of Zora's to which not only she but also her author may be subject herself—those of allowing one's "illness" to run one's life. One can see the struggle to move beyond it, however. In a passage found midway through the book, Rango says that if Djuna's heart is breaking over Zora's hypochondria and over her relationship between Rango and Zora, her suffering will lead to good: "for the artist is like the religious man, [who] believes that . . . trouble will bring not sainthood but art, will give birth to the marvelous" (85).

In the next paragraph, the author's desire slips out of role to interrupt the narrative fabric by demanding recognition of her character as metonymous to herself: "(Thus goodness is a role, too tight around me; it is a costume I can no longer wear. There are other selves trying to be born, demanding at least a hearing!)" (85). Set in parentheses, the passage constitutes an important moment in Nin's process of working through. Fiction itself, analogous to the narrative properties that the ego uses to keep the unconscious at bay, proves too tight a "role" for Nin. On one hand, Nin perhaps achieved only a degree of the artistic goal she set for herself to "give birth to the marvelous." On the other hand, the author protests, both within and outside this role, that achieving the marvelous is a matter of becoming attuned to a way of being *beyond* one's fictions.[25] Here, inside her too-tight role as novelist, Nin switches from third to first person to demand "at least a hearing" for the possibility that she can be an artist beyond the conventional forms, a notion at the heart of her later statement of literary credo in *The Novel of the Future* (1968). Nin's resistance to the demands of the literary establishment—that literature provide a surface plot and conform to readers' expectations of anterior reality and a logical linearity—shows her conscious counterpart to her unconscious desire to frustrate the terms of reality imposed upon her by a system to which she was not satisfied subscribing.[26]

Nin intercedes further as the *Heart* continues, erasing all doubt about the voice of the paragraph narrated in first person. Now the voice of the "I" passage addresses Djuna directly: "Your past history influenced your choice, Djuna; you have shown capabilities to lessen pain and so you are not invited to the fiestas" (86).[27] Two additional paragraphs explain the logic of this passage: the authorial voice points out that others have identified Djuna with her role as helper and continue to hold her to the past because they are "scandalized by an alteration" (86). Next, the narrator gives an order: "Face to the wall!" Djuna must not let Rango see her rebellion. When the third-person narrator resumes, it is to relate that Djuna has discovered something important about herself: she has loved Rango because he lived out her own repressed childhood wishes and desires, including her anger at her parents' cruelty, related several pages earlier.

No evidence in Nin's published diaries or in Bair's biography points to an occurrence in Nin's childhood that mirrors the actions of Djuna's mother. Djuna remembers her mother pretending to be drowned, or disappearing on purpose in a crowded street, hiding behind a pole until her daughter is frantic with the games of "loss . . . which seemed like tragedies to Djuna the child" (83). From a psychoanalytic perspective, these threats represent the fear of loss itself, which motivates the ego to ward off repression. This fictional working through of the issue of loss itself leads Nin into another thematic repetition in the middle of the novel, as the story functions as a veiling of that loss. This happens as the narrative moves from authorial instruction to its next stage, a rather long series of Djuna's responses to Zora's theatrics, her "special theatre of exaggeration" (98), based closely on Nin's relationship with Helba Huara. For over twenty pages, Djuna laments Zora's fatalism and Rango's refusal to take her illnesses for what they are when even the doctors recognize Zora's hypochondria. Djuna wears herself out tending to Zora, trying without avail to live up to the ego ideal she has constructed for herself.

Finally, Djuna decides upon another course for overcoming Rango's psychological blindness to Zora's manipulations. In the hope that Rango will "see her with new eyes" (155), Djuna agrees to study revolutionary philosophy and to prepare to join the party of political rebels to which Rango is committed. She insists she is doing this out of a belief that social change "'must begin at the base, in relationship of man and woman'" (155), for here are the only roots that humans have (154). She tries to overlook "the rigid dogmas" and to see the constructive essence of the socialist agenda.[28] An optimistic view becomes difficult when Rango must indict a fellow member for a supposed treachery and afterward is sick in Djuna's arms. He begins to drink, and the stories he brings home to her worsen. He continues to get drunk night after night, and she escapes into "astronomy" and dreams (159).

The situation becomes so bad that when Sabina appears again, Djuna tries to make a match between her and Rango. The plan does not work: "Rango fled from Sabina's intensity and violence" (162). Djuna feels herself disintegrating. The image Nin uses to portray Djuna's multiplicities of self is Duchamp's *Nude Descending a Staircase:* "Not one but many Djunas descended the staircase of the barge, one layer formed by the parents, the childhood, another molded by her profession and her friends, still another born of history, geology, climate, race, economics, and all the backgrounds and backdrops" (163). The passage continues for five additional lines, ending with "and all the places where a human being is wounded, defeated, crippled, and which fester . . ." (163–64; ellipses in original). This sentence is followed by two paragraphs in which Nin imposes her own theory of the split self on the work whose presence at the 1913 Armory Show brought into art criticism a wide range of speculation on the coexistence between perceptual subjectivities within the self.[29] She would return to this theme, at the end of her next novel, to portray a similar layering and psychic disintegration in Sabina. Modernist art finds particular emphasis in Nin's last two novels, where links between the visual and musical arts, as well as between sculpture and the physical environment, provide access to the body's memory of trauma.

The Four-Chambered Heart reaches its denouement when Djuna, tired of Rango's fatalistic tendencies and Zora's theatrics, attempts suicide. Djuna pulls up a plank and lies beside her sleeping lover "to wait patiently for death" (177). In the interim, a stream-of-consciousness review of her life takes form as a prose poem, its images condensing several of the themes in Cities of the Interior: the labyrinthine search for self, relational difficulties and the quest for an impossible unity, and the anxiety brought by war (178–86). As an image of Djuna's parents appears and she recognizes them for human beings rather than as authority figures, she suddenly changes her mind and calls out to Rango. "Only children and adolescents know this total despair," she decides, "as if every wound were fatal and irremediable" (186). Like many a good story, this one ends as its protagonists escape from near-death and emerge at daybreak to be awed by the dawn as symbol of the potentiality that lies before them. Djuna and Rango's imminent breakup is implicit. The last image, however, invokes Nin's own potential movement away from despair. A fisherman on the quay has reeled in a doll and holds it out for Djuna to see:

It was a doll.
It was a doll who had committed suicide during the night. The water had washed off its features. Her hair aureoled her face with crystalline glow.
Noah's Ark had survived the flood. (187)

In "Birth" and in the Diary, Nin describes her stillborn child in a way similar to the way she describes the doll in this passage. As Djuna regards her own aborted suicide, its many layers of affect and meaning resonate to include those of Nin's attempt to acknowledge her own future in relation to the past.

CONCLUSION

In this chapter I have shown how writing the first three installments of her "continuous novel" helped Nin to grow as an artist as she confronted an internal conflict between artistry and her interpretation of womanhood as a kind of metaphorical mothering. Writing *Ladders to Fire* (1946) and *Children of the Albatross* (1947) provided Nin a way to continue the confrontation of the past that is required in psychoanalysis. Despite her sometimes compulsive use of repetition, the first two novels show that Nin was achieving some success in mourning past traumas and reconstructing their significance in a way more in keeping with her own desire than that established by a patriarchal system of signification. She also refined her writing style and her theories about gender.

By the end of the third novel, *The Four-Chambered Heart* (1950), Nin's writing shows a great deal of artistic and personal growth. Nin's work after 1950 shows her having moved through an impasse in her therapy and effectively mourned her relation to her father as well as the abortion that sixteen years earlier reinforced her belief in life as traumatic and fraught with almost insurmountable difficulties. Approximately two-thirds through her lifetime, Nin had proved to herself that she "had survived the flood." Now, she must gather her ideas into coherent form to write the final two installments of her "continuous novel." Whether she knew it or not, the process of doing so would bring her safely home—to a self she could accept and, most important in terms of her literary achievement, to her diary. The last two volumes would also establish her as an important, though somewhat obscure, Modernist writer.

5 | Catharsis and Healing in *A Spy in the House of Love, Seduction of the Minotaur,* and *Collages*

So *this* Trans—trans*mission,* trans*position,* trans*cendence*—is vi-
tally necessary not only to our human life, but also to our creativity.
And creativity is so necessary to our human life because it shows us
the capacity for change. At a certain moment in politics, when we feel
hopeless and incapable of changing our outer realities, we must re-
member that; and it will in time produce human beings who will not
create this infernal outer reality that we are traversing at this mo-
ment. . . . We have to believe that there is a continuity, that life has
a continuance. And the artist is the one who taught me that. First of
all the musicians taught me how to be consoled, how to be released
from the present, so that you can gather your strength again or main-
tain the spiritual strength which is going to carry you through the in-
ner journey.

—Anaïs Nin

THE LAST TWO NOVELS in Nin's *Cities of the Interior* series, as
well as her final novel that followed this series, show a mature Nin striving for
and often achieving a literary form that combines aesthetic distance and
boundaries with acknowledgment of the unconscious and a corresponding
fluidity of style.[1] Although the fourth novel, the self-published *A Spy in the
House of Love* (1954), often uses repetition in ways less revitalizing than compulsive, it shows Nin experimenting with technique in a way that places her

at the center of the Modernist enterprise. In particular, her attempts to achieve the compositional structure of a musical piece—while drawing on the depiction of a multiplicitous self that she admired in Duchamp's *Nude Descending a Staircase*—show that she was on the verge of establishing her own identity as an artist apart from her sense of others' expectations. *Spy*'s critique of the cultural tendency to see women as interchangeable others is perhaps its most important theme, while its treatment of Sabina's anxiety about her deceptions in the name of love provides a most revealing view of the author's response to the "trapeze" she enacted for over twenty-five years as she divided her life between New York and Los Angeles, between Hugh Guiler and Rupert Pole.[2]

It is the fifth of the series, *Seduction of the Minotaur* (1961), that constitutes real progress for Nin in both technical and thematic advancements. The ending of this novel brings Lillian, one of Nin's alter egos, to an important realization of her tendency to superimpose past images upon each other, in a way she believes she has done to her detriment nearly all her life. While writing Lillian into an awareness of how she has unconsciously eroticized a memory of past abuse and given it power over all her relationships, Nin made a significant shift in her own patterns and, to a large extent, resolved the masochism with which she had been struggling for years.[3]

Nin's resolution finds evidence in her bringing her "continuous novel" to a close, shortly after Lillian's realization, and going on to produce a last novel whose touch is lighter and whose innovative techniques are more whimsical than those of her previous works. This novel, *Collages*, is certainly not her best fiction, but it shows a willingness to let go of the past even as it asserts that, as the story "Ragtime" also declares, nothing ever ends. In this way, Nin embodies in fiction the philosophy about literary form she had been developing in her diary and criticism, namely, that she could both inscribe the formal limits of fiction as a stay against psychic chaos and retain her emphasis on the flux of life.

She also puts into practice in her last novels a distinction she makes in *The Novel of the Future*, a distinction important to her own need to find boundaries in art, between "the paintings of the insane and of the artists" (*Future* 138). Art, she maintains, is born of a disciplined vision and of formal control, whereas the expressions of the insane are more explosion than art. Although Nin herself believed she had lost artistic control in *A Spy in the House of Love* (*Future* 138), she achieved it in the two novels that followed, where her long-term commitment to developing formal boundaries in fiction finally paid off. *Seduction of the Minotaur* and *Collages* show Nin at the far end of a continuum from the explosive near-insanity that she depicted in *House of Incest* as representing her early reactions to trauma.

The five installments of *Cities of the Interior* and the sixth and final novel, *Collages*, are difficult to categorize, in part because of their fluid boundaries. They show Nin developing a clearer set of boundaries herself, not to the extent that she adopts a normative or obsessive stance, but in the sense that she develops the defensive mechanisms she needs to tolerate her existence with a greater degree of joy than she had been able to maintain earlier in life.[4] Commercially unsuccessful as Modernist art, Nin's novels also tell a story that challenges the conventional basis for evaluation of literary success in the first place. All contain moments of insight that make their reading and teaching well worthwhile despite their faults of compulsive repetition,[5] self-referential status,[6] and lack of realism.[7] They are the work of an important, though flawed, writer of insight and courage, one whom Bair has called a "*major* minor writer" of the twentieth century (xviii).

INTERLUDE: DÉDOUBLEMENT AND THE EROTICS OF GENDER IN *A SPY IN THE HOUSE OF LOVE*

The fourth *Cities* novel, *A Spy in the House of Love* (1954), is the most experimental of the "continuous novel" series. In it, Nin forsakes almost all "surface context" and chronological linearity for a "spatial" structure (Jason 60), employing frequent flashbacks and a lack of transitions that often make the action difficult to follow. At the time of its publication, some critics objected to an innovative character Nin named the Lie Detector. They especially objected to the novel's lack of contextual signposts, which makes his identity nebulous. Others, according to Bair, "believe [*Spy*] is her finest novel" (272).[8] Bair, in particular, believes *Spy* shows that Nin was ahead of her time in developing the motif of the split self.[9] The Lie Detector, for instance, is partly a projection of Sabina's fears and fantasies and partly the internal "watcher" with whom Nin struggled during the nearly ten years it took her to write the novel. He represents also the internalized analyst Nin believed must be integrated into a novel about psychic disintegration in modern culture (*Future* 139–40). Apart from its status as a literary work of art, *A Spy in the House of Love* marked a significant step for Nin in her process of narrative recovery from trauma. If, by the end of *Spy*, Sabina has disintegrated into a shapeless mass of conflict and anxiety, Nin has at least made an effort through writing this novel to leave that part of herself behind.[10]

Despite Nin's own acknowledgment that *Spy* is not one of her best (*Future* 138), the novel cannot be dismissed as bad art even when certain descriptions seem particularly inane.[11] *Spy*, in fact, boasts several dazzling passages, such as that describing Sabina's response to Stravinsky's *Firebird*, which she considers "her [own] unerring musical autobiography" (*Spy* 56). Nin combines Sabina's sense of her own identity with the Stravinsky piece, in whose "first sensual footsteps . . . she recognize[s] . . . the adolescent stalking of emotion, . . . the echo of . . . presence, not yet daring to enter the circle of frenzy" (56). The description continues over two more paragraphs whose synchronizations of color and emotion anticipate those of the next novel, where Nin believed she had finally achieved a synthesis of "the interpretations, the knowledge, the vision of the analyst within the novelist" (*Future* 140).

It is in the later *Seduction of the Minotaur*—where Nin's emphasis on music as well as the visual arts as a means of ordering experience coincides with a unified style—that Nin brings one of her alter egos to self-realization and to an effective closure. Nin's use of Duchamp's *Nude Descending a Staircase* in *The Four-Chambered Heart* to portray Djuna's sense of disintegration and Sabina's response to the same work in *A Spy in the House of Love* foreshadow the visual arts theme that becomes dominant in *Seduction*. Sabina believes she can see one of her many split selves in Duchamp's futurist painting. She wishes her husband would add additional silhouettes and dimensions to his image of her. As it is, she thinks, he has welded her to the past, continuing to put his arms around the girl he married rather than allowing his idea of her to expand into a synthesized whole made up of her cumulative selves as she has changed over the years (*Spy* 107–8). Besides this reference to the visual arts, music provides both structural and thematic emphases in *Spy in the House of Love* as Sabina searches in vain for the balance that Lillian finally achieves in the conclusion to Nin's "continuous novel."[12]

SUPERIMPOSING THE PAST: MOURNING AND
ORDER IN *SEDUCTION OF THE MINOTAUR*

Seduction of the Minotaur is probably the most important of Nin's novels in terms of her narrative recovery. Its links among the visual, musical, and literary arts bring real trauma to play in ways that echo the quality of writing Nin had admired in Lawrence thirty years earlier and portrayed in *House of Incest*. Here, her belief that writing can provide a form of self-analysis finds expression in the way painting, sculpture, and photography join music as art forms conducive to Lillian's mourning the past. The tropical Mexican setting aids her in the process by allowing real memory of past trauma to pass through her psychological lines of defense.

The novel calls attention to the way that process parallels the blending of aesthetic lines in Modernist art. Several Modernist painters—Man Ray, Chirico, Matisse, Braque, Gauguin, Diego Rivera, Orozco—orient Lillian toward a philosophy of being that mirrors Nin's own sense that her life was itself a work of art. Nin's philosophy of literary self-making was partly a "refusal to despair," partly a quest to re-make herself in her own image as opposed to remaining identified with images of herself constructed of projected assumptions of what others thought of her. She expresses this idea when Lillian sees the Mexican sky as "an infinite canvas on which human beings were incapable of projecting images" (*Seduction* 15–16). *Seduction* moves from the opening image of a "ship that could not reach the water" (5) to a healing resolution and thus mirrors Lillian's healing process. The novel ends with Lillian's journey home from Mexico to rejoin her family in the United States.

According to Nin in *The Novel of the Future*, she based the opening image of the grounded ship on a visit she made to Brittany to see a house Guy de Maupassant once lived in. Part of the local architecture there included remodeled fishing boats that had been brought inland by storm-time flooding and left stranded after the water receded. Residents would sometimes awake to find these stranded ships lodged permanently in the soil on their properties. Gardens around the area were full of such structures, which their owners had turned into guest houses or utility buildings (*Future* 20). During her weekend in Brittany, Nin asked if she could stay in one that had ended up behind the de Maupassant house. Her hosts would not hear of it and insisted she stay in the main house. That night she had a dream that she had slept in the guest house after all. During the dream, a river came to life beneath the boat, carrying her on a twenty-year journey "while husband and friends called out to [her] to stop" (*Future* 21). Nin uses the anecdote to show the connection between dream and action, for the upshot, she says, was her deciding to look for the houseboat she eventually found and rented.

The incident also reveals a common strategy Nin found to improve on an undesirable reality by fashioning one more to her liking. As the recipients of stranded boats in Brittany would make the best of the situation by using them for practical purposes, Nin remodeled them in her dream where she granted herself the wish to sleep in the boat guest house. More to the point of *The Novel of the Future*, the dream permits an escape from the house associated with de Maupassant as a proponent of literary realism and allows Nin to pursue her quest toward a literary style more in keeping with her unconscious trajectory. After all, a fishing boat belongs not in a garden at all but in "its proper sea bed" (*Seduction* 5), to which Lillian, we are told at the end of the novel's first paragraph, has determined to restore this ship "once and for all" (5).

Shortly arriving in the town she has privately named Golconda, Lillian realizes that the "waterless" dream routes are gone. She has come to forget the past but ends up mourning it instead, remembering wounds that have, as her newfound friend Dr. Hernandez puts it, imbedded themselves in her flesh like a splinter that cannot be ignored (28). The splinter image points to the somatic experience of psychological wounding and a corresponding linguistic texture that Nin recognized in D. H. Lawrence's novels. In *The Novel of the Future*, Nin describes the theme of *Seduction* as "balance between outer and inner, between past and present, between psychological reality and nature" (*Future* 140). Lillian achieves this balance through a corporal, material basis of perception by internalizing the Mexican rhythms and landscape the way a painter shapes a visual image or the way a sculptor molds the body. Nin presents Diana, one of the novel's minor characters, as comparable to a painted image in a work by Rivera or Orozco (*Seduction* 33). It is Lillian who becomes self-creative, by applying artistic techniques to consciousness. The possibility of doing so is a theme that runs throughout the book.

In its attempt to capture the rhythms of music in language in a way that shows the links among perception, a consciousness rooted in the physical body, and art, *Seduction* also reflects some of the aesthetic concerns of Nin's fellow Modernists, including her admirer Wallace Stevens.[13] In her own search for a synchronic moment in art, Nin's writing from *Seduction* onward reflects what the humanist critic Daniel R. Schwarz has described as Stevens's "effort to play colour off against sound" (Schwarz 34). In a discussion that illuminates Nin's emphasis in *Seduction* on what she called "synchronization," for example, Schwarz refers to Kandinsky's theories of "synchronism." Kandinsky, one of Stevens's influences, "believed that 'colors and forms could be the equivalents of musical harmonies' . . . [and that] colour and light could be harmonized like musical instruments" (Schwarz 34).

In a similar way, Nin combines sounds with color: "Every tree carried giant brilliant flowers playing chromatic scales, runs and trills of reds and blues. . . . The houses were covered with vines bearing bell-shaped flowers playing coloraturas" (*Seduction* 12). She also fuses the color schematics' evocative sounds with local flavors: "The guitars inside of the houses or on the doorsteps took up the color chromatics and emitted sounds which evoked the flavor of guava, papaya, cactus figs, anise, saffron, and red pepper" (12). The atmosphere itself sculpts Lillian's body and especially her awareness of it. As she walks through the town, "a procession of images marching through the retina" makes her "more aware of her body. The swimming, the sun, the air, all contributed to sculpture a firm, elastic, balanced body, free in its movements" (90).

As a result, Lillian's focus on suffering and repetition begins to shift. She arrived "not free" (28), a "fugitive from truth" and wondering if she was forever "'condemned to repetition,'" to "'re-experience the same drama over and over again'" (29). Instead, she finds that the atmosphere and the culture help her to relinquish the double exposure of memory that has become a mental habit for her (80). Before her arrival in Mexico, this double exposure left Lillian unable to escape her mother's judgmental eyes or her father's image, to which she always returned through relationships with men like him (75).[14] But here she finds that the warm tile under her feet as she dresses for dinner and the scents of carnation and honeysuckle adrift on the night air as she walks from her room to the terrace reveal her neurotic preoccupations as "out of scale and absurd" (16). Lillian ceases "defending against her own nature in Mexico" (*Future* 69). "The atmosphere of Mexico was in itself *conducive* to a slower rhythm, time for reflection, and the people seemed to live in greater harmony with nature and with themselves" (*Future* 142).[15]

Numerous passages show a connection between the visual and musical arts, on one hand, and a perceptual reality rooted in the body but apprehended in language, on the other. Linking rhythm to the visual realm, *Seduction* provides comment upon Modernist painting in terms of both physical and psychological landscape and its associative images. The narrator comments that the relation between Braque and Matisse paintings and old-fashioned still lifes, in terms of color and textual arrangement, parallels the relation between the local environment in Golconda and the presentational patterns of flowers on the dresses of some of the natives in the dance halls (*Seduction* 105). She invokes Gauguin's work as a model for capturing in language a sense of the body's rhythms. This language is separate from one made up of words (34–35).

Nin gives the body itself emphatic importance from the opening pages when Lillian arrives in Golconda to find her skin breathing differently than at home. The atmosphere attests to the "dignity and importance of the body" (6). Even the airport customs officers convey a bodily sense of authority in their appearing without shirts. In a passage that reveals Nin's own attempts to find balance in literature between structural boundaries and stylistic fluidity, the custom officers' smiling expressions suggest to Lillian that the nature of authority is itself more fluid here. Theirs is "a physical vision" (6), Lillian thinks, repeating a phrase Nin used to describe the texture of Lawrence's writing. Nin's portraying these father figures as smiling and protective, rather than harsh and threatening, also shows Nin using her author's prerogative to reorganize the wounding elements of her past into artistic form.

Acknowledging and coming to terms with her need for boundaries, Lillian incorporates a corporal perspective linked to art and music. The narrator distinguishes that perspective from a tendency to overanalyze. "It was not only the music from the guitars but the music of the body" (14) that Lillian encounters upon her arrival. Jazz, in particular, allows her "to embroider on all her moods" (43). For the mature Nin, jazz improvisation came the closest of all art forms to represent the way she believed writing could be used to improvise a self-myth not dependent on the accumulated memories and attachments of the past. Its turns of phrase and revitalizing repetitions encouraged her to live in the moment rather than to engage in the habit of *dédoublement*. An example of Lillian's new ability to become engulfed in experience through art and landscape appears about midway through the novel as she watches a sunrise:

> Just as music was an unbroken chain in Golconda, so were the synchronizations of color. Where the flowers ended their jeweled displays, their pagan illuminated manuscripts, fruits took up the gradations. Once or twice, her mouth full of fruit, she stopped. She had the feeling that she was eating the dawn. (49)

In passages like this, the blending of landscape imagery with color chromatics provides Lillian, a musician herself, the aesthetic merging she needs to counter a sense of psychological fragmentation. The real memory of past trauma expresses itself gently enough through the body that her resistance to healing can be overcome. At other times, music itself provides the impetus to reflect on the significance of the tropical environment and to return to a physical awareness, as when she listens to a jazz band playing at the Black Pearl, where she has been hired to play. "Because the hiss of the sea carried away some of the overtones, the main drum beat seemed more emphatic, a giant heart pulsing. The more volatile cadences, the ironic notes, the lyrical half-sobs of the trombone rose like sea spray and were lost" (17).

Several additional passages in *Seduction* show Nin at a high point in her career as a writer, having worked through her issues in fiction while also becoming, as Wilson had described her some years earlier, a very good artist. The novel's narrative breaches are also operative. In particular, they show how narrative interruptions function like speech in an analysis, where the stories an analysand tells often reinforce his ego fictions until the narrative fabric can be interrupted and the speaker helped beyond his self-myths to encounter the excluded parts of being. For example, we see Nin's desire for a unifying perspective emerge to interrupt the story at the point just before Lillian realizes that her presence in Mexico can help her, unlike her mother, to accept the "flaws, spots, stains, wrinkles" in life (88). Writing-as-analysis has worked in this instance. Just as a key moment in an analysand's speech can act as a signal for the analyst to guide the speaker to acknowledge the repressed parts of his being, so Nin's desire for a totalizing vision finds a statement, first about the relativity of vision itself, then about the character's separating from mother-as-ego-ideal, and finally about the character's movement beyond perfectionism. Lillian's movement mirrors Nin's own.

Part of Lillian's acceptance of experience on its own terms involves an acceptance of death. *Seduction of the Minotaur* is the first of Nin's novels to portray the death of an important character, Dr. Hernandez, who serves as a kind of spiritual counselor to Lillian. In *The Novel of the Future*, Nin writes that Hernandez's death represents "the first time I accepted a physical death. It was frequent, natural, and consistent with life in Mexico. It also forced Lillian out of her evasions" (*Future* 141).[16] In the novel, Dr. Hernandez is a doctor of Spanish and Indian heritage who long ago, as a condition of his medical education, agreed to spend a year practicing medicine in the local town of Golconda. He resisted the experience at first, reading French novels and occupying his thoughts with future plans. But he, as Lillian does several years later, became enamored with the locality and with the native people there. Unlike Lillian, he eventually loses interest in moving on and decides to stay. Lillian meets him just after she arrives at the airport, when she shares a taxi into town with him and two other men. Lillian and Dr. Hernandez remain friends, until he is shot by drug dealers he has refused to cooperate with.

Although Nin's writing has often been criticized as being precious or self-absorbed, her depiction of Lillian's grief is poignant and real. Lillian's sense of disbelief as she approaches the scene of the accident, her distancing mechanisms as she holds the hysterical Mrs. Hernandez, the way that she inwardly protests the terms of his death—these details corroborate Nin's sense that she has portrayed something different and cathartic for Lillian. Especially important is that Lillian, with some convincing argument from Diana, must realize that Dr. Hernandez played into the games of the drug dealers who killed him. When she sees that his death was probably preventable and thus a form of fatalistic self-determination, she realizes that she, too, has been complicit in a course of emotional, if not physical, destruction. This is an important idea in the novel, and for Nin in general. As if to mark its significance for Nin's restoration to a sense of integration, a passage returning to jazz rhythms and themes—Nin's signifiers for wholeness and artistic reconstruction—marks Lillian's departure from Golconda.

A critique of American consumerism that immediately precedes Lillian's return to the States points to another distinction both Lillian and Nin are making. Lillian strives to distinguish between aspects of "home" that she will accept and elements of her American culture that she will not.[17] Similarly, Nin, who resisted Americanization and became a citizen only in 1952 (Bair 587 n. 31), objected to the values of a culture in which she eventually made a permanent home.[18]

Nin foreshadows the ending of the novel by imbedding within her narrative a rejection of an interpretation of culture and of the value of art that hurts her and, by extension, her characters. The motif appears early, when Lillian takes the taxi ride from the airport with Dr. Hernandez and two other men. One of the others turns out to be Mr. Hansen, an Austrian who, unlike Dr. Hernandez, has not been warmed by the Mexican culture and speaks with an authoritative air. The other man is Hatcher, an engineer "who had come . . . years before to build roads and bridges and had remained and married a Mexican woman" (*Seduction* 10). With his leathery skin, his sandals, and linen clothing, Hatcher is more acclimated to the Tropics than Hansen is, but Lillian muses that "on him the negligent attire still seemed a uniform to conquer" rather than a sign of submission to the atmosphere (10).[19]

Later, when Lillian takes a small trip to visit Hatcher and his Mexican wife at what she imagines will be a simple homestead representing an American's assimilation to indigenous culture, she finds instead a monument to consumerism. Although the living is simple inside the main house, Hatcher keeps a storehouse stacked with supplies of American products such as cans of asparagus and cling peaches, medicines, reading materials, even crutches just "'in case

[he] should break a leg'" (80). As she begins shortly afterward to regain "her own vision" (89), Lillian comes to see the commercialism of a culture that encourages its citizens to be so dependent upon material goods that they cannot let go of their fear and the related theme of one's staying always outside experience as obstacles to true growth. Even Dr. Hernandez ironically becomes commodified through his refusal to participate in another kind of trade—the exchange of illegal drugs. Like Hatcher, though much more beloved, Dr. Hernandez serves as a catalyst to Lillian's growth. Recognizing his flaws helps Lillian accept her own. Loving his memory despite those flaws helps her move toward recognizing that she can give and receive love without demanding perfection.

Another of the novel's critiques of American commercialism appears as a kind of parodic imitation of a scene from a Hemingway novel. Nin includes a bus ride over the rugged landscape (68–78), similar to that in *The Sun Also Rises.* There are also two references to bullfight scenes in her narrative (43, 68). In addition, Lillian refuses the "male-only" protocol of a street celebration and, like Lady Brett, dances into the festivities, swept along by men who are surprised but delighted by the spectacle of the American woman who does not have to "conform to their traditions" (65). Afterward, when her companion, Michael, stands disconcerted and upset by her breach of conduct, Lillian responds with one of the book's gestures toward Nin's gender theories. She asks him, "'What is it . . . ? . . . Did you mind that your fantasy about a world without women was proved not true?'" (66). Nin's critique, then, is not only of the commercialism that renders her psychological stories less valuable on the market than, for example, those of her masculine contemporary Hemingway, a writer whose style could hardly be less different from Nin's, but also of the normative fear of woman that many feminists have seen as the root of the patriarchal repression of women.

Ultimately, the relevance of this idea to Nin's narrative recovery lies in her rejection of any subjugation to the terms of another's story. Nin's insistence on writing her own story as a woman finds particular emphasis in *Seduction of the Minotaur*'s cardboard-cutout theme. In *Spy,* the cutout image appears as part of Sabina's response to Duchamp's *Nude* (*Spy* 107). In *Seduction,* the cutout motif first appears just after Lillian has been made the dupe of a scheme: she has "rescued" an American tourist from prison by giving him money to buy his release. Afterward, the image of various psychological prisons such as anxiety and fear haunts her throughout the novel until she works her way to her own freedom. Before she finds out that the "prisoner" conned her, Lillian feels "immensely light, as if she had freed a part of herself" (*Seduction* 42).

Her lack of familiarity with the local landscape contributes to this sense of freedom, causing a needed but uncomfortable disorientation, like those provoked by the best of Surrealist images. One such image she thinks of is a large cutout of a Coca-Cola bottle, placed in the bullring before a fight she witnessed. The bullfight itself seemed a "gross surrealist dream" (43). Lillian thought the advertising image of the Coke bottle was to be used to incite the bull to charge, but right before the fight six attendants come into the ring, shoulder the enormous cutout, and take it away as "publicity's defeated trophy" (43). The "rescued" Coke bottle reveals the novel's resistance to debilitating generalization. It also reveals Lillian's illusion about having rescued another rather than herself, much as the younger Nin often tried to "mother" other artists rather than nurture her own art.

Coca-Cola becomes a metonymy for both American consumerism and the reduction of women to images, in a later passage, where we meet an ex-violinist named Edward. Married and divorced several times, Edward represents the reductionist gaze of one who sees others as interchangeable, "walking posters, like one-dimensional cut-outs" (55), a metaphor that echoes the advertising-image theme of the Coke bottle in the bull pen. The cutouts and the product itself link these passages: Edward has made his living doing various jobs, recently distributing Coca-Cola calendars throughout Mexico, where, to his surprise, the people love them and display them proudly. Nin's description of the pictures on the calendars is as of a Surrealist advertising nightmare. A female sacrificial victim who looks "like Gypsy Rose Lee," for instance, dwarfs the volcano, protruding behind her like a giant breast (52). The word "calendar" appears once before in the passage, when we learn that Edward keeps track of his past "calendar of events" by determining whom he was married to when an event occurred.

His multiple marriages and divorces, from which he has several children, provide another example of interchangeability and the substitutive nature of his relationships and those he represents. Both terms—"interchangeable mother" and "substitution"—appear in the passage (53). Another telling trait is that when Edward drinks tequila, he launches into drawn-out lectures repudiating art. The Coca-Cola calendar operates metonymously between Edward's character and the bullfight passage to link commercialization with the totalizing impulse inherent in constructions of women and others that render them interchangeable. A second connection appears to establish advertising copy and art as opposites. With her parodic characterization of Edward, Nin deals a critical blow to the reductionism in American critical taste, which she held to be responsible for her novels' lack of commercial success.[20]

A particularly interesting turn in the Edward passage involves a woman to whom he is attracted and whose "perfect image" his children fear because of its potential to leave their father "spellbound" and neglectful. They need not worry; this "airline beauty queen" chooses an injured ex-marine as a partner, a man who (like Hemingway's Jake Barnes, except he served in World War II rather than in World War I) has suffered an injury too terrible to name, not visible from the outside. All we know is that he is "damaged inside" from an atom bomb experiment for which he volunteered. Once again, Nin treats psychological damage in the context of twentieth-century anxieties, linking here (as she does in numerous places throughout her fiction and diaries) the real effects of identificatory limits violation with a wider sphere of threat. The American airline beauty's attraction to her damaged lover is based on a similarity between them, which Lillian sees, and sees through. She believes the couple's rather stiff facades and automatic body language are disguises as much as any others' demeanors and that their dissociative personalities result from their lack of self-awareness (55).

The protective illusion people create so that others cannot read their souls or recognize their vulnerabilities is one of the connecting links to the next passage, in which the bullfight theme finds treatment. On the bus to San Luis to visit Hatcher, Lillian considers the bullfighter and wonders why she was so attracted to his fury at the bull during the fight. Her answer comes in the form of a little girl on the bus whose description matches in significant ways the portraits of Nin's stillborn child that appear in the *Diary* and in the short story "Birth." As Nin mourns her own past, this text shows her willingness to delve, like Lillian, into the memories she has repressed. Lillian considers the transparency of the child with "heavily fringed . . . eyelashes" in light of "Her own little girl at home," who also had this transparency (70). In an earlier image that is reminiscent of Nin's stillborn aborted child, Lillian noticed the tenderness of a small Mexican child, Maria, who is "small for her age, delicately molded, like a miniature child" (11).

Lillian also draws a connection between memory and painting when she reflects that in "the eyes of most Mexican painters, these finely chiseled beings with small hands and feet and slender necks and waists become larger than nature" (11), whereas Lillian sees them small, with tenderness. The representation of a small, finely chiseled child as a sentimental painted image calls attention to the novel's earlier distinction between the still lifes of old-fashioned painters, which Nin depicted as devoid of imaginative transformation, and the vibrantly sensual paintings of the Modernists. With this distinction Nin strives for an artistry she has theorized, one that for her will take the place of and be superior to biological mothering. She perhaps misses the mark, but she creates in art a character who effectively grieves for Nin what Nin could not. Through Lillian, Nin once and for all mourns—rather than denying the need to mourn—the loss of the child "she had once been" (71) and the child whose loss she chose deliberately in 1934.

As Lillian remembers her past on the flight home from Mexico, she relives many additional elements of her past. Among the most difficult issues is her coming to terms with a nearly lifelong masochism. Like Nin, Lillian consciously seeks "the Minotaur who would devour her" (111). Lillian is surprised to realize that "now that she had come face to face" with the internal source of fear she has avoided for so long, "the Minotaur resembled someone she knew" (111). Like Nin, Lillian was rejected by a harsh father, one whose only form of physical expression with his children was a nearly daily ritual of marching the children up to the attic to spank them. In her memory of the punishments, Lillian has "two distinct emotions: one of humiliation, the other the pleasure of intimacy" (111). The feared place of punishment and pain became linked in her mind with ritualized touch, "the only caress she had known from her father" (112–13).

As the flashbacks proceed forward to Lillian's early adulthood, she recalls an additional, more literal scene. She remembers straying into an arcade in Paris and slipping a penny into the slot to watch first one and then another erotic movie clip in which a maid and several schoolgirls were being spanked by men. The first is punished to "atone for the accident" of spilling soup on her employer. In the second clip, the teacher becomes angry at his students' mockeries and demands that they come up one by one to be spanked, "just as Lillian and her sisters and brothers were lined up and made to march up the stairs" (112). At first Lillian wants to flee in order not to feel the pain of the past. But she then is overcome with a sensation of erotic pleasure and wishes she could trade places with the girl in the film (113).

As she reflects on this during her flight, Lillian realizes she has carried the overlaying of pain and pleasure into her adult relationships, expecting not physical but emotional pain from men and receiving it from many lovers (see also Henke, "Lillian Beye" 142–43). She decides the reason she has rejected her marriage is that her husband, Larry, does not cause her the pain she has unconsciously been seeking. This realization shows her there is a logic to her masochism and therefore a solution. Like a cell isolated from its diseased counterparts in a scientific laboratory, she thinks, she is "capable of new life" (*Seduction* 113). She wants to erase "the grooves etched by the past" and shed the "plaster cast" of a "self-created myth" to which she has become habituated (114)—all images that reflect Nin's own analytic goals (Henke, "Lillian Beye" 144).

Whether Nin achieved these goals is debatable. With Lillian's realization that her interpretation of the past is within her own powers to change, Nin makes an important statement about the possibilities for gaining a relative freedom from suffering through acknowledging and coming to terms with repressed parts of oneself.[21] The remaining pages of the book are filled with Lillian's flashbacks and self-observations as she considers her future, returning, in a final astronomical conceit, to be "born in the molten love of the one who cared" (*Seduction* 136). She sees the plane as the "solar barque" of an Egyptian myth cited earlier in the novel, taking her to Larry as source and sun rather than to the moon as a symbol of continued self-mirroring. More important, Lillian's flight "home" represents her own powers of interpretation and points to the excluded parts of her being as source of the balance she has sought and achieved.

Lillian's journey is a singular one. It takes her back to husband and daughters only after she has reached an understanding of the problems inherent in her marriage, most notably that both partners have engaged in illusions of unity rather than in simple caring for each other; her recognition of her own mental habit of superimposing many layers of the past upon her image of Larry helps her move beyond an obsession with a totalizing relationship and allows her to return on her own terms.

Seduction of the Minotaur stands as the novel in which Nin worked herself out of some debilitating attachments to dead letters of the past. It was the first book, she says, that she wrote without dependence on the diary (*Future* 140). In it, she brought to fruition many of the literary innovations she associated with artistic transformation. A quarter of a century after publishing her first work of fiction, Nin ends her "continuous novel," demonstrating in the process that she had effectively established fictional borders within which to mourn. Although she held fiction up as an ideal, she would abandon her belief that it was a higher art than autobiography. Her last novel, *Collages* (1964), portrays her ambivalence toward the opposition she had established in her diary between fiction and diary writing and her movement toward an understanding that both forms of literature reflect only partially the nature of truth.

POSTING THE MODERN:
ARTISTIC *JOUISSANCE* IN *COLLAGES*

As Nin anticipates publishing her diary as a work of literature whose status *as* literature would continue to challenge conventional definitions of what constitutes a literary work, the line between art and life was particularly relevant. *Collages* replaces the devastating effects of identificatory border-erasure evident in Nin's early work by underscoring what Lillian realizes at the end of *Seduction:* that life is fragmentary and often painful, but that those who are willing to confront the monsters within and to reframe those monsters' significance in their lives can establish a creative perspective with which to live more healthily and with more love (*see also* Henke, "Lillian Beye" 144). Nin's belief in the psychoanalytic process finds metaphorical expression in her penultimate novel's redefinition of trauma as a region from which one can emerge, rather than as a perpetual prison for the heart and mind. Her final novel speaks from that release.

The structure of *Collages* also participates in the questioning of artistic categories and genre boundaries typical of Postmodern theory, even as Nin remained thoroughly Modern in her emphasis on structure as an organizing element in art. In particular, Susan Sontag's belief that art in mass culture could be seen as modifying consciousness itself (Hutcheon 249) is echoed in Nin's belief that true art must be born of a disciplined search for meaning within a labyrinthine layering of selfhoods constructed by nature, biology, history, culture, and language. This idea finds fictional form in *Heart's* treatment of Cubist perspectives of modern womanhood. It takes structural expression in the wavering boundaries between the installments of Nin's "continuous novel," between the elements that comprise *Collages,* and between art and life.

In her dedication of her last novel to "R.P. . . . the real gardener" in her life, Nin calls *Collages* a "humorous book." Although Hinz calls it "the most satiric and objective of all her works" (Hinz 61), Nancy Scholar and others have questioned whether there is a truly comedic element in the novel (Scholar 127; Jason 69–71). Their inquiry—along with another somewhat negative reception of the work (Jason 69)—reflects Nin's difficulty in achieving an ironic point of view and negotiating the linguistic subtleties that non-native speakers of English may find difficult to master.[22] Relative to her other works, however, *Collages* is refreshingly lighthearted, even in its refusal to deny a current of sorrow in the world at large.

Related to its treatment of boundaries and choice, its theme is that one may transform authentic human grief from despair into art. Its title reflects the way that one of its characters—named for and based on Nin's friend, the collagist Jean Varda—pieces together various fragments of material into mythological women.[23] The primary female character of *Collages* is also an artist, Renate, who is modeled upon one of Nin's friends, Renate Druks. Nin considered her "'an amusing woman but a bad painter,' but she liked the way Renate lived life with bravado and zest" (Bair 408).

Some critics have accepted the implication of the title and consider *Collages* more a collection of short stories with a common thread than a novel (Evans 178; Knapp 18). For example, in the early sections, Renate's experiences are central. By the middle of the book, her role has shifted from protagonist to participating observer or subject of observation. By *Collages'* ending section, Renate has been replaced as a major character by Judith Sands (a writer whose characterization was inspired by Djuna Barnes but who also may represent Nin).[24] The shifting perspectives, the lack of a unified narrative voice, and the eclectic mix of vignettes support the title idea that a work of art as collage can represent modern life in ways that motivate one to go beyond that representation and beyond the totalizing tendencies of the ego.[25] For the first time, Nin produced a book that was neither modeled on herself nor about a distressed, neurotic woman seeking relief from emotional suffering. Rather, *Collages* was modeled on one whose otherness Nin did not try to appropriate.

The increased degree of aesthetic distance in *Collages* reflects that Nin had truly moved away from stifling interpretations of the past. It also shows that she was learning to adopt a healthier attitude toward negative critical response to her work. The issue of "good" versus "bad" art (a subject treated with some depth in *Seduction*) appears in *Collages* as an extension of Nin's belief that one's life itself can be made a work of art. *Collages* also reflects Nin's idea that critical assessments of the visual as well as the literary arts are often based on subjective prejudice, shifting critical taste, and misunderstanding of the works' intentions (Hinz 84). As Nin matured, she was able to gain some distance from the critical rejection that had followed her throughout her career. She was still prone to respond to negative reviews—either directly, by writing to the reviewer, or indirectly, in *The Novel of the Future* and the *Diary*—but *Collages* demonstrates her ability to stand back and laugh in her own way at what she perceived as her own and others' failings.

Renate's response to her young lover's irresponsibility and narcissistic antics mirrors Nin's attitude of acceptance without masochism. A truly funny scene demonstrates this shift in Nin's behavior, especially in its parodic relation to earlier episodes in Nin's fiction. One scene Nin parodies in *Collages* is the one from *Ladders to Fire* that shows Lillian's suffering in response to Jay's story about the two pianos in the rain. Nin personalizes the scene, as she continues to personalize all his flights from responsibility, until she is finally able to take leave of him emotionally at the end of *Seduction of the Minotaur*, when she puts his egoism in perspective by reflecting on the way his paintings portrayed "everything . . . larger than nature," as if he was "trying to match his own extravagances" (*Seduction* 116). Djuna in *The Four-Chambered Heart* feels similarly hurt by Rango's irresponsibility, and she depends on his general passivism to ensure he will sleep through the suicidal crisis she creates near the end. Only her own change of heart saves her.

In *Collages*, Nin parodies both scenes with a farcical European sailing trip Bruce and Renate take at Bruce's insistence. The journey is fraught with small crises for the inexperienced sailors: Bruce has learned to sail by reading "directions from a book" (*Collages* 23). Shortly into their trip, he becomes tangled in cords and must call to Renate for help. When they decide to leave the roughness of the sea for the calmer rivers, they cannot make the boat travel a straight line, and Bruce receives a ticket for ruining an historical bridge, which he protests he "'didn't know . . . was historical'" (24). Eventually, they must put the boat on a train where its caulking melts in the hot Mediterranean sun. When they put the vessel into the water again, it is full of holes. It sinks. Rather than taking these failures personally, though, the exhausted Renate takes a wider view than Nin's former characters. She sings a song from childhood as she helps to rescue the boat, insisting that "'From now on our travels will have to be inner voyages. You are only fit to be the captain of Rimbaud's *Bateau Ivre*'" (26).

Another parodic scene puts Jay's larger-than-life paintings in humorous perspective. When Renate's house catches fire, Bruce rescues a huge painting of himself that Renate made when, at the beginning of their relationship, he demanded she stop all other work to paint him. It is a life-sized depiction of Bruce as Pan. As Bruce carries it down the hill away from the house, it covers his whole body so that only "two feet showed below the frame, two feet in shoes just below the naked feet of the painting" (28). The reader can share Renate's mix of dry amusement, resignation, and humor at the spectacle of "a walking painting with feet" approaching the astounded firefighters below. The disruption of expectation that Jay appreciated in the sight of two pianos on a rainy New York City sidewalk is superimposed by this image, which provides a similar disruption (but to better effect) and at the same time highlights the process by which Jay and Bruce project their own images at their partners' expense. The difference, of course, is in how their partners react.

Sharon Spencer points out that, even when Bruce's faults are more cruel, Renate, because she is "far more healthy and mature" than some of Nin's earlier characters, "accepts what [Bruce] can give" without making him the focal point of her full, rich, creative life (Spencer 115). Bruce's cruelty appears when he writes stories about his past for Renate to read. He particularly wants her to read them when she is curious about his bisexuality or his past. One story involves a form of sexual sadism whose aftereffect Renate finds worse than the sadistic sexual act. She learns that a young man in Mexico, caught naked in the woods when he and Bruce were beating each other with switches, ended up being arrested and imprisoned, perhaps for life, because Bruce cleared himself by accusing the boy of stealing his watch. Renate throws this story and the box in which Bruce left it into the ocean, as if to refuse his attempt to manipulate her emotions with his stories. One can wonder at the efficacy of Renate's action while recognizing that the principle Nin affirms in Renate is the ability to use an artist's ability to shape the materials of life into a livable reality and to transform the ugly and traumatic into meaningful expressions. For Spencer, Renate's "combination of a creative attitude toward people . . . and her devotion to the art of painting make her the single figure in Nin's fiction whose life expresses the values described in the Diaries as specifically feminine" (Spencer 115).

While portraying Renate as specifically feminine, however, Nin moves beyond the gender opposition that occurs earlier in her career as novelist. Varda's characterization places an insightful, artistic man in a central position and, along with Renate's portrait, makes explicit a change in the notion, which Nin expresses as early as *Ladders to Fire,* that gender is a matter of whose eyes one looks through. By this point, a healthy perspective is an artistic perspective, regardless of gender. Whereas Nin's early depictions of gender are often as of polarized opposites, *Collages* puts forth a less gender-based portrayal. In her last novel, Nin looks beyond rigid categorical principles to find a perspective in keeping with an evolving being's need for innovation and joy.

That need finds multiple expressions in *Collages*. The enhancement of the ordinary appears in the characterization of Count Laundromat, a potentially anonymous person who is brought to significance when Renate pays attention to his personal history. In another section, Renate's painting "the friendship of women and animals" (40) appears an alternative to artistic cruelty. Another scene shows transformation taking an imaginary turn when an old man becomes a seal. Renate's experiences as a nightclub hostess to earn extra money include an incident about a man who turns the tables of expected reaction when he insists his angry partner be given the best wine goblets in the house to break, and a story about a cook who channels an acquired American "giganticism" into the creation of specialty dishes.

The important vignette involving the collagist Varda portrays his teenage daughter's rebellion against her father's vision. Her experiments with hallucinogens show her a way to see the world differently. But because Varda, rather than moralizing, discusses the drug's effects on perception, his daughter emerges from the cocoon of rebellion to see with her own eyes, rather than through drug-induced vision, the transmutations of color, light, and images her father's collages make available to those who are willing to see.[26]

In an ending that "may well be prophetic" (Spencer 115), Nin returns to the interrelated themes of gender and artistic transformation. Judith Sands, a character clearly meant to represent Nin, is an author whose works have been neglected by critics and public alike and who has become a recluse. One day Dr. Mann, a scholar and a collector of art who makes yearly trips to the States from Israel, visits her apartment. He has read her books; he knows she is an important writer despite the public's rejection. His name itself shows that Nin believed in "man's" potential to grow and to learn beyond traditional masculinities. Dr. Mann insists, among other things, that the distinction between "women" and "men" are "mock distinctions." He tells her he has recognized this truth in her books. For himself, he has not decided whether to "write as a man or a woman" (*Collages* 115). He believes he is a true-life version of her characters and believes she denies him a part of himself by not agreeing to see him.

Finally, after Dr. Mann has pleaded from outside Judith's closed door for days, she lets him in. After they meet, he takes her to the Museum of Modern Art to witness one artist's interpretation of technological angst. The art piece appears to be a pile of assorted objects covered with snow, wired to explode at a key moment. As the public watches the exhibition, the artist, Tinguely, sets its performance in motion. A baby carriage escapes but circles back; a piano bursts into flames; a balloon emits gases and vapors with dramatic bursting. The structure rumbles, sputters, protests, and explodes as the "new kind of destructive, death dealing instrument" (*Collages* 119) carries on to exhibit automated painting of artists' names upon rolls of paper only to immediately consume the list back into itself "in desperate inversion" (119). Later, all but a few of the names are destroyed when the sculpture spits them back out and they catch fire. The scene goes on, but the structure, programmed to perform its suicide, is taking too long. Finally, Tinguely must intervene before the fire chief stops the action. He gives it a kick, bringing the symbolic destruction to a swift closure as the media photographers capture only the artist's final kick on film.

It is a marvelous passage, one that captures Nin's sense, shared with other Modernists, that urbanization and technology were changing the nature of life, of art, and of media-conditioned responses to both. Spencer implies that the narrator is indicting Tinguely for "nudging his own brainchild to death" (Spencer 116). Certainly the images of self-destruction are operative on many levels. As Nin takes leave of novel writing for good, she emphasizes her own resistance to such self-destruction.

After the exhibition Judith, Renate, and Dr. Mann return to Judith's apartment. The name "Judith Sands" is among those on Tinguely's machine that has not burned, signifying that her art has lasting potential. The novel ends when she agrees to show her visitors an unpublished manuscript, and Renate begins to read from it the same words as those that begin *Collages*. The ending of the novel is circular, a no-end that once again challenges conventional borders, showing Nin's ambivalence toward formal boundaries. Ultimately, her ending shows her conscious choice to choose a permeable and elastic literary form in which to express her idea that art was inextricably bound to lived experience.

Collages is, in a sense, Nin's love letter to those who helped her along the way as well as a good-bye to her career as novelist. The fiction that had occupied her for three decades was behind her. The diary she afterward considered her true life's work was waiting to be born as a published work. Yet, even as she ended her career as fiction writer, Nin thematized in her last novel the issue of formal boundaries by ending with a paradoxical refusal to end. Unlike earlier refusals, this one shows Nin drawing a permeable line between past and present, between fiction and diary, and between traditional art and the novel of the future. Accepting the fluctuating nature of that line was part of her healing.

CONCLUSION

None of the six flawed but insightful novels Nin produced between 1946 and 1964 has yet fulfilled Nin's hope that they would establish her as a literary innovator of stature equal to that of Joyce, Proust, Lawrence, and the other Modernists with whom she identified. Her hope of gaining public recognition for her work would indeed be fulfilled during her lifetime, but most of it was inspired by the *Diary*, whose first volume appeared in 1966. Although a handful of critics have written in-depth studies of Nin's fictional works, it remains to be seen whether Nin will emerge at some point in the future of literary criticism as a novelist of distinction. Nin's growth as an artist and as a human being, though, is clearly established in the progression from *Ladders to Fire* to *Collages*.

As an artist, Nin gains distance and objectivity and enhances her craft. As she learns to relinquish the role of wounded daughter, Nin moves out of an unhealthy attachment to the past, becoming more able to make appropriate distinctions, to let go of perfectionism, and to accept her own flaws, as well as those of others. She uses the formal constraints of writing fiction to separate ego from ego ideal, even as she challenges these formal constraints in constructive ways in order to come to terms with her own desire. Nin's long, painful process of mourning her father's hold on her eventually led her to a position from which she could reclaim her self and her diary as her own. The latter would not remain her own for long. Once it was published, *The Diary of Anaïs Nin* became as much her readers' as her own. But the self she had created in the process—a self staked out apart from patriarchal and paternal dictates—would remain Nin's best work of art. Whether it was a work of fiction or nonfiction is, by this point, a rhetorical question.

6

Narrative Recovery and Narrative Authenticity in *The Diary of Anaïs Nin*

The women's movement, in its different and sometimes contradictory aspects, has, for the past few years, deeply shaken the social habits and the cultural tradition of the modern world. Propelled by this movement or disturbed by what it has left untouched, research on women has recently begun to appear. It took its first steps modestly, but it has become increasingly daring in the various domains of writing and the social sciences, abandoning the vindictive discourse of a modish and already out-dated feminism in order to attach key areas of ideology or of knowledge and to analyze them from a new vantage point—the point of view of women.

—Gisèle Halimi

IN 1966, NIN'S DREAM OF PUBLISHING her diary came true.[1] After numerous rejections from other publishers, Harcourt Brace Jovanovich issued *The Diary of Anaïs Nin (1931–1934)*. Six additional volumes emerged at regular intervals over the next fourteen years: *Volume 2 (1934–1939)* in 1967, *Volume 3 (1939–1944)* in 1969, *Volume 4 (1944–1947)* in 1971, *Volume 5 (1947–1955)* in 1974, *Volume 6 (1955–1966)* in 1976, and *Volume 7 (1966–1974)* posthumously in 1980.[2] Nin considered the fifty-five-year project, which she had worked for over thirty years to make public, her masterpiece. Many critics have concurred. Considering her autobiographical writing as having the greater value, for instance, Franklin and Schneider judged that Nin's thirty-odd year effort to gain recognition as a fiction writer had been misdirected (Jason 67). With the publication of the *Diary,* Nin's resolution of her conflict over the issue of formal aesthetic boundaries was made complete. Having worked out her narrative recovery in fiction, she could embrace its source material—her diary—as having equal, or greater, worth. Paradoxically, it was only by working through the fiction first that she could claim the *Diary* as her tour de force.

In the early 1930s, Henry Miller had predicted the diary would make her famous someday; and it did.[3] "The literary world, having ignored Anaïs Nin for the past quarter century, suddenly perked up, and the attention she craved all those years descended in a deluge" (Bair 479). Nin's life changed almost overnight as fan letter after fan letter arrived. Her perception in the public eye was transformed from a little-known coterie writer of abstract fiction to a spokesperson for the conscience-raising movements of the 1960s, especially women's studies:

> I don't know what a "radical feminist" is, but I *am* a feminist. . . . And what I discovered, when the diaries came out, were the thousands of women in lonely little towns who had no one to share their aspirations with; who had some creative disturbance and restlessness and felt that they had potentialities but did not know how to develop them and were very much lacking in self-confidence; who were apt to invest in the people around them the faith that they should have had for themselves.
>
> Now, it is true that I believe liberation is never achieved by one segment of people; it has to be simultaneous and it has to happen to all of us. But I also think that men have learned from woman's great quest for her identity, have learned that we have to peel off the programming, the conditioning, the education, the taboos, and the dogmas that have been inculcated in us. The restrictions were stronger for woman because the pattern was very rigid and very limited, and she was shut in within her personal world. (*A Woman Speaks* 35)

For the rest of her life, Nin remained at the center of a devoted circle of readers who found messages of hope and inspiration in the *Diary*'s emphasis on personal growth, though she also often fell under fire of feminist objection to her particular kind of femininity.[4] Their loyalty to her extended beyond that usually afforded a writer. Anaïs Nin became, for many women as well as men, a universal mother figure, one who answered their questions and their letters and continued to inspire them with the *Diary,* college lectures, and speeches.[5]

Nin died in 1977, a cultural heroine, the object of awards and recognition beyond expectation. Her honors included her induction into the American Academy of Arts and Letters in 1974, as well as inclusion in both Judy Chicago's *Birth* series and the United Nations' "The Year of the Woman" (Bair 503, 504). The critical approbation with which critics would increasingly view the *Diary* would come, for the most part, after her death.

According to Nancy Scholar, the early volumes of the *Diary* are Nin's finest works. The later volumes, in Scholar's opinion, provide a negative impression, offset only by the posthumously published childhood diaries that "are full of precocity and charming ingenuousness which engage us as the journals of the older Nin often do not" (Scholar 131). In her analysis, Scholar, the critic who claims that Nin is best at the art of seduction, criticizes the seductive appeal she finds engaging in Nin and loses interest in the maturing writer who moves away from a seductive role. By contrast, Spencer writes that "a definite progress can be traced from the first published Diary to the sixth" (Spencer 164).[6] She argues that whereas some critics have called Nin narcissistic, the evolutionary movement of the diary "invites us to re-examine superficial attitudes toward the myth of Narcissus in favor of the deeper interpretation offered us . . . by the living portrait of the artist" (Spencer 158).

Like Spencer, I find that Nin's writing reveals a progressive movement from the self-preoccupation found in the early diaries to a wider perspective in the later writing, characterized by increasing flexibility and a willingness to acknowledge personal shortcomings. The later volumes also show Nin's movement away from polarization between others and self, between fiction and diary, between life and death. Having discussed the first three volumes in earlier chapters, I turn now to Volumes 4 through 7 to trace how Nin draws these important, and wavering, lines in pursuit of a narrative recovery from trauma in terms of a Modernist and feminist remaking of the self.

A BETTER REALITY: *VOLUME 4 (1944–1947)*

Nin expresses in the opening of Volume 4 that—with her tremendous need for external approval increasingly satisfied after *Under a Glass Bell* had brought her a long-sought recognition—she wonders if "the outer life" will overtake the inner realm of the diary. Immediately after saying that the diary is taking a lesser role in her life than her publishing career, she begins a series of entries about her weakening relationship with her analyst, Martha Jaeger. These passages reflect her desire to retain the storyteller's mastery over her own self-myth. Nin is still struggling here with the relation between neurosis and creativity, afraid that if she becomes completely "cured" she will lose a great deal of her particular sensibility. It is an interesting concept in light of her attachment to her own status as wounded daughter. Now, as in her previous therapies, she begins to separate herself emotionally from her analyst; this time it is not by trying to seduce her analyst, but by casting Jaeger in the role of a mother-figure who cannot function in any social setting beyond the clinic. To reject this maternal role is also to separate ego from ego ideal, lessening her identification with the sacrificing style of her own mother.

Her next passage reflects her increasing sense of independence. Reiterating the artist's power to author herself, as well as emphasizing her own analytic abilities, Nin interprets her Haitian friends' belief in ghosts as internal guilt. When she states that *"we are the authors of the ghost"* (4: 14) she asserts her particular credo that one can create a livable world by rewriting the script to one's life drama. By attributing responsibility for the authorship of one's internal dialogue to the individual, she uses writing not so much as a metaphor for life as a way of living. Although she credits Jaeger with liberating her from her "savior role" (4: 15), Nin strives to retain authorship over herself. She further divests the analyst of control by becoming concerned about her as a friend and writing that Jaeger lost her analytic power when she pressured Nin into joining a discussion group and resorted to "'banishment and excommunication'" when Nin refused to join (4: 15). This use of religious terminology conveys that Nin places Jaeger and the church under one category, in which she places any other (including critic or analyst) who supposes too much mastery over Nin's story.[7] Having made some progress in exorcising the father within, Nin takes pains to refuse his place to any other.

Nin continues to claim rights for herself, not over others necessarily although she was talented at getting people to do what she wanted, but over her actual writings and her personal life drama. One such claim is her assertion of literary prerogative in terms of style. Nin recognizes some value in the critics' complaints that her fictions do not provide a "realistic" view of life, but she also challenges these critics as being limited, while she holds to her belief that the normative reader is shortsighted. Jaeger agrees, telling Nin her belief that an appreciation of Nin's writing requires an understanding of the unconscious. Nevertheless, Nin admits that she does need to "synthesize and organize" (4: 17) her material. This is an important distinction of the mature Nin who had overcome a "youthful exuberance" often characterized by a lack of distinction between inspiration and well-ordered art (*The Novel of the Future* 11; Hinz 86–87). "The truth is," she writes, "I get lost in the richness of the diary . . . in . . . the labyrinth" (4: 17).

Yet the labyrinth is assigned a high value. "I am still in [it]" she writes in April 1946, "and I must be willing to get lost before I am saved. It is only when I abandon myself that I am saved" (4: 143). With this gesture toward a Christian theme, Nin draws a connection between the absolving function of analysis and the role of diary as confessional, as well as between her diary and the unconscious, to which she, as the artistically feminine (by her own accounts), has access.[8] She rebels against the call for realism, writing that she is not attempting to portray "objective reality" (4: 122) but to bring clarity to a felt reality. The role of modern literature, she argues, is to function like an analysis in providing a means to access a structure whose core "has to be searched for, like the opening of the labyrinth" (4: 102).

One fear Nin expresses at this point about her self-recognized increasing maturity is that she will become rigid. She acts out this concern through a number of affairs and friendships with men significantly younger than she. Much as she expresses fear earlier that overcoming neurosis will take away her poetic powers, she becomes afraid that if she lets go of her youthful exaggerations, she will become like Wilson, whom she loathed beyond compare. According to Bair, Nin associated Wilson with "every negative thing she ever thought about herself" (Bair 311). When she portrays him in unfavorable "colors . . . the brown of philosophy, the gray ashes of scholarship, the dreary traditions" (4: 105), Nin asserts a reconstructed mastery. "I am aware that it is I who choose my characters," she writes, reiterating that her own life is a story over whose characters she has at least imaginary control (4: 97). "In Edmund Wilson I sought reconciliation with the father. Or was I seeking to conquer the father?" (4: 97). The question answers itself. But she continues to ask it, and she continues the pattern of repetition evident in her fiction of the late 1940s and 1950s.

She also continues to formulate what she had long ago decided was the root of her pain: "The first person I gave myself to, my father, betrayed me," she writes, "so I split. . . . I split, split, split, into a million small relationships" (4: 139). Nin sees her relationship to her parents as also having structured her fear of talking in public. As a child, she decides, she internalized the belief that her parents would love only a self molded to their expectations.[9] As an artist, she says, she exposes her real self, which is different from the identity presented to parents. This exposure is frightening for the possibility that others, like her parents, might reject her.

It is here that the mothering metaphor Anaïs Nin formulated in Volume 2 comes to fruition. Commenting on the psychoanalytic idea that "the poet [is] the one in whom the child's sensitivity survived in the adult" (4: 99) and linking the idea of artistic self-creation with literary myth-making, Nin, like Freud, sees a metaphorical relation between children and artists.[10] Freud implies that the artist's laxity of repression allows him greater access to his childhood memories and wishes as well as to unconscious desire. Many such memories and wishes, he writes, are repressed by the nonartist for their socially unacceptable—erotic or aggressive—content. Similarly, Freud explains that the meaning of dreams often remains obscure to the dreamer because dreams provide distorted expression of wishes of which the dreamer is ashamed and has repressed from consciousness. Daydreams or fantasies operate by the same process though to a lesser degree, and the underlying wishes must also be subject to concealment from the daydreamer himself (148–49). Freud's comparison of creative works to dreams and daydreams may again explain the difference between the artist and nonartist; while the nonartist replaces child's play with dreams and daydreams that provide his consciousness a necessary shield from the erotic and aggressive nature of his wishes, the artist (less subject to the repression of these wishes) retains into adulthood at least partially conscious awareness of them and thus has greater access to them as the source material for creative works. Nin draws repeatedly on such memories, creating a present by reformulating in writing her relation to the past. Her line of inquiry about creativity and childlike consciousness stems from a related discussion: she contrasts Wilson's "laws engraved on stone" (4: 95) with the style of her "transparent children" (4: 96), those young writers with whom she associates and identifies, as fictionalized in *Children of the Albatross*.[11] She writes that their presence lightens her existence and changes the world "from an oppressive, definitive, solidified one to a fluid, potentially marvelous, malleable, viable, as-yet-to-be-created world" (4: 95).

What is significant for Nin is the authorship of self she sees in the analogy: "both live in a world of their own making" (4: 99).[12] Nin's quest for a real self engages the artist's prerogative in reconstructing the unconscious basis of an identity; she strives for a self-myth that will provide her a porous, yet protective, medium for living, one that is neither rigid like that of Wilson's realism nor lacking in structure. With this thinking, Nin battles with a conflict between a welcomed maturity of vision and a feared process of emotional aging by imagining the best of both worlds for herself. Her role, she decides, can engage the transparency of her young artist friends, as well as the self-composure she needs to respond to an increasing acceptance of her work, as manifested in invitations to lecture students, give readings, and autograph copies of her books.[13]

Eventually, Nin would incorporate the tension between age and youth into her theory of literary form, depicting, in Volume 7, a moment of suspended animation in which a writer can capture both time and an eternal moment. Here, we can see her developing this line of thought as she considers the formlessness she valued as a stay against rigidity in terms of mental health. She later links her notion of structured fluidity to a concept of artistic discipline. "What is the difference," she writes in an entry labeled "Summer, 1946," "between the fragmentation I see around me, and the plurality the German writer Novalis considered a sign of genius?" Again, Nin answers her question with a question: "Is it that rich personalities have many aspects, but do not fall apart?" (4: 157). This question-answer represents Nin's attempt to formulate solutions concerning the "whys" of creativity without systematizing them in a rigid pattern of tightly held creeds. By leaving the question open, Nin leaves room for exploration, even while settling for a temporary answer. She entertains plurality while accepting a formulation that will enable her to retain a sufficiently unified "self"—a concept at the heart of her later idea of a synchronic moment in art.

In "January, 1946," Nin again addresses the disparity between the concrete reality demanded by American critics and the psychological reality on which she believes her characterizations are based: "The real wonders of life lie in the depths. Exploring the depths for truths is the real wonder which the child and the artist know: magic and power lie in truth" (4: 12). Nin's "truths" point to unconscious desires as the motivating forces behind human action. She creates fictional characters who reflect an emphasis on these forces, rather than on more externally oriented ones such as socioeconomic conditions and physical environment. She asks, in a response to Diana Trilling's caustic reading of *Ladders to Fire:* "How can one spend the length of a novel making something real which appears unreal to the central character?" (4: 121). She writes that her stories are not the case histories Trilling suggested but instead are the embodiments of her belief in the psychoanalytic premise that "it is the unconscious which rules and shapes our lives" (4: 139). Her storytelling, she adds, encompasses "a new vision of the unfolding of character" (4: 139). Her intuition, she believes, allows her to glimpse her own unfolding character as she works, through analysis and writing, to iron out some of the old fold lines.

Meanwhile, despite the progress she is making toward "health," this balance alternates with relapses of suffering. When her working day ends at five o'clock, she sinks into a depression that she likens to death (4: 166). When she sees other people leaving their offices to hurry home to loved ones, she is choked by a sense of rootless anguish (4: 166). In "February, 1946," she wonders whether her ability to discern more than others do constitutes a kind of madness. "Is it possible," she asks, "to see THROUGH a party at the inner reality, as if people were transparent, and discover that . . . they were not there, but only pretending to be there?" (4: 132). In addition, she feels that every person she reaches out to in hopes of establishing "a big friendship" seems less committed than she, answering her letters with terse, ungenerous responses (4: 166). Besides Trilling's, some of the responses she objected to were those of other literary critics, with whom Nin always had a strange relationship, writing to refute anything negative she perceived in even neutral or positive reviews (Bair 561 n. 28). Because her fictional characters are thinly disguised representations of her own identificatory issues, criticisms of them were criticisms of her, at least in her mind. Their pain was her pain, hers to defend as well as to work out. Nin quotes, for instance, Jacqueline Ford's comments on *Winter of Artifice:* "'It hurts too much. . . . [for] there are [no] interruptions . . . from . . . deep feelings. It's unbearable'" (4: 129). Because Nin uses her fictions to work through her pain rather than to cover it up, they function as recreated aspects of her own unconscious structure. Her task as a novelist, she writes in "April, 1946," is to "re-create the world" (4: 154), that is, her world and her relationships to it.

Several pages of the *Diary* here are devoted to a description of the trip west that Nin says she took on the advice of "a young American from the West" whom she met at a cocktail party in New York. (We learn in later publications that this man was Rupert Pole.) He convinces her that she should see much more of the States than just New York, where life for her has been "harsh and abrasive . . . like the climate" (4: 196–97). Supported as it is in the editing for publication by changes in factual details, the trip as she presents it in Volume 4 represents a venture into a new territory analogous to her inner reconstructive work. She writes near the end of Volume 4 that the excursion gave her respite from the depression she had often felt in New York, and that if she had not had the chance to see the rest of the country, she might not have been as eager to become a permanent American resident (4: 222).

Nin incorporates this idea in the ending of *Cities of the Interior*'s last installment, *Seduction of the Minotaur.* The ending of Volume 4 is, like that novel, set in Acapulco, which Nin describes as a place with velvety-soft winds, where "the sea [is] as warm as a mother's womb" (4: 224). As Lillian in *Seduction,* she considers how the design of one's life "comes from within." But the next morning, as she takes a swim in the tropical sea, she regains her faith that "a new woman would be born here" (4: 225). It is as a woman that the *Diary* indicates Nin will return to the States, not as a hurt little girl fleeing with her mother and brothers from her father, nor as a patient identifying with and eventually seducing her analyst, nor as a substitute mother for various friends and lovers. After a period of gestation, the woman to reemerge will be Anaïs Nin, but one who is stronger and perhaps closer to freedom.

THE BODY'S RHYTHMS: *VOLUME 5 (1947–1955)*

As Franklin and Schneider point out, this volume of the *Diary* is the most fragmented of the seven volumes published, a trait they attribute to Nin's frequent travels, the increase in lectures she was giving in various locations, her illnesses (some of which required surgeries), the death of her parents, and the uneven reception of her literary works. All these events led to increased depression and difficulties in maintaining the freedom from suffering that she had acquired during the years covered by the previous two volumes (Franklin and Schneider 237–51). Despite the occurrence of what might be considered relapses into hysteria, Nin perseveres in her refusal to succumb to painful circumstances. As Volume 5 opens, she is still in Acapulco, where she continues her efforts to "leave the past alone except to fictionalize and transform, and turn sorrows into tales" (5: 46).

She emphasizes creativity as a choice one can make to overcome sorrow; she also implies that psychic structure is alterable, even escapable. Yet she also acknowledges that some aspects of her identity may never be changed (5: 5). With health as her goal, she uses her vacation to move away from self-absorption in order that she might return to her "self" with a different perspective. She also returns, through memory, to childhood in order to be reborn. She remembers that her childhood gave her the spontaneity and "predisposition for pleasure" (5: 6) before numerous losses caused her to look at life as suffering. This imaginary return to childhood, though, is less a reflection of the way she actually responded to life during childhood than it is of desire to be a spontaneous, flowing being—much as Lillian decides it is her *interpretation* of the past that has bound her to suffering. Even as a child, Nin reports, she was haunted by her father's misrecognition of his children's feelings and thoughts, such as those manifested in the games she and her brother played. One of these games was born of the "childish need of a secret house within a house," which she and her brother found under a round library table covered with a heavy, green cloth (5: 52). Nin interprets their play as a way to create a place of their own, apart from their parents (5: 52), a metaphor for the structural realm of fiction in which she, as an adult, strives to meet that need.

As she goes on to describe the rest of her stay in Acapulco, Nin continues to link the physical environment and the body itself to a consciousness of mobility. For instance, she describes the atmosphere as having the "continuity of music which makes the blood rhythms pulsate" (5: 10). The emphasis on flow is represented by Nin's recurring dream of a grounded boat, which cannot reach the river. But, like her fictional counterpart in *Seduction,* she is encouraged by her progress toward joy and writes that she believes her dream of pushing a stranded boat would never recur (5: 10). She attributes this feeling to "the fusion of [her] body with nature" (5: 10) and to "the healing separation from our dissonant and harsh Western life" (5: 10). When Nin makes her "brutal" return to New York, she writes that she has left behind a house she bought in Mexico. Knowing the house awaits her reminds her that she has a place of her own, which represents her ability to stake out her own position. That it is a physical place is important for her association of the physical body and its sensations with consciousness.

In "February, 1948," Nin has returned to New York to attend to "unfinished tasks and responsibilities" (5: 22). We know from Bair's account that she returned many times to New York, living a "trapeze" life between the City and Los Angeles, between Hugh Guiler and Rupert Pole. In this volume, she portrays that the most important of these duties is her continuing self-creation. While facing her daily routines, she finds it helpful to remember the Tropics as reassurance "of the existence of life and joy," which has been, throughout much of her life, "the unattainable state (except intermittently). [Happiness] was the unknown land" (5: 22). Increasingly, though, the harmony she achieved there is retained in her conscious life, and she writes: "The deep life runs securely like a river and the rest is adornment. I no longer fear the shallowness of my father when I give time to take care of my body, lie in the sun, swim, learn to drive a car" (5: 26). This passage condenses several poignant themes. The "deep life," an existence lived closely to the level of unconscious desire, "runs securely," or flows without danger of becoming damned, the fear of which is reflected in Nin's recurrent dream of a grounded boat. Here reign mobility, fluidity, and the ability to encompass the flux of a human awareness.

When Nin returns to her mothering metaphor to describe artistic creativity, this time it is with a stronger sense of independence from cultural expectations. She cites a myth she remembers about the image sleeping within the block of marble until it is awakened by the sculptor. The artist, Nin writes, is "not so much inventing . . . [the image] as delivering [it] from its prison" (5: 31). The sculptor Cornelia Runyon (whom Nin describes meeting in Zuma Beach, California, in "Spring, 1948") epitomizes, for her, the feminine creator. "Her work, I believe, is the opposite of an act of will," Nin writes. "It is an act of creativity which remains rooted in nature, more like an act of giving birth" (5: 30–31).

Nin strives to be just such a sculptor in writing, freeing the sleeping (repressed) self-image by delivering it from the trap of neurotic repetition. This was the artistic act that found expression in Lillian's journey toward freedom from *Ladders to Fire* through *Seduction of the Minotaur*. Despite her progress, the process is painful. Nin suffers again from fear and introversion, writing that she must not burden others with her secret pain (5: 34). Even Nin's conscious recognition that her anxiety is linked to her father does not alleviate the suffering. In much psychoanalysis, an analysand holds back some of the most relevant and painful material until the end of a session or the end of an analysis. Similarly, Nin seems to encounter some of the most poignant pain and to make some of her greatest strides in the last volumes.

Nin reports a dream about giving a lecture that further shows her quest for freedom. In the dream, forgetting that the audience does not speak French, she writes the speech in her native language and must translate it as best she can during delivery. Just before giving the talk, she kills a tarantula. When she knocks it to the floor, it splits open and offers up seeds "like those of a watermelon" (5: 86). She interprets the spider, like the other creatures that have been appearing in her dreams around this time, as her "feeling about the reviewers, the critics, the people who have derided [my] work" (5: 86). It is significant that she interprets the pests not as the people themselves but as her *feelings* about those who "represent the dangers I incurred when I decided to expose [my] work to their criticism" (5: 86).

On some level, Nin recognizes that her reaction to criticism of her work poses a danger but that confronting the reaction by killing the spider, or by unraveling its existence as a construction, frees the seeds of creative potential from their encasement in neurotic fear. Her character Lillian in a similar way comes to recognize her attachment to pain as being self-constructed. That

Nin's speech is written in French points to a link she perceives between her literary work and the formative influence of her childhood. At this time, she has been turned down for a Guggenheim, and the four finished components of her "continuous novel" have received harsh reviews. Nin attributes their lack of acceptance to the American literary climate, in which the human soul is dismissed and ugliness is the only criterion for realism. She wishes to return to France where, in her view, people were more accommodating of the artist and where there was more personal freedom (5: 87). When in the dream she writes the lecture in French, she condenses the wish for a more approving milieu with the desire that her literary reflection of her unconscious structure be recognized as art.

In this volume, as in earlier ones, Nin traces her fear of disapproval to her relation with her parents. This connection is evident throughout her lifelong diary, but it is in Volume 5 that Nin analyzes in depth the effects of parental influence on her present position. When she receives the news that her father has died in Cuba on October 20, 1949, she feels, appropriately in terms of her emphasis on the somatic nature of emotional trauma, "the loss in [her] body" (5: 51). Her most painful memories involve his ceaseless faultfinding. "Why did he always seek the flaws in others, why were his blue eyes so critical?" (5: 51), Nin asks.

Revisiting her sense that psychoanalysis is the only tool for responding to the "pitfalls from which art cannot save us" (5: 170), she reports that she has begun another analysis, with Dr. Inge Bogner (who was to remain her analyst until Nin's death in 1977). When her mother dies three years later, Nin incorporates her grieving into the analytic process, by which she is still, at the age of fifty, coming to terms with her stifling psychic inheritance. With both parents deceased, Nin recognizes that she has let their dictates create dualities in her (5: 184). In an important move toward a healthy distance from past effects, she asserts that true maturity involves compassion for one's parents (5: 188).

Although she is not at this point fully freed from the effects of parental influence (as probably no human is), her diary entries of this period show that she has progressed far from the fragility that characterized the early diaries. Nin brings this volume to an end with her consideration of psychological healing and its relation to the effects of music and writing upon the physical body. Emotional pain, she reiterates, "attacks the body" (5: 51). Memory, normally associated with thought processes, "stirs in the blood obscurely at certain spectacles" (5: 37). "The body carries cells of memories down through the ages, in the same way it transmits physical traits" (5: 38).

But music eases the pain, giving "an entirely novel and modern expression" (5: 240) of fluidity that is otherwise inaccessible, even through drugs. She describes, for instance, "the color of [Harry Partch's] music, the fluidity" (5: 241) as a therapeutic experience, a way—like writing—to "transmute our sorrows into beauty" (5: 170). Choosing an active rather than a passive role, Nin thematizes her reworking of old family myths. She has lost interest in those old myths, she says, because people need to create their own myths (5: 193). She writes that psychoanalysis and writing, together, keep her working to rewrite her own legends (5: 171). "I have to go on in my own . . . disciplined, arduous, organic way of integrating the dream with creativity in life," she writes. "What can be more wonderful than the carrying out of our fantasies, the courage to enact them, embody them, live them out?" (5: 262).

COMING TO TERMS WITH DEATH:
VOLUME 6 (1955–1966)

The first several entries of the sixth volume reflect Nin's continuing desire to embrace an active role and to escape the traps of an existence based on others' desire. In the first entry, dated "Fall, 1955," Nin summarizes the "extraordinary change caused by analysis," saying that it has been a "month without depressions, anxieties or nervousness" (6: 8). Yet the period is also marked with a sense of constriction. During the first analytic session that she reports here, Bogner attempts to convince Nin that she herself creates her own traps and binds herself unnecessarily to responsibilities. Bogner repeats a phrase that Nin used in an earlier session to describe her feeling that she is "'living in a cast'" (6: 7). This issue, Nin reports, "clarified the truth that freedom is an inner attitude, habit, easier to acquire than one imagines" (6: 7).

The results of her new mental habits are less tension and an ability to handle the conflicting pressures of everyday life. "I can do housework half a day, write half a day, and still go out at night" (6: 8), Nin writes, and she reports that she is now able to attend parties without anxiety born of the fear that those attending might reject her work, and therefore her. When she says, "I have overcome the neurosis at last" (6: 8), she means not that she is "cured" in any totalizing sense, but rather that she is now able to live on a day-to-day basis without the kind of disabling mental anguish that has often accompanied her. Now, she tells Dr. Bogner, "'When the buses are full and pass me by, I do not sit on the curb and almost weep at the inhumanity of the world, the overwhelming struggle even to get home'" (6: 12). When she is able to hear ships' foghorns without being devastated by a real sense of loss associated with the trip to America that separated her from her father, Nin attributes this change to the element of personal transformation in her concept of artistic creativity. "We have a right to select our vision of the world," she asserts, and hers is "a deliberate choice" (6: 12). "Isn't the miracle in the interpretation of events, in this transformation of nostalgia, regret, longing into hope and faith?" (6: 11).

As she interprets the past, Nin more clearly defines her desire and learns to recognize her unconscious role in the choice of symptoms and to consciously exercise a relative mastery. For instance, she reports that when she is coming down with a bout of bronchitis, she can see the ways that as a child she associated illness with affection received from her mother. She also notes that it was during an illness, when she was at her "lowest ebb" during recovery from appendicitis that her father abandoned the family (6: 16).

Nin also makes a connection between the bronchitis-induced loss of voice and the "downward pull" of anxiety and depression she experiences as a response to the confinement she feels in being geographically rooted by another's profession, rather than her own (6: 16). This statement reflects the way her family of origin had to move repeatedly because of her father's tours. It also refers to Nin's relationship with Pole. While leaving out of the *Diary* all mention of Pole and her husband, Nin pinpoints the nature of many a woman's geographical restriction to her partner's career. "For a neurosis such as mine," she writes, "to take roots means to be rooted to a situation of pain . . . so . . . there is an impulse to remain mobile" (6: 15).

Nin's association of stability with stasis indicates the degree to which she still links subjugation to male desire with loss of creative power. She dramatizes this conflict in the *Diary* by playing one statement off against another. For example, she writes, "Every moment you can choose what you wish to see, observe, or record. It is your choice" (6: 12), but the rebuttal comes several pages later: "But then a woman's life is always derivative in the sense that the man's profession creates the initial place, frame, atmosphere, design of the life" (6: 14).

The passages from Volume 6 that portray Nin as a woman striving for independence from a patriarchal system undermine the image Scholar presents of a would-be artist playing at poverty to enhance her persona. Nin makes clear that, as she struggles for her own professional identity, she is continuing to feel the real effects of an early psychic wound. During analysis, Nin weeps over the topic of money, puzzled that, although she has worked very hard, she earns so little (6: 19). Shortly afterward, Nin states she has suffered "a total loss of freedom" (6: 23) in her decision to stay within the boundaries of a protective and yet confining situation. Yet she perseveres in her effort to live creatively on the side of freedom. For her this means to transform ugliness into beauty and unpleasant circumstances into a livable reality. If America is hostile toward the artist (6: 24), she writes, the most productive response to its rejection is to "combat negativity and loss of hope with assertions of creativity" (6: 25).

A dream Nin reports under "Winter, 1956–1957" reflects her effort "to organize and reconstruct [her]self" (6: 27). In the dream, Nin is watching three girls swimming in a pool. The girls are similar in age to her neighbor's children, whom she has babysat on occasion. Nin identifies with the oldest one who, at eleven, is the same age as Nin was when her father abandoned her. Nin calls the children out of the water and dries them off, but the oldest one catches a chill and dies of cold. Nin links her death to a lack of love. As the dream continues, Nin goes to scatter the girl's ashes off a ledge but decides not to when she sees that what lies below is a bottomless abyss. She does not want the remains to be lost "into infinity, irretrievable" (6: 70), a detail that she interprets as her own desire not to be metaphorically buried where she cannot "reconstruct [her]self" (6: 70). The dream also shows that Nin still mourns the child she was and the child she aborted in 1934. Nin's effort to restructure her life surfaces as she considers the way the past has shaped her being and anticipates her actual death, which she feels is fast approaching.

As Nin considers her art in relation to life and death in "Spring, 1961," she writes that she does not believe in an afterlife and that "the gift artists make to the world is a selfless one ultimately" (6: 263). She goes on to clarify that what she means by "selfless" is the disappearance and vanishing of the "core and center" (6: 263). If an artist's "words or music continue to enter others' blood streams they are no longer identifiable" (6: 263). As she prepares for death, Nin re-creates herself each moment by theorizing a literary form that is fluid enough to accommodate the opening of each moment to its future. She asserts that writing is the only occupation which *give[s] you back the life which is flowing away from us every moment"* (6: 244).

Nin ends Volume 6 by linking the personal style of the diary as subjective literary form to the transpersonal and cultural. "My span may seem smaller" than those who write objectively, she writes, "but it is really larger because it covers all the obscure routes of the soul and body seeking truth" (6: 400). She also suggests that she has accepted the cost of seeking truth and of mourning loss: "It would be simpler, shorter, simpler not to seek this deepening perspective" and to "lose myself in the simple world of war, hunger, death" (6: 400). That the final word of Volume 6 (the last volume Nin herself prepared for publication) should be the word "death" is itself an affirmation of Nin's life. It shows Nin accepting paradox and limitation while maintaining that art, particularly literature and music, provides ways to transcend what is most painful in life.

A decade and a half earlier, in her self-published pamphlet *Realism and Reality* (1946), Nin had compared her writing to the sculptor Brancusi's "bird in space" (14). "As the [sub]title implies," writes Evelyn Hinz, "it is neither bird nor space that the artist is interested in but the interaction of the two—the impression of flight. Nin is striving for a similar unique effect" (Hinz 68–69). In diary writing and, to a lesser degree in her own brand of fiction, she believed at the end of her life that she had achieved this effect. Similarly, in a "continuous" writing project, she had found a way to reconcile the need for boundaries with the desire to be free of too limiting a literary form. Now, as Nin journeyed toward death as the ultimate boundary, she strove to capture in writing a sense that time and the eternal were inextricably linked in the artist's work. For Nin, of course, the true artistic medium was one's own life, including death.

TOWARD AN EPIPHANIC ART FORM:
VOLUME 7 (1966–1974)

The last volume of the expurgated series reads more like a writer's notebook, appointment book, and record of correspondence than as a conventional diary. Shaped into book form by Gunther Stuhlmann, Volume 7 follows Nin through lectures and readings during a period that was professionally more fulfilling than any other part of her life. Nin was blessed in her personal life as well, surrounded by good, true friends, including her brother Joaquín Nin-Culmell, who taught music and served as distinguished department chair at Berkeley. Her devoted partner, Rupert Pole, with whom she had at last found a lasting happiness in love, was by her side. It was also a time of great physical suffering, however, especially after 1969 when her cancer symptoms began in earnest to ravage her body (Bair 496).

It is Nin's writing about her suffering and her impending death that gives this volume its power, particularly toward the end of the book where her earlier thoughts about literary form converge with an epiphanic sense that time is both flowing away from her and leaving her suspended in a full sense of the value of each moment. The volume is shaped skillfully enough to indicate this theme throughout. For instance, in a passage near the opening, Nin describes a point of balance between the temporal and the flowing natures of art in her description of Japanese architecture as "frozen music" (7: 11). Emphasizing the physical effect of language, the comparison shows Nin striving to capture in literary form what she describes later in the volume as a moment of suspended awe. Her "frozen music" analogy provides an ideal model for her writing. It is reminiscent of the synchronizations she describes in the later novels of *Cities of the Interior* whereby the forms and colors of Modernist art and jazz music provide a permeable model for accessing one's inner patterns.

These images of suspension coincide with her continuing efforts to transform suffering both into art and into an artfully constructed life, her own kind of "writing the body."[14] Whereas in her early work, writing the body appears as a particularly feminine form of creativity, Nin's later work emphasizes a kind of attitude she believed would characterize the writer of the future.[15] This future writer would maintain a relationship with the ego and with the physical body that, she believed, many women shared with writers such as Lawrence and Proust, musicians such as Debussy and Partch, and painters such as Duchamp.

Throughout Volume 7, Nin continues to emphasize the relation of gender difference to writing style, a relation that continues inseparable from the writer's overall attitude. She writes, for instance, that "'the primacy of the intellect and the atrophy of sensuality'" noted in civilization by Freud "applies more to men than to women" (7: 313). For the most part, however, Nin ceases to use terminology denoting gender to describe differences in artistic tone and uses terms such as the "modern" writer and the writer of the future, which she opposes to "traditional" artists. As she continues to formulate a theory of creative difference, she also strengthens her emphasis on attitudinal fluidity rather than on biological gender differences.

Writing as a form of therapy also continues as a major theme in Volume 7. Nin describes her illness in terms of a void reminiscent of earlier volumes, as an "undertow of depression which lies at the bottom of my life, ever ready to suck me down" (7: 192). Again, she resists being engulfed by her pain and once more finds comfort in both writing and music. She compares her writing to music, a symbol not only of art for her but also of the good parts of her childhood that, she writes, "was nourished on music" (7: 237).

As she anticipates her physical death, she uses this analogy to take her out of a linear progression of time. Writing that the "life current" belongs to other, younger writers now (7: 217), Nin embraces the very flux that propels her toward physical death. She writes that the diary "is true to becoming and to continuum" (7: 109). She strives to take a path of nonresistance, believing that "life heals you if you allow it to flow" (7: 232).

A visit to Bali in the last several years of her life inspires her last written images (Bair 486). Near the end of Volume 7 she writes that Bali's tropical culture has reinspired her faith in artistic transformation (7: 335). Here, she writes, she has again found freedom from anxiety in music, which creates for her "an atmosphere of . . . sensuous mysticism" (7: 313). This description is recognizable from the later *Cities* novels. Her mysticism, of course, is not of dogmatic spirituality but of a type of relation toward that which lies at the edge of intellectual comprehension.

Nin particularly liked the tones produced by an instrument called the gamelan, which she says may be "impossible to describe except in terms of a shower of gold, a rain of silver" (7: 327).[16] By using imagery suggesting precipitation, Nin counters the sense of impending doom that she earlier described as a "precipitation toward death." She leaves, in the last pages of the diary, simultaneous impressions of a captured essence and a healing flux, using another musical analogy to describe their paradoxical coexistence:

> In music I feel most deeply the passing of things. . . . The note that was struck, and vanished, carried away with its sound the things that are precious . . . [leaving] an echo of things that are gone. Between it and the . . . note that is com-

ing, there is a space that holds a loss and an emptiness. Music holds the movements of life, the chained incidents which compose it, the eternal melting of one note before another to create song. (7: 340)

Nin's letter to the world takes the form of such a song, for as Volume 7 insists toward its final pages, the note is left reverberating. Ultimately, Nin embraces the paradox that literary form can provide both boundaries and fluid permeability. Like a musical composition that seems to end and then comes back with another strain, Nin's diary defies an ending. It has its final word, but for Nin, "notes fly so much farther than words" (7: 340). Nin ends her life story with a note to herself: "Let me think of death as the Balinese do," she writes, "as . . . a joyous transformation, a release of our spirit so that it might visit all other lives" (7: 336). Among the lives Nin visits, of course, are those of her readers, many of whom continue to find a way to address their own desires within the structure of her writing and to confront the issues of authenticity and identity as analogous to her works' constructions.

CONTRACT AND COMMUNITY IN THE *DIARY*

Even before her death and before the publication in the late 1980s and early 1990s of unexpurgated portions of Nin's work, the primary critical concerns about the *Diary* were the issues of narrative authenticity and (as Franklin and Schneider suggest is perhaps more to the point) editorial responsibility for the shaping of the work (169). Both issues are offshoots of Nin's boundary theme, dealing with the line between fact and fiction as well as that between art and life. It was the issue of authenticity that became the focus of substantially more critical debate after unexpurgated (or less expurgated) portions of Nin's diaries were published as *Henry and June: From the Unexpurgated Diary of Anaïs Nin* (1986), *Incest: From "A Journal of Love"; The Unexpurgated Diary of Anaïs Nin, 1932–1934* (1992), *Fire: From "A Journal of Love"; The Unexpurgated Diary of Anaïs Nin, 1934–1937* (1995), and *Nearer the Moon: From "A Journal of Love"; The Unexpurgated Diary of Anaïs Nin, 1937–1939* (1996).[17] Many readers found particularly shocking the gap between *Incest*— which describes Nin's affairs with Allendy, her father, and Rank, as well as the abortion of a six-month fetus—and the early volumes of the *Diary.*

Even when only the series published as the *Diary* was available, critics picked up on its status as Nin's self-mythology. Franklin and Schneider conclude that "because of the careful selection, arrangement, and structure, the *Diary*, while possibly being faithful to the original manuscript, fits more into the category of a new and created work of art rather than being simply a reproduction of Nin's private journal" (Franklin and Schneider 172). For these critics, the conversion is a strength. They judge the *Diary* more successful as literature than Nin's fiction, "because it is rooted more firmly in an identifiable and substantial context" (172).

Other critics have found problems with the *Diary*'s context and structure. Wendy DuBow's argument in 1993 that the early publications defy "one of the central tenets of successful narrative," the "filling in of factual gaps" (DuBow 28) in a way that would establish cause and effect relationships, echoes that of earlier critics such as Scholar, perhaps the harshest of Nin's critics regarding the issue of narrative authenticity. In her monograph, *Anaïs Nin* (1984), Scholar expresses particular annoyance with Nin for manipulating the events recounted in her diary expressly for the purpose of creating a self-image. Most bothersome to Scholar are the unanswered questions: Where did Nin get her money? Who were her lovers? Who was the father of the stillborn baby she bore? In addition, Scholar seems indignant that Nin's writing contains mention of a maid when she was supposed to be living near poverty and that Nin "magically" acquired a house without making herself accountable for how it was purchased (Scholar 21–22).

Whether one considers the early or the later publications or a combination of both, Nin's emergent and many-layered story works to question literalist views of identity and of truth in ways that may well make readers uneasy. Scholar's questions would be answered in *Incest* and *Fire,* but her criticism gives the impression that the answers themselves are not the point. Her anger, mirrored by others in response to the unexpurgated *Incest,* is directed specifically toward an elusive "truth" that is presumed to be lurking somewhere behind the scenes in her works.[18] Her anger reflects a more generalized human malaise in relation to all that is inarticulable and impossible in life.[19] Nin's work suggests that no self, after all, is a unity, and the fragile human ego can only provide a compensatory set of self-myths whose unity exists as metaphor, or substitutive cohesion. By thematizing these issues and playing with them in ways that grant a narrative *jouissance* beyond phallic certainty, Nin's diaries provide performative if not narrative gratification.[20]

Still, Nin's expurgated diaries capture much of the truth of her life even as they defy a strictly literal interpretation of authenticity. In many cases, the "unexpurgated" volumes simply expand on issues already acknowledged in the *Diary,* such as Nin's admission that she used seduction as a tool against patriarchal power. In Volume 4 this admission comes in reference to Edmund Wilson. As if in passing, she mentions Otto Rank in the same passage, as a basis for comparison. While *Fire* makes the nature of Nin's relationships with both men explicit, Nin acknowledges the seductiveness in both versions. In fact, it would be hard to miss the sexual overtones of Nin's account in the earlier-published volume.

Similarly, Nin's relationship to her father is clearly, to read the *Diary,* over-sexualized. Careful readers have always questioned the basis of Nin's attachment to her father. Many had already suspected what the unexpurgated volumes of *"A Journal of Love"* make explicit, hearing and reading between the lines of the work Nin published during her lifetime an affectivity beyond the words themselves. *Incest* complicates the issue by "revealing" that Nin's boundary issues were far more than psychological and that, during the summer of 1933, Nin became lovers with the man she felt had abandoned her as a child (*Incest* 208–15). Yet if narrative authenticity is in doubt, even *this* story is subject to fictionalization.[21] As Joanne Rock points out:

> Even if the "Father story" were an invention by the diarist to interest Dr. Otto Rank or a self-indulgent fantasy, it still presents a problem for the reader. Does the choice of an incestuous relationship represent the ultimate act of free will and sexual liberation for the writer, or is this too an illusion? (Rock 38)

Rock's point, specifically referring to the father-daughter relationship in Nin's work, echoes a more generalized statement by Franklin and Schneider that "To ask whether the *Diary* is fact or fiction is to miss the point; whether these events happened or are delusions does not help to answer the questions raised above [regarding 'editorial responsibilities,' 'questions of genre,' and 'the function of time, composition, and organization upon the finished product']" (Franklin and Schneider 169).

The importance of the story in the present is that it bears an analogous relation to the self-myths Nin constructed for herself. In her writing, she thematized her own and the general human tendency to self-mythologize as something to work through and acknowledge. Whether "truth" or fiction, the account of Nin's relationship with her father represents an extreme crossing of limits, of a kind that is characteristic in adult survivors of childhood betrayal. Contemporary critics dismayed by a sense that Nin's omissions in the *Diary* constitute a kind of literary breach of contract between author and her reading public have much to explore in pinning down the significance, much less the veracity of, Nin's incest story.[22]

Besides Nin's relationship with her father, the stillbirth or abortion controversy (see chapter 3) has given some readers particular pain. Suzette Henke, in "A Confessional Narrative," has written about the way Nin's emotional pain around the issue is implicit in many places through the extensive intertext made up of her published fiction and diary volumes. This is another indication that the "truth" of Nin's writing as published during her lifetime has been there all along. Nin's desire to make the whole story known after her death gives the lie to the notion that the *Diary* is a lie. Her request that her complete diaries be published eventually makes it possible to put her "lies" in the context of social constructs such as marriage and motherhood—whose definitions are themselves comprised historically, socially, and linguistically and are thus called into question by Nin's refusal to honor their encodings.[23]

Nin's work often embodies a sense that truth is singular, fluctuating, and momentary. Wisdom, Nin implies, may come as an acknowledgment that the human self, like the best works of art, is comprised at the border of what is known—and constructed over the gaps between what can be embodied in language and what eludes it. Together, Nin's expurgated and unexpurgated diary volumes say that wisdom is episodic and momentary. Read in conjunction, they speak especially to the therapeutic potential of writing and the possibility that even someone seriously traumatized early in life can engage in a process of self-making and work through early issues to remake a life into art.

CONCLUSION

Many questions remain about the nature of Nin's early experience, of course, as well as about the degree to which she effectively mourned and moved beyond it through literature. Some of these questions will be answered when additional unexpurgated portions of Nin's diary are published. Others will remain unanswered and unanswerable. The material available now makes clear that there was a significant reason besides marketing considerations that Nin chose the period of her life beginning in 1931 as a starting point for the *Diary*. In particular, that year constituted her entry into the analytic process of delving into the past in order to come to terms with and eventually let go of repressed pain and unhealthy attachments. The fiction and criticism Nin published between that time and the end of her life constitute a process of narrative therapy, through which she employed literary form as a means of instilling much-needed boundaries in her life even as she developed a theory of literary creativity that allowed her to retain the elements of fluidity she associated with both a feminine principle and an understanding of the unconscious forces that shape humans' lives.

Part of Nin's quest for an authentic and unviolated self involved her portrayal of the human ego as a work of fiction. Her journey also engages the artist's prerogative in reconstructing the self and the feminist aims of doing so outside the social roles prescribed by patriarchal law. As a writer who anticipated a Postmodern emphasis on plurality, Nin embraced the paradox that literary form can provide both boundaries and fluid permeability, eventually engaging both fiction and diary writing as continuous projects wherein she could reconcile the need for boundaries with the desire to be free of too limiting a literary form. As a Modernist, she understood the self as fragmented but found a permeable model for accessing one's inner patterns in the forms and colors of Modern art and jazz music. Her own quest for a synchronic moment in art took her theories of creativity beyond the polarization of gender where they had started, while maintaining Nin's emphasis on the physical texture of language so central to her first critical study.

Most important, Nin's work shows that as she worked toward relinquishing her attachment to the wounding elements of the past, particularly in terms of her father, she grew as both an artist and a human being. Nin was never fully able to leave her past behind, and she continued throughout her lifetime to experience anxiety, as well as to engage in behavior that intensified her malaise. The progress she did make, however, is significant. Through writing, Nin found not only a way to survive but also a way to make that survival meaningful. The notes she left on the nature of literary healing, Modernist self-making, and feminist reconstruction will reverberate for a long time to come.

Notes

INTRODUCTION

1. Epigraph is from *Introduction to French Poetry* (Appelbaum, N.Y.: Dover, 1969), 136, 137.

2. I am far from the first to suggest that the artistic process was therapeutic for Nin. In *Anaïs Nin,* for example, Bettina Knapp writes, "*House of Incest* was the outcome in large measure of Nin the patient and the psychotherapeutic sessions working in conjunction with Nin the artist" (Knapp 44). Suzette Henke has, since 1985, explored the process of "scriptotherapy" employed by Nin and other women writers; her research forms the basis for her work-in-progress, *Re/Constructing the Subject: Women's Life-Writing and Narrative Recovery.* For the term "narrative recovery" itself, we are indebted to Daniel Morris, who used it in his essay "'My Shoes': Charles Simic's Self-Portraits," *a/b: Auto/Biography Studies* 11.11 (spring 1996): 109–27.

The phrase "narrative therapy" has come into recent usage among clinical psychotherapists. See, for example, Michael White and David Epston, *Narrative Means to Therapeutic Ends* (New York: W. W. Norton, 1990); and Jeffrey L. Zimmerman and Victoria C. Dickerson, "Using a Narrative Metaphor: Implication for Theory and Clinical Practice," in *Family Process* (1994): 233–45.

3. Because Nin had clearly specified in her will that the details of her past that could hurt or embarrass her husband, Hugh Guiler, were not to be published until after his death, many of the most basic facts about her personal life (including marital status, the nature of her many liaisons with men including her father and Henry Miller, and the fact that she aborted her child in 1934) were left out of the versions of her life published as *The Diary of Anaïs Nin* between 1966, when Harcourt Brace published the first heavily edited volume of the diary, and 1980, when Volume 7 of this series was published posthumously. But 1986, the year following that of Guiler's death, brought the publication of *Henry and June: From the Unexpurgated Diary of Anaïs Nin,* the portion

of Nin's unexpurgated diary on which Kaufman's film was based. A second volume of the unexpurgated series, *Incest: From "A Journal of Love": The Unexpurgated Diary of Anaïs Nin, 1932–1934*, was issued in 1992. Then the year 1995 brought *Fire: From "A Journal of Love,"* described on its jacket as "the previously unpublished, unexpurgated diary 1934–1937." *Nearer the Moon: From "A Journal of Love" : The Unexpurgated Diary of Anaïs Nin, 1937–1939* appeared in 1996.

4. Noel Riley Fitch's *Anaïs: The Erotic Life of Anaïs Nin* (1993) sparked additional interest in Nin's life and work, especially in the veracity of the self-portrait Nin had painted in the expurgated volumes of her diary. In 1995, Bair's *Anaïs Nin: A Biography* provided a fuller perspective on her controversial life, whose many conflicting portrayals (and about which scores of important details have been only recently made available to scholars) have left readers in the dark. Nin's diaries are owned by and housed at UCLA; however, Rupert Pole, Nin's second "husband" (she never divorced her first husband and thus was never legitimately married to Pole), is the sole executor of her estate, deciding "to whom they should be accessible" (Bair 518).

5. Although Nin's questioning boundaries such as those between art and life and between fiction and autobiography at times reflects Postmodern concerns, I shall show that she remained thoroughly Modern in her self-reflexive use of literary form to foreground the reconstructive nature of art and to provide a stay against psychic chaos.

6. Among book-length studies of Nin's work, Knapp's and Spencer's in particular draw on psychoanalytic concepts to put Nin's literary accomplishment in a wider context of theoretical affinities and self-exploration. Both emphasize Nin's engagement in a therapeutic literary process. Henke has written a particularly cogent Freudian account of Nin's character Lillian Beye. A number of additional articles by other authors delineate Nin's relationship to various psychoanalytic schools of thought. For additional bibliographic information about the use of psychological themes in Nin criticism, see Philip K. Jason, *Anaïs Nin and Her Critics* (esp. 92–93); unless otherwise noted all parenthetical references are to this work.

7. Bair has shown that this story of the diary's origins is somewhat less than factual, since Anaïs and her father had been exchanging letters for some time before she sailed with her mother and brothers to New York in 1914, and they continued to do so even as she began a diary in a notebook her mother had given her as a distraction (Bair 29–30).

8. In "A Confessional Narrative: Maternal Anxiety and Daughter Loss in Anaïs Nin's *Journal of Love: Incest*," Suzette Henke writes that *Incest* "exploded like a bomb on the feminist community, many of whose readers felt shocked by [its] frank portrayals" (Henke 71). The bombing metaphor is apt; Nin's work is replete with images that link her past trauma to the effects of bombing, in a way that illuminates the connection between incest and nuclear development excellently presented and convincingly argued by Jane Caputi in *Gossips, Gorgons, and Crones: The Fates of the Earth*. Caputi writes, "The effects of incest, like the effects of radiation, are insidious, long-term, and transmitted through generations. They lie harbored in the victim until they later erupt into disease and disorder, just as toxic and radioactive waste lies 'safely buried' until it leaches out into the environment and affects all life-forms." See her chapter "Unthinkable Fathering" (117–40). For sources on the long-term effects of incest, Caputi cites Ellen Bass and Laura Davis, eds., *The Courage to Heal: A Guide for Women Survivors of*

Child Sexual Abuse (New York: Harper and Row, 1988); Gail Elizabeth Wyatt and Gloria Johnson Powell, eds., *Lasting Effects of Child Sexual Abuse* (Newbury Park, Calif.: Sage Publications, 1988); and E. Sue Blume, *Secret Survivors: Uncovering Incest and Its Aftereffects in Women* (New York: Ballantine, 1990).

9. Throughout this study, I use italics—the *Diary*—to refer to any of the seven volumes published as *The Diary of Anaïs Nin* (1966–1980). Otherwise, I use the common nouns "diary" or "diaries" to refer to diaries in general and to Nin's unpublished diary.

Nancy Scholar was among the first to argue, in her monograph *Anaïs Nin,* that Nin manipulated the events recounted in her diary expressly for the purpose of creating a self-image. Noël Riley Fitch and Deirdre Bair have written extensively about Nin's fictionalizing of her life for presentation in the diary. Miranda Seymour's review of Fitch's book—"Truth Wasn't Sexy Enough" (*New York Book Review,* 17 October 1993)—is among the most condemning perspectives; its subtitle, "Anaïs Nin's Diaries Were a Fraud and Even Her Marriages Were Lies," echoes a number of earlier critics' concern with the validity of Nin's narrative as it emerged over the years. For a full description of responses to Nin's work, see Jason, *Anaïs Nin and Her Critics.*

10. Alice Miller's *The Untouched Key: Tracing Childhood Trauma in Creativity and Destructiveness* (New York: Doubleday, 1988), 73.

11. Bair states that among the most common responses to her research was the notion that Nin, because she "lied" in her diary, did not "deserve" to be the subject of a literary biography (Bair xvi).

12. In his introduction to *Landscape and Power* (Chicago and London: University of Chicago Press, 1994), W. J. T. Mitchell distinguishes between the Modern and Postmodern views of landscape, placing more directly representational aspects of landscape in the realm of Modernism and characterizing the abstract use of landscape as signifier as a Postmodern usage. Nin's concept of landscape as the central grounding of selfhood in an interior psychological realm belongs in the first category. For her, this landscape was the place one could go to escape the meaninglessness of pure abstraction and reflection.

13. Nin placed her own work in their ranks, while believing (as Suzanne Nalbantian has pointed out in *Aesthetic Autobiography: From Life to Art in Marcel Proust, James Joyce, Virginia Woolf, and Anaïs Nin*) that her work went beyond their novels in providing a psychoanalytic model for dealing with themes of fragmentations and splitting (Nalbantian 177). My own view is that Nin's intentions and her aesthetic achievement are somewhat at odds on this point. The quality of her work does not surpass the quality of those she was competing with. At the same time, her work deserves more recognition than it received during her lifetime, for both its aesthetic accomplishment and its importance in capturing psychoanalytic themes.

14. Nin, in *The Novel of the Future,* parodies Stein's repetition of "rose," seeing it as a call for a blunt and conventionally realistic use of language in literature. But her affinity with Stein lies in her challenge of conventional literary realism. See Wendy Steiner, *Pictures of Romance: Form against Content in Painting and Literature,* 177–78.

15. Steiner argues that "twentieth-century art took so long to attempt multi-episodic narrative painting because the delicate balance between representationality and self-reflexiveness in cubism was tipped for so long toward abstraction" (Steiner

182–83). Steiner cites *Cameraworks* by David Hockney and Lawrence Wechsler (New York: Knopf, 1984) and observes that, like David Hockney, Nin saw Cubist art as being "'about the real world'" (183). For Nin, reality was better depicted by resisting the conventions of literary realism and narrative chronology than by employing them.

16. Steiner distinguishes between narrative (as the temporal depiction of events founded on the assumption that chronology matters in the creation of meaning) and design (as the mechanical repetition of images that points to the nonreferential and noncontextual world promoted in commercial culture). Pop artists' play "at the boundary between narrative and design inevitably poses the issue of value" (Steiner 177). Similarly, Nin plays with boundary issues to question the basis of value, even as she affirms the existence of an enduring and universal meaningfulness of existence. In my chapters on Nin's last works of fiction, I show how she draws on Modernist and Postmodern works of art to make this assertion.

17. Nin's decision to begin the *Diary* series with material written in 1931 (rather than the "real" beginning of her diary, which she started writing at the age of eleven) signifies the importance of this period in her life. I place Nin's entry into the psychoanalytic moment—by which she could begin to come to terms with the past—in 1931 (see chapter 1). It was also the point at which she became established as a writer.

18. Nin's perspective on feminism is best represented by her comments collected in *A Woman Speaks: The Lectures, Seminars, and Interviews of Anaïs Nin*, and the "Women and Men" section of her *In Favor of the Sensitive Man, and Other Essays*. See Bair (particularly 493–95) for a discussion of Nin's relationship with feminism.

19. In *Feminine Sexuality: Jacques Lacan and the école freudienne*, Lacan also described the woman as radically Other and fundamentally related to the Real (the impossibility in life). Women's *jouissance* is addressed to the Other, according to Lacan, whereas normative male *jouissance* is directed toward others. By going beyond the human relation, as Lacan describes, a woman will experience herself as intricately more complex than either the angel, whose image society asks her to present, or the monster, which exists as one aspect of any speaking being. A normative woman (a female subject who identifies with law and strives to be the woman a father or husband expects her to be) is one who does not "go beyond" phallic *jouissance* (*Feminine Sexuality* 141).

20. This book spans most of the works Nin brought to publication during her lifetime and the diary volumes that were published after her death. Because my plans include a separate study of Nin's erotica, I have not included them in this study.

21. See Dominick LaCapra's "Canons and Their Discontents."

CHAPTER 1: NARRATIVE OPENINGS

1. A significant and growing focus in D. H. Lawrence scholarship is on the way his writing intersects with women's studies issues. After Simone de Beauvoir's discussion of Lawrence in *The Second Sex* (1953) and Kate Millett's in "D. H. Lawrence and Tradition," in *Sexual Politics* (1970)—both portrayed Lawrence as an indisputable misogynist whose literary characters provide a straightforward mirroring of his own anti-woman positions—several critics have called for a reassessment. In *D. H. Lawrence and Feminism*, Hilary Simpson writes, "From the very first, Lawrence's work has been a focus for the discussion of sexual relationships and roles" (Simpson 13). Simpson's

book moves beyond the impasse created by approving and disapproving feminist readings of his theories and fiction, to place Lawrence's formulations of gender difference and the relations between men and women in historical context. Carol Siegel, in *Lawrence among the Women: Wavering Boundaries in Women's Literary Traditions* (epigraph from p. 125), argues that, although "Lawrence's position is usually understood as antithetical to women's literary traditions" (1), his relationships with women writers— including contemporaries such as H.D., Katherine Mansfield, and Virginia Woolf— and their responses to his work show that, however irritating they may have found his depictions of and theories about women, his was a voice to be heard. "We should look as skeptically at feminist descriptions of Lawrence that reduce him to a symbolic Other as we do at patriarchal reductions of women writers," writes Siegel (6). Her book also includes a discussion of Nin's study, which she characterizes as endorsing an essentialist position.

    In *Anaïs: The Erotic Life of Anaïs Nin*, Noël Riley Fitch writes that the "title of her first novel, *The House of Incest*, and scenes in four pieces of fiction [three stories from the erotica and a scene in *Children of the Albatross*, in which Djuna, abused as a child, describes "'a shattering blow' to her body"] say it all. Señor Joaquín Nin y Castellanos . . . seduced his daughter. This fact is impossible to prove conclusively, but it is borne out by her subsequent behavior." For sources on lifetime effects of childhood trauma and sexual abuse, Fitch cites Alice Miller, *Thou Shall Not Be Aware: Society's Betrayal of the Child*, trans. Hildegarde Hannum and Hunter Hannum (New York: Farrar, Straus and Giroux, 1984). See also Bair (17–18; *Nearer the Moon* 207) for an unpublished diary passage in which Nin writes an account of the early sexual abuse she later believed to have occurred at the hands of her father when she was a child.

    2. Gunther Stuhlmann writes that "few of the people, including Miller, was 'famous' at the time we started actual work on finding a publisher. . . . In fact, Hiram Haydn, her editor at Harcourt, asked me to take out Artaud since nobody knew him here and we could save some 25,000 words" (G. S. to D. R-A., letter, 5/10/97).

    3. According to Stuhlmann, Nin opened the *Diary*—at his suggestion—with her becoming a writer, that is, when the Lawrence book made her public (G. S. to D. R-A., letter, 5/10/97).

    4. According to Stuhlmann, her choice of Lawrence as her subject was to some degree accidental—"she grabbed the opportunity when [Edward] Titus mentioned that he was looking for a Lawrence book while turning down her fiction" (G. S. to D. R-A., letter, 5/10/97). See also Stuhlmann's essay "Edward Titus et al." in *Anaïs: An International Journal* 7 (1989): 113–18.

    5. According to Stuhlmann, Anaïs "always maintained that her father had left Spain to escape from military service" (G. S. to D. R-A., letter, 5/10/97).

    6. Until he abandoned his young family for good in 1913 and ordered them to stay at his parents' home in Spain, Joaquín would often ask Rosa and the children to follow him and his work. By the age of ten, Anaïs Nin had lived in Havana, at least three cities in France (Paris, St. Cloud, and Arcachon), Berlin, and Brussels. After a time at her paternal grandparents' home in Barcelona, she found herself traveling to still another city, New York, where, in addition to the French and Spanish languages of her early years, she would learn the language to which she would commit all her adult writing—English.

7. Bair points out that, of the five members of the Nin family, Anaïs was perhaps the least talented in music, or the least committed to learning to play a musical instrument, though she would later try to emulate the rhythms and forms of music in her mature writing. It was her talent at creating stories, concocting elaborate costumes, and staging small dramas of her own making that, early in her life, manifested her true artistic calling.

8. The City remained Nin's home until 1925 when she returned to Paris as a married woman. New York would become a temporary residence several times afterward as well: from November 1934 through mid-June 1935 when she worked as a psychoanalyst under the supervision of her mentor and lover, Otto Rank; for several months early in 1936; from 1940 until 1947; and then alternately through the early 1970s as she traveled between the East and West coasts, between Hugh Guiler and Rupert Pole.

9. Bair points out that Nin's shift to English coincides with the moment when she began to consider her daily journal writing as a diary (Bair 531 n. 14)—a point that contradicts somewhat Nin's later account of the diary's origins. The shift was a practical necessity at the time (G. S. to D. R-A., letter, 5/10/97).

10. Stuhlmann points out that learning English was an additional separation from her father, since he did not know the language. It "also reflected her new circumstances" in that she had had little formal schooling in either Spanish or French (G. S. to D. R-A., letter, 5/10/97).

11. Bair lists Emerson, Robert Louis Stevenson, Frank Swinnerton, George Meredith, the children's writer Eleanor Hodgman Porter, and the diarists Eugénie de Guérin and Marie Bashkirtseff among Nin's early readings. Nin's favorite journal at that time was *The Delineator*, which combined feminist thought with sewing patterns (Bair 43–46, 50).

12. Hugo eventually took engraving lessons and (as Ian Hugo) developed a following for his engravings. His "first artistic success" was a solo exhibit at the New School in November 1941. He also made a number of small films, including *Ai-Ye* and *Bells of Atlantis* (Bair 275, 335, 352).

13. Not long after they met in 1931, Anaïs would become Miller's muse, mistress, and patron, giving him not only her devotion and passages of her own writing, which he used in *Tropic of Capricorn* and *Black Spring* (Bair 154, 195–96), but also her typewriter, and half the household allowance that Hugo allotted his wife. With part of this money, Anaïs paid for an apartment for Miller at Clichy (with roommate Fred Perlès) and at 18 Villa Seurat. For several weeks in 1932, Hugo's earnings were also spent on Miller's wife, June, with whom Anaïs engaged in an unfulfilled flirtation with lesbianism—an episode perhaps best known through Philip Kaufman's film *Henry and June* (1990), based on a book by the same title published in 1986 as the first volume of Nin's "unexpurgated" diaries. She would later support Gonzalo Moré and his wife, Helba Huara, as well as others whom she referred to as her "children."

14. Once Hugh, Anaïs, Rosa, and her two sons were established in France, it was Anaïs's brother Thorvald whom the elder Joaquín sought out; the middle Nin child was so confused by his father's attention and his mother's being so angry that he was sent back to Havana, where an aunt had found him a job. Thorvald and his sister were never to experience a meeting of minds, about their father or about anything else. Bair de-

scribes an encounter Anaïs would later call Thorvald's "Inquisition" when he angrily confronted her at her home in Louveciennes (which she and Hugo had acquired in November 1930). Thorvald arrived in the middle of the night and verbally attacked his sister for what he believed was her duplicity regarding her letters to her father and to the rest of the family (Bair 112–13). They would meet again in 1936 in New York, a meeting Nin fictionalizes in *Winter of Artifice.* Their last encounter would take place in 1965, when Nin asked her brother to confer about passages to be published in the *Diary;* at that time he was still an angry, bitter man who, until his death in Texas in 1991, would resent his sister's lifestyle and writing (Bair 475–76). Thorvald did not allow Nin to keep him in the published diary.

15. The Guilers' sex life took some months after their marriage to begin and ever afterward fell short of Anaïs's expectations and needs (Bair 65).

16. By 1931 she had read Freud, Adler, and some of Jung's work, making her motto Jung's advice to "proceed from the dream outward" and theorizing in her writing how Modern writers like Joyce and Proust captured dream imagery (Bair 110).

17. René Allendy told her in 1932 that her desire to excel in the arts stemmed from a desire to show herself superior to men and that if she had achieved success in writing she would not have been interested in dancing (Bair 147).

18. According to Stuhlmann, Anaïs used the term "made love" in her original diary to report "flirtations in broad daylight, as it were. . . . It was one of [her] English-language quirks" (G. S. to D. R-A., letter, 5/10/97).

19. Stuhlmann writes that "Erskine apparently did not 'turn her down' [as in Bair's account. Nin] had a crush on [Erskine] but they only 'met' once in New York when both made feeble advances and [Anaïs]—who knew about his mistress—did not find his way in 'real life' as appealing as her fantasy, which she tried to work off . . . [later] in her 'John' novel, eventually abandoned" (G. S. to D. R-A., letter, 5/10/97).

20. Anaïs and Eduardo had been close companions as teenagers in New York until his mother, Rosa's sister Anaïs (named for her mother, the youngest Anaïs's maternal grandmother), fearing he would marry his cousin, forbade the teenagers to see each other. By 1929, Eduardo had moved to Paris and had come out to his parents as a homosexual man—though he tried to convince Anaïs that his homosexuality stemmed from his unrequited sexual passion for her (Bair 135).

21. Jason points out that, besides a "patronizing and revoltingly sexist review" by Waverly Root and a dismissive comment in the *Times Literary Supplement,* the 1932 edition of Nin's book on Lawrence received very limited attention. The introduction to the Swallow edition in 1964 brought slightly more critical notice, along with Harry T. Moore's praise for the texture of Nin's work. Of the "critics who fashioned the six book-length studies of Nin's work, only two consider it important enough to warrant extended treatment" (Jason 29). Hilary Simpson gives Nin two lines, and I have also found brief references to Nin's book in Arnold Armin's *D. H. Lawrence and America* (London: Linden Press, 1958); a footnote reference in Yudhishtar's *Conflict in the Novels of D. H. Lawrence* (New York: Barnes & Noble, 1969); and a two-line mention in Harry T. Moore, *The Priest of Love: A Life of D. H. Lawrence,* Rev. Ed. (New York: Farrar, Straus, and Giroux, 1974). In addition to Siegel's *Lawrence Among the Women: Wavering Boundaries in Women's Literary Traditions,* Sandra M. Gilbert's "Feminism and D. H. Lawrence" (in *Anaïs: An International Journal* 9 [1991]: 92–100) also establishes the

value of Nin's Lawrence study to feminist criticism. Recent publications that discuss Nin's response to Lawrence include Leo Hamalian's "Anaïs Nin: A Spy in the House of Lawrence" in his *D. H. Lawrence and Nine Women Writers* (Madison and Teaneck, N. J.: Farleigh Dickinson University Press, 1996), 86–99; Jane Eblen Keller's "Living à la Lawrence" (in *Anaïs: An International Journal* 15 [1997]: 12–25); and Suzette Henke's "Androgynous Creation: From D. H. Lawrence to Djuna Barnes" (in *Anaïs: An International Journal* 15 [1997]: 85–94).

 22. Evelyn Hinz argues that Lawrence's influence on Nin was not as great as might be imagined. Jason points out that, as a Lawrence scholar herself, "Hinz was perfectly positioned to value Nin's first book for what it is and to warn against measuring it by assuming intentions Nin never had" (Jason 28).

 23. Reception of Nin's critical ideas, like that of her fiction, has been hampered by several complications, including her inability to accept criticism. Jason writes that a "narrow circle of enthusiasts" have echoed Nin's need for unmitigated praise, protecting her status under a kind of "jealously maintained glass bell" (Jason 10). Bair's biography provides much insight into Nin's response to any critical work that was not "unmitigating hagiography" and her insistence that reviewers write only positive comments about her work (Bair 464–65, 480–81).

 24. For Siegel, Nin's study is valuable to the study of Lawrence's reception because it provides a transitional response (Nin identifies with Lawrence, whose depictions of the historical period they shared "coincide with hers") and because Lawrence's "rebellion opens ground that [Nin], as a woman artist, is prepared to occupy" (Siegel 125). By setting up a context of Lawrence's influence on Nin, Siegel draws attention to the issue of shared objectives. The problem of essentialism, however, again interferes. Siegel believes Nin implies that she is "superior to [Lawrence] because she believes that the femininity, which is the best part of his work, would naturally be the essential part of her own" (Siegel 125). However, since Nin's formulations of femininity in terms of writing are not exclusive to women (but rather are based on an attitude toward conventional gender identity roles, in a similar way to Lacan's distinguishing feminine *jouissance* from the masculine), Nin would not have considered herself superior to Lawrence.

 25. Nor does her theoretical position reinforce the binary oppositions that Anne Rosalind Jones, in "Writing the Body: Toward an Understanding of *L'écriture féminine*," suggests may perpetuate phallocentric definitions of gender without providing for the kind of paradigmatic shift in social relations called for by many American and English feminists (Jones 369–71), although Siegel and others have objected to Nin on this account. I agree with Jones that, "if one posits that female subjectivity is derived from women's physiology and bodily instincts as they affect sexual experience and the unconscious, both theoretical and practical problems can and do arise" (Jones 362). Yet, rather than positing a "female subjectivity" as primarily "derived from women's physiology and bodily instincts," Nin's ideas often echo Lacan's on the materiality of language—the way that the literary use of language can embody unconscious structure, through which gender distinction comes into play as an effect of a secondary (rather than a primary) signification.

 26. It contains a kind of aesthetic appreciation that, according to Carol Siegel, "could probably have been written only by a woman who became a writer too late to

see him as a competitor and too early to hear of him as an acknowledged master" (Siegel 120). It also contains several omissions and minor (but seemingly careless) errors. My complete discussion of Nin's relation to Lawrence as I read it from a Lacanian perspective appears as "*L'Écriture féminine* and Its Discontents: Anaïs Nin's Response to D. H. Lawrence" (*Lawrence Review* 26 [1997]: 197–226).

27. Bair writes that, of the women Nin cited here to show that "women-artists were now succeeding in the world of men, . . . only Amy Lowell was a near-contemporary, and Ruth Draper was truly modern. Conspicuously absent was Virginia Woolf, whom she thought 'over-intellectual' and indistinguishable from Rebecca West: 'each write[s] like a man and I don't like it'" (Bair 102).

28. See my article "Anaïs Nin's Mothering Metaphor."

29. Jason cites Millett's "Anaïs—A Mother to Us All" as one example of an appreciative feminist stance toward Nin. It is interesting, however, that Millett's view of Lawrence in *Sexual Politics* could not be further removed from Nin's.

30. For Lacan, it is the hysterically positioned subject (male or female)—as well as the mystic—who incorporates the mobile and fluctuating nature of existence. After situating feminine *jouissance* "on the side of the mystics," Lacan asks, "Might not this *jouissance* which one experiences and knows nothing of be that which puts us on the path of ex-istence?" (*Feminine Sexuality* 147).

31. Nin's *The Novel of the Future* (1968) centers around her ideas about the relation of the feminine to a synchronic moment in art.

32. For discussions of male hysteria as a response to war, see Elaine Showalter, "Rivers and Sassoon: The Inscription of Male Gender Anxieties" and "Male Hysteria: W. H. R. Rivers and the Lessons of Shell Shock."

33. Bair reports that the communication began again shortly after Anaïs and the Spanish composer Gustavo Durán spoke at a recital about Joaquín Nin. Durán told the daughter that her father missed his children, to which she replied that Durán should invite Joaquín Nin to visit her "'the next time he is in Paris'" (Bair 167). She invited Durán and another artist to her house a few days later, hoping that they would describe "her fairy-tale house" to her father so he would want to come. "The ploy worked," Bair writes, and several days later "she received a letter from her father" indicating that he "wanted more than anything not to see [the house] but to see *her* in it. She was like a teenager with her first invitation to the prom" (Bair 167).

34. Nin's affair with Rank would last through early 1935, ending for good only several months after she abandoned a pseudo-career as a lay analyst under his supervision in New York. She would process her experiences as analysand and analyst in a second novella in the book eventually known as *Winter of Artifice,* which she and Miller arranged to have published (with Hugo's money) in 1939.

35. A manuscript by the working title of "Alraune" was under way by late 1932. By November 1933, Nin had established the points of division: "Alraune I" became the prose poem she would publish in 1936; "Alraune II" eventually became her second published fictional book (Bair 184), a book different in format and content from the collection of novellas published as *Winter of Artifice* by Alan Swallow in 1961. As early as February 1935, Nin also refers to her "Father story manuscript." Gunther Stuhlmann notes: "Anaïs Nin's Father story, much revised under different manuscript titles, including 'The Double,' eventually became the title story in *The Winter of Artifice* (three

novellas, published by the Obelisk Press in Paris in 1939)" (*Fire* 23 n). In March 1935, Nin reports receiving rejection letters for a story called "Chaotica," which Stuhlmann notes was apparently an early version of "The Voice" (*Fire* 44 n), one of *Winter's* three novellas. The "Father story" that Nin refers to in her diary of 1934–1937 was titled "Lilith" in the volume published by Jack Kahane's Obelisk Press in 1939, financed by Nancy Durrell.

36. Mark Bracher, in *Lacan, Discourse, and Social Change: A Psychoanalytic Cultural Criticism,* suggests that learning to analyze and to articulate on one's own terms a set of master signifiers (ideals around which identity is structured) is the key to living a more healthy interface with the world. Once the "master signifiers" (those unconscious identifications around which one's alienation has been structured unconsciously in terms of law and desire) have been identified, or "mapped" in the analysis, one can go through the important process of separating from them and forming new identifications more in keeping with one's desire. This happens, according to Bracher, as the analysand moves through four discourse structures. (1) University Discourse—that which emphasizes the "factual" history of one's life, knowledge, and consolidation of the "ideal ego (the point from which one experiences oneself as lovable)" (Bracher 69) through sought reinforcement of one's value through others'—including the analyst's—approval. (2) Master Discourse—that which aims toward "an autonomous, self-identical ego" and which "keep[s] fantasy . . . in a subordinate and repressed position" (Bracher 59). Examples of master discourses are political, philosophical, and even psychoanalytic meaning systems, in fact, any use of language to establish an authoritative certainty that reinforces the fixity of the ego. In this stage of analysis, the analyst often tries to provoke the third discourse structure, (3) Hysterical Discourse of the split subject, and then to reveal, in the ruptures in the analysand's narrative, "the underlying fantasy . . . which functions as a bedrock meaning for the analysand" (Bracher 71) and to expose what has been repressed, so that the patient can alter the ego ideal by assigning different values to the elements around which he or she has structured the ego ideal. Then (4) Discourse of the Analyst—according to Bracher, it is only with this discourse structure that one can come to acknowledge, claim as one's own, and prioritize the repressed parts of one's being that beforehand have been "excluded from symbolization . . . and suppressed by the discourse of the Master" in order to establish new master signifiers (Bracher 68). It is this discourse structure that I believe Nin can be seen moving through, albeit intermittently, toward the end of her life, especially as she came to publicly advocate an embracing of creativity beyond gender and beyond literary realism.

37. The difference between these early writings and those published in the 1930s and afterward concerns her increased ability, in the later work, to overcome not only a literal silencing of the past but also the silencing that occurs when discourse is used to avoid confronting trauma rather than to give it voice. The adolescent romanticism and melancholic sentimentality of the early diaries is not wholly abandoned either in Nin's adult diaries or in some of her adult fiction, but (as I shall demonstrate in this chapter) the degree of denial lessens.

38. Gunther Stuhlmann points out that Nin says herself at the opening of *House of Incest* (originally published as *The House of Incest*) that everything she knew "was contained in this book—which was prophetic indeed!" (G. S. to D. R-A., letter, 5/10/97).

39. Jane Caputi links the importance of finding a voice with which to outcry in-

cest with that of revealing the betrayals of trust at the heart of nuclearism: "making genocidal bombs isn't taboo, but speaking out against them is. So, too, as many observers note, incest is not really taboo in our culture, but speaking out against it is. . . . Indeed, in order to thwart both child sexual abuse and nuclearism, we must gossip, or in the phrase commonly used by survivors, 'break silence'" (Caputi 130–31).

40. Nin began *House of Incest* in 1931 and published it in 1936. It was during the middle of this process (July 1933) that Nin's "seduction" of her father took place.

41. That Nin rejected her father's influence shortly after their affair (as fictionalized in her next fictional work, *Winter of Artifice*) shows her "taking leave." This is not to say, however, that she ever achieved total freedom from the effects of her father-trauma. On the contrary, her lifelong struggle to combat neurosis highlights the traumatizing effects on a child of an adult's abuse or neglect. At the same time, Nin's rejection of many cultural norms (role of mother, monogamy, deference to husband, and so on) may be seen as a rejection of patriarchy itself.

42. Both *The Diary of Anaïs Nin* and *Henry and June* portray the themes of fragmentation, disunities of selves, the need for narrative invention, and Nin's and June Miller's reliance on imagination as a way to piece together the disparate elements of the psyche. The difference between June and her, Nin writes, is that June remains unconscious of the role of self-construction through tale-telling, while Nin herself is self-consciously embracing the role of inventor creator: "June and I have paid with our souls for taking fantasies seriously, for living life as a theatre, for loving costumes and changes of selves, for wearing masks and disguises. But I know what is real. Does June?" (*Diary* 1: 22).

43. See *Diary* (1: 22, 51–52), for instance, for Nin's discussion of June Miller's tendency to lie and for Nin's drawing a parallel between lying and costuming. See also *Henry and June:* "I cannot tell the whole truth simply because I would have to write four journals at once. I often would have to retrace my steps, because of my vice for embellishment" (208).

44. I use the "father function" in the Lacanian sense of a differentiating principle through which language and law occur as the intervention of symbiosis. Thus, "father" is not necessarily a male person but one who carries out and represents this function. Caputi points out, however, that "both incest and nuclearism are perpetrated primarily by men" (see 313–14 n. 6).

45. For Lacan, the Symbolic (cultural and linguistic) patriarchal constructions of identity cut language off from its signifying function—castrates it, as those whose identities are structured around the phallus as image of power, autonomy, and ego are "cut off" from awareness in varying degrees proportional to the rigidity of their unconscious fixation on this image. Those wounded in the process of identificatory structuring can relate to and make sick attachments to words as dead objects (rigid, divorced, devoid of life). In Lacanian theory, neurosis stems from the subject's temporal identification with such "dead letters."

46. Caputi's point is that the violation of trust and function by the incestuous father is linked in the popular imagination to images of destruction and the violation of public trust that accompany nuclear thinking. The pre-atomic *House of Incest* demonstrates the earth-shattering effects of incest in a way that highlights the aptness of the image.

47. Correspondingly (according to Ellie Ragland-Sullivan in *Jacques Lacan and the Philosophy of Psychoanalysis*), Lacan taught that the possibility of freedom from neurosis lies in the subject's "effort to overcome its own internal, libidinal alienation" (Ragland, *Philosophy* 63).

48. The image was inspired by Helba Huara, the dancer married to Nin's lover Gonzalo Moré. Helba was also the model for Zora in *The Four-Chambered Heart.*

CHAPTER 2: BREAKING SILENCE

1. With his daughter in the audience, Joaquín Nin collapsed on stage during a concert in Paris in 1939. He recovered enough to travel to Cuba a short time later, where he resided until his death in 1949.

2. Stuhlmann points out that the book published as *The Winter of Artifice* was so completely different from the *Winter of Artifice* discussed in this chapter that the notion of "successive" editions could be misleading. In addition, the "failure" of *The Winter of Artifice* ought, he writes, to be understood in light of the following facts: "*The Winter of Artifice* was apparently not reviewed in Paris because the war broke out and her publisher, Kahane, died that day . . . —nobody had expected to make any money of it. Nancy Durrell had backed the printing cost for Kahane." The Paris edition of *Winter of Artifice* got one review in the United States, in an obscure magazine; the 1942 U.S. edition received three reviews (G. S. to D. R-A. lettler, 5/10/97). My emphasis in the chapter is on Nin's successive attempts to write fiction successfully.

3. All textual citations from *Winter of Artifice* in this chapter are from the Swallow edition. According to Jason, Benjamin V. Franklin and Duane Schneider's *Anaïs Nin: An Introduction* was the first interpretive study to "make use of the publication history of *Winter* . . . [and] to base their interpretative discussion on the 1961 (Swallow edition), thus . . . attend[ing] to 'Stella' as part of Nin's final plan for this book whereas earlier critics either ignore it or treat it separately from the titles with which Nin eventually associated it" (Jason 43).

4. See Jason (23) for a discussion of Nin's relationship with feminism.

5. The lack of clear boundaries between early versions of one work and another—as well as numerous changes in the editions between one publication and the next—makes the publication history of *Winter of Artifice* confusing, to say the least. According to Jason, the book was first published by Obelisk Press in Paris in 1939 as *The Winter of Artifice* (the definite article was later dropped). This version contained three long stories or novellas: (1) "Djuna," which was dropped from all editions beginning with the one Nin self-published in 1942; (2) "Lilith," which was later rewritten and left untitled in the edition Nin self-published in 1942, then called "Djuna" as one part of a single two-part story, "Winter of Artifice," in the Dutton 1948 edition of the collection of stories entitled *Under a Glass Bell,* and then called "Winter of Artifice" in the Swallow version of *Winter* published in 1961; and (3) "The Voice," which was also rewritten and included as part of the two-part version of "Winter of Artifice" included in Dutton's 1948 version of *Under a Glass Bell* but separated from it in the Swallow edition, where it is the third of three novellas (Jason 39). The edition of *Winter of Artifice* published in 1961 by Swallow thus contains rewritten versions of material originally published between 1939 (when the first version of *Winter* was printed by Obelisk) and

1946 (when Dutton's *Ladders to Fire* was published containing the story called "Stella" that in the Swallow edition of *Winter* appears as the first of three novellas).

6. See *Fire* (234) for one of several passages establishing the link Nin saw between the diary and psychoanalysis.

7. See *Fire* (esp. 234, 240, 248, 376, 382, 390) for passages in which Nin links diary writing to her "disease" (240).

8. Bair's statement that, with Rank "doubling as lover, she made no progress in her own therapy" (205) may be applied to both Rank's and Allendy's treatment. In both cases, Nin ended up over her head in the treacherous waters of hysterical posturing, even while recognizing her tendency to engage in such posturing. Her recognition may be seen in passages such as the following: "The danger of schizophrenia is to seek another shock to awaken, to seek pain" (*Fire* 212). On a similar note, Nin writes later in the same volume of her resistance to closure (*Fire* 310), a trait linked to hysteria.

9. Bair suggests that Rank's "infatuation" with Nin—at a time in his life when his professional judgment might have been impaired by depression and loss—was the reason for his lapse: "When . . . Rank met . . . Nin, his marriage was foundering, he was in serious financial straits, and he was himself in the midst of an emotional crisis" (Bair 188). Citing Elizabeth Roudinesco, *Jacques Lacan and Company: A History of Psychoanalysis in France, 1925–1985*, trans. Jeffrey Mehlman (Chicago: University of Chicago Press, 1990), Bair goes on to explain that "the rules governing relationships between analysts and patients were not as clearly defined as they are today" and that it is thus "not surprising" that Rank and Nin mixed therapy with sex—following (it seems to me) a general tendency to hold Nin to a different standard of accountability than is applied to those she seduced. About Rank's setting Henry Miller up as an analyst and sending patients to him, Bair writes that Rank's "willingness to send innocent people to . . . Miller can be attributed only to the depth of his infatuation with Anaïs Nin" (208).

10. In "Dora and the Name-of-the-Father: The Structure of Hysteria," Ragland writes, "while sexual desire is always at issue in any story of suffering, its role is symptomatic, not causative." And symptoms are "ego stories" that "take part in the denial of unconscious truths that cannot be faced" (Ragland, "Dora" 7, 15).

11. Ragland has explained that Lacan revised the Freudian notion of transference as a dynamic, by which the "presupposition of a unified relationship between analyst and analysand" could be traversed (*Philosophy* 123).

12. It is completely normal, of course, that the analyst, as a human being, should want this recognition. The key is what he or she does with that desire. A successful transference can be used, Ragland writes, "to lead both analyst and analysand beyond narcissistic fixations, aiming the analysand toward knowledge of his or her Desire, and away from the personhood of the analyst" (Ragland, *Philosophy* 123).

13. Ideally, an analyst "works at dissolving symptoms and traversing Imaginary (ego) fantasies" (Ragland, "Dora" 216). But both Nin's male analyst lovers become supporting characters in the script of her personality and thus failed, to a significant degree, to help her delve beyond the surface nature of the ego. What is especially important about Nin's inability to find relief from her suffering in Allendy's or Rank's treatment, then, is not so much that they repeated what she believed was a paternal betrayal, but that she was not helped through their treatment beyond the narcissistic identifications with that betrayal. Jonathan Scott Lee, in *Jacques Lacan*, has explained

that Lacan's point about countertransference (as opposed to the emphasis of object relations theory) "is simply that it is the *effects* of the countertransference on the analytic
dialogue (rather than the quality of the analyst's lived experience of countertransference) that are of central importance to psychoanalytic practice and theory" (Lee 34; my
emphasis).

14. For example, in *Fire*, Nin expresses gratitude to her husband when she
writes, "Hugh is my axis. . . . I owe Hugh everything, all my strength and courage to
live out other things," and refers to him as "My sweet, young father" (*Fire* 148). She
also realizes that, by casting the husband as father and Henry Miller as child, she loses
a mate: "and so I shall die without a love equal to me, a love that will be as old as I am
today" (153).

15. Nin similarly acknowledges her seductive powers in Volume 4 of the *Diary*,
when she describes her relation to Edmund Wilson, with whom she had an affair in
1945. She saw Wilson as a father figure, whom she wanted to "enslave and abandon
first" (4: 143).

16. The experience of early sexual traumatization is a "shock" whose effects often reverberate through the rest of a victim's life. Jane Caputi compares the destructiveness of such shocks to that which accompanies nuclear bombing and traces a number of expressions that highlight such a link.

17. According to her account in *Incest: From "A Journal of Love,"* Anaïs Nin's affair with her father took place in the summer of 1933 in the south of France. See also
Bair's account (167–76).

18. Nin's belief that Henry would not resist the sexual offer of an analysand indicates that the issue of the proper handling of countertransference was foremost in her
mind (see *Fire* 217). In the same passage she writes that she, by contrast, *would* resist;
however, Bair indicates that Nin "actually lay on her analytic couch with one man while
Rank was in session in the next room" and that she wrote she wanted to betray Rank
in this way (Bair 206).

19. On one hand, passages such as this one seem not to have much bearing on
the actual relationship between the diary and the fictional treatment of the paternal issue. The title novella of the collection that would eventually be published as *Winter of
Artifice*, for instance, does not bear a great deal of stylistic similarity to that of Nin's diaries—expurgated or unexpurgated. However, the various references to what Nin calls
her "Father" story in the diary of the period 1934–1937 are important, because they
show Nin coming to realize the effects her relationship to her father have on her everyday life and her need to work through the issues *in fiction* in order to distance herself
from these effects. This need is linked in her mind to distancing herself from the diary,
even as she imitates its structure.

20. She also strives to integrate "the eternal" with "the temporal" and "individual creativity" with "our historical world" (2: 348)—a goal she would achieve, to large
extent, only much later.

21. Although Wendy DuBow, in "The Elusive Text: Reading 'The Diary of
Anaïs Nin, Volume 1, 1931–1934,'" argues that the early publications defy "one of the
central tenets of successful narrative" (28), the "filling in of factual gaps" in a way that
would establish cause and effect relationships, I think the narrative "gaps" in both versions of Nin's story perform important functions (see chapter 6). They express the uses

and the limits of authorial intention and illustrate the way an author's unconscious desire can often slip through the disguises of language to reveal as much in what is left unsaid as in what is said.

22. Similarly, the published unexpurgated version portrays a woman vacillating between the desire to be an artist and an unhealthy need to subjugate her own artistic goals to the sexual and artistic needs of several lovers. It is to *her own* interpretation of others' needs that she subjugates herself.

23. Nin's rebellion against Allendy's interpretations may be understood as what Jonathan Scott Lee defines as negative transference, the analysand's aggressive or belligerent reaction to the analyst, which stems from images of the fragmented body revived in the analysand in the course of the analyst's helping him or her to "recognize what he is" (Lee 25–26). Such negative transference indicates that the ego is hard at work to maintain its illusions.

24. A proponent of *l'écriture féminine* might see in this passage the possibility that Nin was trying here to forge a way to retain what she sees as a feminine position, even as she resists the limitations traditionally associated with this position, and was adhering to aspects of her identity that she was not willing to forgo—such as fluidity, relationality, interiority, and intuition. However, the limitlessness of the subtext of this passage may just as likely involve some of the negative neurotic characteristics such as dependency and masochism that, for Nin, have hitherto gone hand in hand with femininity. Such masochism was a bedrock trait of her problem; Allendy himself linked her "'consistent desire to be punished, humiliated or abandoned,'" to her "having loved her father too much" (Bair 142–43). The theme of masochism with an underlying sadism was the subject of a later analysis Nin pursued with the analyst Clement Staff, between 1945 and 1951 (Bair 305, 359).

25. Stella's problems reflect Louise Rainer's marital conflicts with Clifford Odets (G. S. to D. R-A., letter, 5/10/97). Nonetheless, the applicability and resemblance to Nin is clear.

26. An account that may be troubling from an analytic perspective is that Allendy apparently used a whip to enhance his excitement during at least one sexual encounter with Nin, an action that (if Nin's story is accurate) may especially heighten the nature of transferential betrayal. See Bair (164–65) for an account of this incident, which Bair portrays as resulting from Nin's decision to "demonstrate her power over Allendy. . . . *She* persuaded *him* to invite her to a hotel" (165; my emphasis).

27. This phrase is especially significant from a Lacanian perspective, because the mirror stage represents the point from which a subject respectively defines an illusory wholeness—based on the image a child sees in the mirror. From that point onward, that image represents an illusory wholeness, based on the idea of a bodily integrity. The mirror stage also highlights the subjective split that Lacan described as existing between the word (signifier) and what the word is meant to represent (signified).

28. Nin's identification with Rank falls into the first of four patterns of narcissistic transference as delineated by Martha N. Evans: (1) identification with analyst as counterpart or twin, (2) idealization of analyst, (3) separation from that ideal (involving the sense of fragmentation that Lee associates with negative transference [25–26]), and (4) finally a "recognition of the *moi*'s source in the Other" (Ragland, *Philosophy* 37).

29. According to Bair, "the first mention that she was considering a career as a

psychoanalyst came in a postscript to Rebecca West written the previous June." Nin had told West that she was receiving instruction from Rank in order to gain independence. "Her only training—if it can be dignified by the term—came in early July, when she attended a few early sessions at Rank's annual institute" (Bair 203).

30. Even the unexpurgated diary does nothing to negate the significance of Nin's identification with Rank as father and her restructuring of an oedipal drama. Instead of "marrying" in reference to the father's image as she did while in analysis with Allendy, Nin's becoming a lay analyst indicates her efforts to *become* (identify with) the father (in Rank's image), in order to stake out a position not based on the models of sacrifice and self-effacement provided by her nor based on subjection to her father's desire. The part of the story that was left out of this version (that Nin and Rank were lovers) only intensifies the significance of what each party in the relationship felt as a betrayal. The other part (that Nin had entered analysis with Rank having already engaged in an incestuous adult tryst with her father, an event that [according to Bair 190] she soon told him) makes unarguable the inextricable linkings between paternal betrayal, psychological wounding, and analytic transference in Nin's psychological landscape.

31. Nin's conception of intellectual thought systems as being masculine makes sense also from a Lacanian perspective. Since, for Lacan, *connaissance* lies on the side of fiction, the pleasure the ego derives from a belief in the "cunning of reason" (*Ecrits: A Selection* 308) is a function of pretense, or repression. Feminine *jouissance,* on the other hand, deals with "a *jouissance* of the body which is . . . *beyond the phallus*" (*Feminine Sexuality* 145), beyond the function of pretense, and which quests for another kind of "truth," for *savoir.* Since *savoir* cannot be attained through the intellect, Lacan distinguishes between knowing and experiencing: "There is a *jouissance* proper to [woman] and of which she herself may know nothing, except that she experiences it" (*Feminine Sexuality* 145). As in Nin's system, *connaissance*—or the ego's knowledge of the systems it creates to maintain the illusion of unity—is seen as masculine. Nin places unconscious knowledge or "truth" (*savoir*) on the side of the feminine. It is the knowledge of a "beyond," an unconscious, with which Lacan also credits the mystics.

32. Nin's decision to seek her own cure in writing fiction as a feminine activity finds parallel in her movement away from an analytic mode, which she associates in the diary with a more masculine process: "I realized once more that I was a writer, and only a writer, a writer and not a psychoanalyst" (4: 41). This statement precedes her declaring, "I was ready to return home and write a novel" (4: 41). Whether this was her primary reason for returning home to Louveciennes near Paris (Bair implies that it was not), *Winter of Artifice* (really a collection of novellas) did follow, a work in which she would try to work out her need for analysis (more specifically, the need for a father transference adequate for letting go of patriarchal identification) as well as her need to reject the terms of analysis as she had experienced it. See Bair's account of her career as analyst and of her continuing "machinations" with several men including Hugh and Henry (Bair 203–10).

33. In my article "Anaïs Nin's Mothering Metaphor," I argue that the womb becomes, for Nin, a metonymy for a linguistically structured unconscious. Rather than supportive of an essentialist position, Nin's mothering metaphor and womb imagery point to the creative application of what is itself creative—or structuring, since humans use language to re-create their existence even as they are structured by it. In this corre-

lation between language and experience, we may see not only the structuring effect of language on identity constitution but also its reproductive effect on sexuality, which is also perpetuated in and through culture.

34. Since the Swallow edition of *Winter* is now standard, I treat "Stella" here. A discussion of it belongs here because the story did not appear in *The Winter of Artifice* and also because its themes reflect Nin's diary writing of the period preceding the printing of the original *Winter* in 1939, particularly regarding the author's efforts to write herself out of a neurotic attachment to her father. See also Jason (43).

35. In Volume 2 of the *Diary*, for instance, Nin links the feminine both to "instinct and intuition" (2: 45) and to acknowledgment of one's dependence on others (234). She links the masculine to "scientific intellectual inventions" (203), to impersonal abstractions (172), and to objectivity and separateness (234). In turn, she draws a connection between these differences between masculine and feminine ways of thinking and her own search for someone to share her sense of the world (62), even as she develops an understanding that "to seek a total unity is wrong," since there "is not one big cosmic meaning for all, there is only the meaning we each give to our life, an individual meaning, an individual plot, like an individual novel, a book for each person" (45).

36. Several critics—including Fitch and Scholar—have argued that Nin, too, remained sick and blind. I want to emphasize her work toward health, which in Lacanian thought is a matter of position and degree more than a matter of finalized cure.

37. The account of a young woman's reunion with a father she has not seen for twenty years is recounted nearly identically in the two mediums, fiction and diary. Neither *Incest* nor *Fire* mirrors the narrative style of Nin's fiction.

38. Nancy Scholar, for instance, has seen "Winter of Artifice" as a "flawed novella which substitutes indirection and innuendo for a full rendering of the father-daughter story" (Scholar 90; cited in Jason 44).

39. Nin's struggle to name her narrator speaks to her difficulty in finding an appropriate fictional identity for representing herself away from her father's and Rank's desire. After naming the protagonist Djuna and Lilith in early versions of the story, Nin finally leaves the narrator unnamed in the Swallow edition.

40. See Volume 2 of the *Diary* for the companion passage to the fiction: "I wrote the last pages of Winter of Artifice. About the last time I came out of the ether to see a dead little girl with long eyelashes and slender head. The little girl died in me and with her the need of a father" (2: 62).

41. Bair interprets Nin's response to her abortion as one of utmost callousness and indifference (200–202). By contrast, I interpret the frequent reference to themes of stillbirth, birth, and mothering in Nin's writing, as well as Nin's air of indifference itself, to indicate the degree to which she was traumatized by her abortion experience. This view is shared by Suzette Henke, whose essay "A Confessional Narrative" provides convincing textual support for this argument. I am troubled by Nin's choice to abort a six-month-old fetus. At the same time, however, I think it important to acknowledge the complexity of her situation before the abortion and the complex reaction to it she experienced for the rest of her life.

42. A similar passage may be found at the opening of *Ladders to Fire*.

43. In my discussion of the short story "Hejda" (see chapter 3), I interpret this kind of seeking in terms of the Lacanian notion of the gaze.

44. For Lacan, perversion involves the fetishizing of any object or relation. That is, when a subject takes another as the solution to his own lack and invests in the belief that a sexual relation—or any object that represents it—can fill up lack, he may be considered perverse. Thus, it is not the gender of Lilith's chosen love object that is at issue, but her inability to tolerate lack.

45. I discuss Nin's account of the stillbirth abortion experience as part of my explication of the short story "Birth" in chapter 3.

CHAPTER 3: EXILE AND (RE-)BIRTH

1. The epigraph is taken from Edward Said, "Reflections on Exile," in *New Worlds of Literature*, ed. Jerome Beaty and J. Paul Hunter, 2nd ed. (New York and London: W. W. Norton, 1994). Wilson's review is of the eight-story version published by Nin as opposed to the now standard thirteen-story version. Franklin and Schneider list "Through the Streets of My Own Labyrinth," "The All-Seeing," "The Eye's Journey," "The Child Born Out of the Fog," and "Hejda" as additions (Franklin and Schneider 56).

2. Stuhlmann considers Wilson's review "lukewarm and backhanded" and points out it was part of another review (G. S. to D. R-A., letter, 5/10/97).

3. Bair reports that by 1944, Miller had reversed their financial arrangements and had begun sending Nin an allowance (Bair 298). However, Stuhlmann writes that Miller sent Nin one check in 1944 after receiving a one-time "windfall" (G. S. to D. R-A., letter, 5/10/97).

4. Nin would fictionalize Gonzalo as Rango in *The Four-Chambered Heart*.

5. Nin says later, during an interview in February 1972, that she considers it a sign of maturity for a woman to outgrow the need for male approval. "But I don't think any of us do," she adds. "There is always someone whose judgment we need" (*A Woman Speaks* 106).

6. Nin's *Diary* description of anxiety echoes Lillian's sense in *Ladders to Fire* that her "nameless anguish" is like "the asphyxiation of pain, the horror of torture whose cries no one hears" (*Ladders* 16).

7. One critic who similarly cites the gain in Nin's artistic control in this collection is Oliver Evans (see Jason 46–47).

8. Paraphrasing Freud's " *'Wo es war, soll Ich werden'* [Where the id was, there the ego shall be]," Lacan said that the human "I" comes into being at the point that the speaker disappears in the process of speaking: "There where it was just now, there where it was for awhile, between an extinction [anticipation of death] that is still glowing and a birth that is retarded" (*Ecrits* 128), that is, whose significance, like human maturity, is delayed. Lacan argued that we live our lives in the future perfect tense, creating the meaning of our lives in the way we tell the stories of our lives in speech, which carries the appearance of inevitability and of anticipation. Nin's momentum from stasis to movement—along with her narrator's movement in the first story of this collection from convention to exile—takes place in the anticipatory status of an "always already" exiled; as author, she moves toward a re-memory of the past (in which she gave stillbirth to an aborted child) through whose narrative form she attempts to come to terms with the conditions of her (universally human) exile from language and her (particular) exile from the father whose abandonment of her anticipates and predetermines in

a practical sense her "abandonment" of her own child.

9. We can recognize the narrative process of *Glass Bell* in the Lacanian critic Jonathan Scott Lee's account of analytical discourse, where he shows how truth emerges in the telling, and how meaning comes into being in story form. Lee writes: "meaning comes in the way that [an analysand's] tale takes the brute and largely unconnected facts as remembered ([Lacan's] 'past contingencies') and strings them together to produce a linguistic creation exhibiting something like the inevitability of plot ([Lacan's] 'the sense of necessities to come')" (Lee 43).

10. See Henke's "Confessional" for further exploration of Nin's "extinguished daughter/self forever mourned" (76).

11. The description that appears in Volume 2 of the *Diary* (118–19) is a compilation of both experiences (see Bair 566 n. 13).

12. As Lee puts it, one moves from one notion (that the unconscious is outside the individual's control) to the notion of the "transindividual" (that the unconscious is outside the individual's control simply because "'language and its structure exist prior to the moment at which each subject at a certain point in his mental development makes his entry into it'" [Lacan, cited in Lee 46]). The difference is between the notion of subjugation to unconscious motivation, in the former, and the notion of coming to terms with the conditions under which one has acceded to the Symbolic in the latter.

13. In the *Diary* (2: 118–19) Nin portrays her choice to live on the houseboat in a way that does not, to any significant degree, call into question her attachment to the imaginary, romanticized nature of her choice. "Houseboat" avoids such romanticization and allows the image to be viewed *as* image, similar to the way an analysand may come to recognize the fictional status of the ego and thus to live more creatively as author rather than as subject of fiction.

14. Prayer, ironically, constitutes an appeal *in language,* in this case an appeal for immunity from the effects of language.

15. For Dominick LaCapra's comments on one's willingness to experience anxiety as a stage in the mourning process, see his "Canons and Their Discontents."

16. The process of confronting terms of her entry into the realm of language that existed before her has shown her a significant distinction, similar to Lee's distinction between (1) a subject powerless in the face of the unconscious and (2) a subject who—though subject to an unconscious structured (as Lacan said) like language—can nevertheless recognize that this subjectivity stems from a point of entry into the Symbolic, which structures subjectivity itself (Lee 46).

17. Nin returns to the idea that early paternal disapproval can lead to a child's inability to find satisfaction with one lover at the end of *Ladders to Fire,* where Lillian's attachment to an imaginary ideal leads to the ever-recurring sense that "'This is not the place,'" followed by "'He is not the one.'" In *Fire,* Nin explores the relationship between her father's disapproving rejection and her own tendency to resist the absolute through several forms of splitting, including a consciously chosen sexual promiscuity. See, for instance, *Fire* (244, 330, 368).

18. This image recurs later in the collection in "The All-Seeing" (*Glass Bell* 74).

19. Other enactments of this theme include, in "The Mouse," the title character's inability to finish singing a folk song (whose first seven notes she repeats over and

over) and, in "Under a Glass Bell," the ending image of a guitar string breaking as the instrument lies at the feet of the protagonist.

20. Jane Caputi, in showing how the twentieth-century popular imagination has been fascinated with images of explosive disruptions, has drawn a connection between (1) individual trauma such as incest and society's failure to protect the child and (2) the twentieth-century social upheavals resulting from technology. On both levels, the lack of respect for boundaries leads to disruption. Nin's use of imagery suggesting disruption and explosion, used to connote individual trauma in *House of Incest,* is carried through her increasing acknowledgment of the link between individual and social trauma in *Under a Glass Bell.* See, for instance, the *Diary* (4: 152) for Nin's link of atomic theory to "inner eruption," and *Fire* (336, 376) for two of many passages in which Nin uses explosive terms to describe her individual traumas.

21. The image follows up on the way that the truth of one's trajectory lies in the speech with which one tells it (Lee 42–43) and the way that meaning comes into being in the same way that, in an analysis, the analysand gives remembered "facts" linguistic form and "strings them together to produce an exhibition of ostensible inevitability characteristic of plot" (Lee 43).

22. Franklin and Schneider also find evidence of Nin's social conscience in this story (58). A difference between their reading and mine is that they believe the narrator, though genuinely concerned about the Mouse, "is unable to participate as fully as she might like in the sympathy and understanding that will bring about the cessation of convenient stereotyping" (Franklin and Schneider 48). In contrast, I read the story to endorse Nin's sense that the social structures that alienate the Mouse can be changed only through one's own recognition of one's place in those structures—and through one's entering a personal labyrinth through which to establish new structures. The narrator's compassion can help the Mouse only insofar as it motivates the Mouse to recognize and confront these issues.

23. In Lacanian terms we can say that all humans are, in a sense, exiled, and some humans are doubly exiled—once by language and again by the secondary effects by which their bodies come to signify "woman."

24. Jane Caputi has observed that blowing the whistle on bombers or incestdoers is more prohibited in our culture than are the acts themselves: "making genocidal bombs isn't taboo, but speaking out against them is" (Caputi 130).

25. Bair documents at least two abortions that Nin had subsequent to the one in 1934 to which I refer (259, 328). I believe Nin's writing shows that the first one, performed at the cusp of the second and third trimesters of pregnancy, was the most traumatic.

26. Stuhlmann believes "glass bell" more likely refers to the glass covering "over a clock which cuts it off from the outside world" (G. S. to D. R-A., letter, 5/10/97).

27. The continuation of this passage, which tells that the Mohican's whirling people around an illusory hub is done through a "breaking all the laws of human life which demand collisions and intermarriages" (*Glass Bell* 45), condemns the kind of rule-breaking that Jane Caputi has argued characterizes the perpetuation and cultural protection of both incest and nuclear weaponry.

28. Evelyn Hinz, in *The Mirror and the Garden,* emphasizes Nin's treatment of necessary distinctions (86).

29. See, for example, Kent Ekberg, "The Importance of 'Under a Glass Bell'"

in *Under the Sign of Pisces: Anaïs Nin and Her Circle* 8.2 (spring 1977): 4–18. See also Nalbantian's *Aesthetic Autobiography* (172–74) and Spencer's *Collage of Dreams* (esp. 187).

30. Franklin and Schneider distinguish between the ragpicker's perspective, which they see as reinforcing rather than suggesting a way beyond disintegration, and the narrator's, which allows her to emerge from her "nightmare" to understand that "the past cannot be recaptured and that one must make the most of the present" (Franklin and Schneider 55).

31. In my paper "Anaïs Nin's 'Poetic Porn': Subverting the Male Gaze," I argue that Nin's erotica, edited by John Ferrone and published posthumously as *Delta of Venus* (1977) and *Little Birds* (1979), may be read as parody, through which she calls into question the patron's objectivizing "gaze."

It was only near the end of her life, however, that Nin reluctantly agreed to the publication of her erotica. She was afraid that the erotica, of which she was embarrassed, would hurt her literary reputation (Bair 513–14). The effect was actually a mixed blessing, for *Delta of Venus* became a best-seller, providing the financial security she had wanted but linking her in the public mind (and perhaps forever) with the genre she considered least worthy of her talents as a writer. Because my plans include a separate study of Nin's erotica, I have not included them within the scope of this book.

32. Karen Brennan, in "Anais Nin: Author(iz)ing the Erotic Body," has pinpointed the theme of oscillation between subject and object roles such as occurs in the first two of these three stories as the narrative technique that, as used in Nin's erotic fiction, makes possible a feminist reading. Brennan discusses Nin's "doubleness" with reference to Nin's account in the *Diary* of her agreeing to write erotica for one dollar per page, during the 1940s, when Henry Miller received an offer to do so from an unknown patron represented by a book collector Henry knew. According to Brennan, Miller felt castrated by the arrangement and eventually bowed out, but Nin (who writes in her diary that she accepted the offer in order to raise money for bills and supplies) did not feel castrated. According to the diary, she got her friends involved in the project as well and, despite their making fun of the patron as a voyeur, produced the pages and collected the pay. Brennan attributes the difference between Henry's and Anaïs's attitudes to their gender positions: whereas Henry is uncomfortable relinquishing masculine control and becoming a literary prostitute for a "voyeur at the keyhole," Nin, as a woman, was able to use the opportunity to perform as both spectator and object and to write erotica that "denies narrative gratification at the same time that it fulfills the erotic promise of a pornographic text" (Brennan 77).

33. Bair writes that Nin considered the baby girl's potential "only for a moment" and quickly "dismissed the thought" (202). I believe Nin's inability to give the matter much *conscious* thought resurfaces often in her work. Henke explores these resurfacings in her insightful essay, "Maternal Anxiety and Daughter Loss."

34. Jason has pointed out that "Appearing twenty years apart, these treatments of 1931–32 will find different readers, as well as readers who lived with one set of impressions for two decades and now have different ones to contend with. Some of these readers will feel cheated" ("Dropping Another Veil" 30). I discuss my own reaction in my article "Narrative and Authenticity—Strategies of Evasion in the Diaries of Anaïs Nin: Then and Now."

CHAPTER 4: REPETITION AND RESISTANCE

1. She would also publish three pieces of literary criticism of particular relevance to her fictional aims: *Realism and Reality* (1946) and *On Writing* (1947) she self-published at Gemor Press; "The Writer and the Symbols" appeared in *Two Cities* in April 1959. All three became part of Nin's expanded statement of literary philosophy in *The Novel of the Future* (1968). Hinz's chapter "Backwards and Forwards" in *The Mirror and the Garden* provides the best available discussion of Nin's critical works. Hinz's thorough discussion of Nin's developing thought includes analysis of the changes in Nin's views and approaches between her Lawrence study and *Future*, as well as a careful discussion of Nin's fiction in terms of Nin's interpretations. The epigraph to this chapter is taken from Hinz, *The Mirror and the Garden* (61).

2. See Jason (56, 58, 59). The novels were first published in one volume as *Cities of the Interior* in 1959. A work entitled *Solar Barque* (1958) served temporarily as the final novel in the *Cities* collection. *Seduction of the Minotaur* (1961) incorporates and expands upon the original *Solar Barque*. In 1974, the "final authorial version" of *Cities of the Interior* appeared in a one-volume edition (Jason 55, 57).

3. Hinz discusses Nin's emphasis on the need for literature to be morally instructive. "According to Nin, it was because America lacked a literature of this quality that 'The Lost Generation' came into being" (Hinz 10).

4. Originally a separate work published at Nin's Gemor Press in 1945, *This Hunger* included "Stella" (later made a part of *Winter of Artifice*) and "Hejda" (later incorporated into *Under a Glass Bell*). The section of the 1946 version of *Ladders* entitled "This Hunger" included "Stella" and "Lillian and Djuna." By the time of the Swallow edition of *Ladders* in 1959, all that remained of the section called "This Hunger" was the part originally called "Lillian and Djuna" (Jason 55–56). Part 2, "Bread and the Wafer," became part of the 1946 version of *Ladders*.

5. In *The Novel of the Future*, Nin discusses the importance of retreating to inner meditative places, "islands within an uncluttered mental space," especially as the pace of life accelerates (*Future* 27).

6. On a single page in the unexpurgated *Fire*, Nin portrays orgasm as dynamite (that is, as a potentially destructive and dangerous force) and, without any transition, goes on to describe an anecdote of a father with his little girl asking, without explanation, "why are his eyes so wet, his mouth so wet, why are her eyes so tired . . . why . . . why this malaise I feel as I pass them . . . ?" (*Fire* 331). In numerous passages throughout Nin's work, there is an implicit link between trauma related to fathers and young daughters, on one hand, and Lillian's and Djuna's inability to reach orgasm, on the other.

7. For Lacan, gender is linguistically overdetermined because the meanings given to "male" or "female" depend on culture's association, on a secondary rather than a biological and primary level, of mother with loss and phallus with power. That is, "mother" does not in any primary sense mean "loss"—nor does "father" or "man" or "phallus" mean "power." Society assigns secondary significance to "phallus" because it is *seemingly* autonomous (rising and falling as if by will) and because it comes to represent the illusion of autonomy that the ego embraces.

8. This metaphor is linked to the illusion of *moi* unity represented by the mirror-stage image of bodily *gestalt* and, appropriately in terms of the Imaginary status of

such human belief in wholeness, to Lillian's vulnerability (in Djuna's mind). "Djuna looked tenderly at her . . . [at] the hidden, secret, frightened Lillian who had created such a hard armor and disguise around her weakness" (*Ladders* 47).

9. Bracher writes that the appearance of shame indicates a breach in the fabric of the ego, a place where a skilled analyst can interrupt the linguistic covering of rhetoric, as the patient tells her story, and thus help her to access the unconscious causes of desire whose repression has resulted in neurosis (Bracher 66). It is unlikely that Nin received this interruption in her analyses, for she quit each one (Allendy, Rank, Jaeger, Staff) for various reasons before she recovered, staying only with her last therapist, Dr. Inge Bogner. Bair describes Dr. Bogner as a "medical doctor with a specialty in psychiatry" who "commiserated and comforted [Nin], even as she tried to help her choose one man or the other" (Bair 353, 355). The effect of Bogner's analysis on Nin was positive in many ways; Nin was extremely grateful to her, crediting Bogner with helping her gain the courage to publish her *Diary*. Still, it is clear that Nin needed to supplement her clinical therapy with writing, working out much of her own analysis in written form, and that the length of this stage of her narrative recovery—sixteen years of writing *Cities*—is linked to her difficulty in separating her ego-fictions from the ideal ego she had set up in terms of an idealized mothering role.

10. Evelyn J. Hinz, in *The Mirror and the Garden*, has characterized this image as the central one for understanding Nin's aesthetics. The mirrors represent the artifice of conventional literary realism, while the garden stands for Nin's conception of reality as a natural, organic process of life and death.

11. Bair writes that to read Nin's diary of the 1940s one would never guess there had been a world war (308). However, the war imagery that abounds in Nin's fiction gives voice to aspects of Nin's personal suffering in terms that link it to a wider sphere of violence and destruction and to imagery of twentieth-century warfare, in particular.

12. The passage containing this description is repeated almost verbatim in *A Spy in the House of Love*, a repetition Oliver Evans has found to have "no strategic purpose" (160), but which I think Nin may have intended as a kind of musical recurrence of theme.

13. Sabina is actually modeled more directly on June Miller than on Nin herself. Portraits of June Miller may also be found in the *Diary* (1: 20–46) and in *Henry and June* (1986), on which Philip Kauffman's film of the same title is based.

14. This characterization places gender, again, in an analogous relationship to language, as Jay and Sabina participate in the erasure of individuality that happens when individual women are reduced to clones of a universal concept of "woman"—a reduction Lacan critiqued in his often misunderstood comment that "*the* woman" does not exist (*Feminine Sexuality* 137, 144).

15. For an explanation of Lacan's "something of One," see Lee (180–82), where the concept of romantic love is treated in terms of its inherent narcissism: for example, "The One that is sought in love is really one's own unity . . . , forever lost as a result of primal repression, of the castration effected by speech and language. What the lover seeks in his beloved is nothing else than his own integral identity" (Lee 181).

16. In the *Diary* Nin also compares the disintegration of the modern self and its representation in the works of Modernists like Proust and Joyce to the "splitting of the atom," a process, she argues, that can release energy instead of destroy it (4: 152). Jane

Caputi's work emphasizes the prevalence of atomic imagery in twentieth-century writing, particularly that writing by survivors of the "unthinkable fathering" (see chapter 2).

17. See Bair's discussion of Nin's relationships with a series of young homosexual men (318).

18. The shame and guilt that Bracher explains are indicators of a movement away from the desired separation (Bracher 66) are also present in Nin's account of Djuna's conflict (*Heart* 82).

19. In the appropriately named unexpurgated diary volume *Fire*, Nin writes about seeking many lovers in quest of an absolute not found in one man but found, instead, in a multiplicity of many lovers (*Fire* 368).

20. For Nin, being an artist like her father meant leaving one's dependents, something Nin—having been on that side—could not bring herself to do (staying married to a man she no longer loved as a husband, for instance, out of both fear and compassion). Her mother had given up her singing career to be a good wife and mother and had been left anyway. Nin struggled for years, wavering between identification with her mother and identification with her father.

21. See Lee (182) on the relation between "woman" and "soul" in Lacanian thought.

22. Nin continues this theme in *Nearer the Moon*, esp. 55–56.

23. Significant in this respect is Nin's statement that not "all the stones tied around my analyzed neck can drown the poet" (*Fire* 369)—indicating that in the process of her analysis, she finds it necessary to resist the dangers inherent in analysis itself. One danger is the coaptation to a totalizing perspective proper to a master discourse system such as psychoanalysis.

24. In *The Novel of the Future*, Nin discusses the relation between subjectivity disguised as rationalism and the fatalism inherent in romantic notions of what literature should be. See Hinz (84, 86) for a concise, insightful analysis of Nin's relation to realism and reality.

25. Similarly, Lacan depicted feminine *jouissance* as the kind of "knowing" that does not deny the body but, rather, goes through and beyond the body to the knowledge that lies beyond notions of autonomy embodied in language.

26. Bracher, too, emphasizes the degree to which Lacan's notion of hysterical structure provides a way for subjects not only to resist but also to protest "the exclusion of part of their being (desires and jouissances) by the master signifiers and the resultant subject positions of women imposed by the patriarchal system" (Bracher 67). Bracher explains that feminist discourse, as an example, may be seen as a verbal counterpart to the bodily symptoms of Freud's hysterics. Nin's repetitions—as well as the kind of narrative interruption that marks an opening in the line between fiction and nonfiction—may be seen in this light of an embodiment of language of a subjective split, not only between the speaking subject and the ego but also between Nin's unconscious desire and the terms of patriarchy.

27. The party motif is repeated so often in Nin's works that one wonders how many times Nin will lament her feeling of exclusion through her characters. Her repetition indicates an inability to move on, even at this late point. Not yet able to separate her own self-myth from an idealized Image of the mother and partner to her Imaginary father she thinks she should be, Nin continues to repeat herself, giving voice many

times over to the dynamics by which the unconscious slips through the ego's covering. Although she shows a tremendous and often fascinating perceptivity about the operation of this dynamic in her own life, her writing indicates an inability to enact her intellectual understanding on the level of form and style in this novel or the next.

28. In a passage labeled "April, 1940" in Volume 3 of the *Diary*, Nin writes a passage that echoes Djuna's perspective in *The Four-Chambered Heart*—that she is beginning to avoid discussions because she no longer believes there is a mass solution to the world's problems, such as that offered by Marxism (*Diary* 3: 28). By "September, 1940" she has refined her position; she asserts more strongly a belief in exploring individuality for answers to general trends and states that certain colleagues' obsession with sociological trends is shortsighted (3: 44)—an obvious reference to Gonzalo. The world's ills, its mass movements and cultural patterns, can only be understood by examining the individual character as a symptom of the whole, she believes. She argues that it is only through psychoanalysis or through literature such as hers, whose characterization is based on psychological premises, that the irrational and violent aspects of society may be understood (3: 46).

29. See, for instance, Daniel R. Schwarz, *Narrative and Representation in the Poetry of Wallace Stevens*, where he discusses the 1913 Armory Show and also Wallace Stevens's fascination (similar to Nin's) with "the possibility of being both protagonist and ironic spectator" (Schwarz 31). Regarding the Armory Show's influence on Stevens, Schwarz (see chapter 5) goes on to quote Joan Richardson's study, *Wallace Stevens: The Early Years, 1879–1923* (New York: William Morrow, 1986). The applicability to Nin's treatment lies in Richardson's statement that "'The various intersecting and juxtaposed forms depicted on a cubist canvas were intended to mirror this constant movement of consciousness, aware of itself, as it observed something external that temporarily focused attention'" (403, cited in Schwarz).

CHAPTER 5: CATHARSIS AND HEALING

1. The epigraph is taken from *A Woman Speaks*, p. 183.

2. Beginning around 1950, Nin used the word "trapeze" to describe her double life between the husband in New York to whom she had been married since 1923 and the Californian Rupert Pole, whom she met in 1947 and married (without divorcing Hugh Guiler) in March 1955. The second marriage was annulled in June 1966 (Bair 373, 612 n. 24), although Pole remained Nin's primary partner until her death.

3. Besides the four analyses Nin describes in the *Diary* (those with Drs. René Allendy, Otto Rank, Martha Jaeger, and Inge Bogner), Nin saw Dr. Clement Staff intermittently from 1945 until 1951. Staff is given two brief mentions in the *Diary*, the first in Volume 6 where Nin praises her friend Frances Brown for persevering through her own courage even when she did not receive "the best of psychological help from Jaeger or Staff" (6: 36). In Volume 7 Nin quotes Staff, "Dr. Staff said in 1947: 'Analysis is like a spiral. The crises grow smaller, less violent'" (7: 232). Bair reports that Dr. Staff's analysis was the first instance when Nin "could not commit what happened in the analyst's office verbatim to the diary." Instead, she made "garbled and muttered comments" about her masochism, behind which "lay 'sadism'" (Bair 305).

4. Both *Seduction* and *Collages* show Nin's increased emotional and artistic

maturity; the latter declares Nin *relatively* free of the affective (hysterical) suffering that plagued her through most of her adult life. Nin was still intensely neurotic in some ways through the 1950s and 1960s, living a lie as a bigamist and often paranoid about criticism. But her writings show that she had learned to survive (if only through sheer willpower) and could feel more sustained contentment than perhaps ever before.

5. The repetitious nature of the first four *Cities* novels, as well as of certain aspects of Nin's behavior, is apropos to a Lacanian view of resistance as "the insistence of an unconscious discourse, which prefers to repeat itself in language or behavior (rather than to know itself)" (Ragland, *Philosophy* 121). The fifth novel shows Nin overcoming this resistance.

6. The novels' flaws are related both to each other and to Nin's movement away from father transference as she strove to create her own patterns in literature as well as in her psyche. It is not surprising, then, that the structure of these works—characterized by a lack of boundaries, which Sharon Spencer considers an "open, dynamic form" (Spencer 36) and Nancy Scholar considers a preoccupation with narcissistic issues (Scholar 109)—mirrors the hysterical structure of their author.

7. Though criticized for not having enough surface realism in her novels, Nin justified the lack as a conscious choice. It was a choice related to her effort to move away from an attachment to the Imaginary father and from a corresponding identification with a perfectly nurturing mother. For instance, having come by this point to associate the critic Edmund Wilson (with whom she had an affair in 1945) with literary realism itself, she writes in the *Diary* that "Wilson's reality holds terror for me . . . and . . . nameless dangers" (4: 84). Nameless because they belong to an unconscious primordial inheritance but perceptible because Nin is progressing toward a conscious understanding of her unconscious positioning, these "dangers" are of being engulfed by the father's name: "Will I be overwhelmed by the power of the father?" (4: 84), she asks. Nin's solution to this feeling of being engulfed is to continue to produce displacements within the boundary of fiction, thereby shifting emphasis away from her personal framework (a structure that imprisons her) and onto an Other she has created to bear the brunt of some of her suffering.

8. I disagree with those who believe *Spy* is one of Nin's best. For the purposes of the present study, especially, I have chosen to concentrate on this novel as an "interlude" because I think it shows Nin working *toward* (but not quite achieving) what she wanted to accomplish in fiction. Consider her comments to this effect in *The Novel of the Future* (138).

9. In an especially insightful passage (one of the few incidences of literary criticism per se in Bair's biography), Bair describes the novel's centrality to late twentieth-century perspectives of the self and credits Nin with creating "one of the first novels to deal with this theme." Typically, however, "Nin is never given credit for being one of the originators of [the theme], nor is her work included among its best examples" (Bair 366). Later, I address how Nin's treatment of the fragmented self anticipates Postmodern theories.

10. In Nin's own behavior, the splitting of the self would rather take on a different form than be left behind. Although Nin's promiscuity ended shortly after she met Rupert Pole in 1947, she remained split between two partners and two homes for the rest of her life; restricting herself to two lovers was Nin's own form of sexual loyalty

(Bair 273). Although Bair's observation refers to Henry Miller and Gonzalo Moré, I find it applicable to Nin's double marriage as well. Again, I am stressing a relative degree of recovery.

11. Consider, for example Nin's description of Sabina and Philip's sexual encounter as the enactment of "one ritual, the joyous, joyous, joyous, joyous impaling of woman on man's sexual mast" (*Spy* 29).

12. Jason, among others, has described the development of Sabina's character both through her relationships with men and "through accompanying allusions to a spectrum of composers, musical works, and style of music" (Jason 62). See Jason, "Teaching *A Spy in the House of Love*," in *Under the Sign of Pisces: Anaïs Nin and Her Critics* 2.3 (summer 1971): 7–15.

13. Stevens placed a subscription for *Under a Glass Bell* in 1944 and remained an admirer for the rest of his life (Bair 293).

14. According to Volume 5 of the *Diary,* Nin sensed herself caught in such a pitfall, unable to shuck her mother's judgmental eyes, even at the time of her mother's death in August 1954. She cites her own failure to relinquish the role assigned her by her mother—that of "a good daughter" (5: 177)—and to stop playing the countering part even while recognizing its source. "Very early," Nin writes, "I was determined not to be like her but like the women who had enchanted and seduced my father, the mistresses who lured him away from us" (5: 182).

15. Similarly, in Volume 5 of the *Diary,* Nin associates changes in her self-concept with the tropical setting of Acapulco. As portrayed in *Seduction of the Minotaur,* language appears less alienating to her in Mexico than it does in New York, because the fluid, relaxed lifestyle of the Tropics allows her to open—in a way that the fast-paced rhythms of the city did not—to a connection between language and the body. Words, which Nin has always felt were insufficient to link her with others, now, she writes, "have no weight" (5: 5). They do not seem heavy to her, do not depress her with their alienating role. She describes them as floating, mixing with the rhythms of the music she hears around her. "Jazz is the music of the body," she writes (5: 5), as she does in *Seduction,* sensing a harmony between words and the real responses of her body to sensory images.

16. Nin was coming to terms with her own mortality, having been diagnosed with a fibroid tumor in 1947 and having an ovarian cyst removed in January 1953. She died in 1977 from a cancer that had started in her vagina.

17. Nin's interest in consumerism and its effect on art and artists is important both to her own work and to critical perspectives such as the psychoanalytic that emphasize choice and the ability of individuals to make distinctions between what they truly need and want, on one hand, and what is marketed to them, on the other.

18. Nin also had to contend with INS regulations, "which, among other points, require five years of uninterrupted residence in the U.S., and 'moral turpitude' was a potential . . . reason [for exclusion]" (G. S. to D. R-A., letter, 5/10/97).

19. This is but one instance of a general toning down in Nin's style: the gender-as-costume motif of the earlier novels in the *Cities* series appears more subtle here than before, and the didactic, editorializing narrator has ceased lecturing her readers on "man's" and "woman's" constructions. Rather (a better novelist by this point), she more often lets the details speak for themselves, and the details—particularly in terms of

costuming—emphasize modes of being-in-the-world over gender.

20. The efficacy of this critique depends, in part, on the Minotaur of the title. Part of the seduction of the half-bull, half-man creature living in the mythological labyrinth involves Lillian's desire to avoid a confrontation with the image of herself and of her relationship with those who have hurt her in the past. When the bus ride jars her, first, to consider the bullfighter (who is a fellow passenger on the bus) as the victim of a "symbolic rape" (*Seduction* 70) and, next, to remember the effect of her mother's gaze (88) and her tendency to be drawn to father-figures like Hatcher (75), Lillian confronts this internal monster.

21. After reading Nin's unpublished diaries, Bair records an entry that indicates Nin believed her father had sexually fondled her during a spanking (17–18). Yet, as Bair's account goes on to point out, the adult Nin had many questions about this image born of "the haze of childhood memory [as she tried] to ascertain what was fact and what was fantasy, and to arrive at the truth" (18). See also Bair 527 n. 25.

Whether Nin was sexually abused as a child is not, according to Nin's own writing, as important as her interpretation of the effect of the past. Nin spent most of her life learning to overcome her wounding by her father and did reach a state of relative happiness that came to fruition during her final years. Her father's death in October 1949 provided a sense of closure to a traumatic relationship whose effects are evident in Nin's writing before and after his death.

22. J. M. Coetze's "Speaking for Language" (*New York Review of Books,* February 1, 1996, 28–31), his review of Joseph Brodsky's *On Grief and Reason: Essays* (Farrar, Straus, and Giroux, 1996), cites David M. Bethea's view—in *Joseph Brodsky and the Creation of Exile* (Princeton University Press, 1944, p. 234)—that "the nuances of ironic humor [are] the very last level of English . . . to be mastered by foreigners" (Coetze 31).

23. "Re-constructing the world" is the theme embodied in Jean Varda's collages, as represented by his characterization in *Collages.* Near the end of Volume 4 of the *Diary,* Nin describes her meeting the original Varda, whom she considers "the only modern artist who creates not the sickly-sweet fairy tales of childhood but the sturdy fairy tale of the artist" (4: 216). When Nin visits him in Monterey, she is impressed with his homemade flag fluttering from a turret atop his house. It is a good image for the self that Nin strives to construct for herself: sturdy enough to withstand the weather but flexible enough to ripple and flow with the changing currents of the surrounding medium, it is flown with a sense of individual pride, but also with the consciousness that it is a symbol whose meaning depends on the cultural system of which it is a part.

24. Franklin and Schneider's study includes the observation that the focus of *Collages* shifts from scenes that feature Renate as primary to those where "she is more an observer than a participant" (Franklin and Schneider 153; see also Jason 70).

25. This idea is foreshadowed by Nin's presenting a similar idea in the *Cities* series where she uses Duchamp's *Nude* as a model not only for Djuna's and Sabina's sense of fragmentation but especially of the multiplicitous nature of consciousness and a circular *dédoublement* of perception.

26. Nin's later writings are replete with her objections to drug use as a means of attaining what she believed could best be accessed through learning to re-vision, for

oneself, what modern culture has repressed. See, for example, *A Woman Speaks* (134–35, 187).

CHAPTER 6: NARRATIVE RECOVERY AND NARRATIVE AUTHENTICITY

1. Gisèle Halimi is cited from "Research on Women," translated by Elaine Marks, in *New French Feminisms*, edited and with introductions by Elaine Marks and Isabelle de Courtivron (New York: Schocken Books, 1981), 211.

2. A four-volume series of *The Early Diary of Anaïs Nin* was also published posthumously by Harcourt Brace Jovanovich: *Volume 1 (Linotte, 1914–1920)* in 1978, *Volume 2 (1920–1923)* in 1982, *Volume 3 (1923–1927)* in 1983, and *Volume 4 (1927–1931)* in 1985. "John Ferrone, at Harcourt, did the slight abridgment of the original French text for *Linotte*, and all the English-written volumes were published uncut and unedited except, of course, [for] the usual in-house . . . editing" by the publisher (G. S. to D. R-A., letter, 5/10/97).

3. Beginning in the 1930s, Miller encouraged Nin to publish her diary. In addition, he promoted it in his essay *"Un Etre étoilique,"* which was published in *The Criterion* 17, no. 66 (Oct. 1937), and reprinted in *The Booster*, December–January 1938, as well as in *The Critical Response to Anaïs Nin*, edited by Philip K. Jason (Westport, Conn.: Greenwood Press, 1996), 147–54. See Bair (242, 569 n. 28).

4. Nin's lecture at Smith College on December 11, 1969, in particular, ended in a self-professed "failure" when "she was hooted and hissed" after giving what her audience considered unacceptable answers to the questions they had asked about her role as Miller's helpmate, and other issues. At Bennington College, Nin received a less hostile but similarly skeptical response to her commencement address in 1971 (Bair 493–94).

5. See Bair's chapter entitled "Being Famous" (479–95).

6. The unexpurgated publications yet to be published will shed more light on the degree to which the progression in the *Diary* was directed in an essential way in the editing process.

7. Bair discusses Nin's rejection of Catholicism and her need for absolution (162, 375–77, 513, 609 n. 48), and her rejection of her brother's offer to call a priest so that she could make a final confession (512).

8. For Nin, the feminine position is one in which corporal issues—such as those involved in her depiction of the physiological, visceral basis to woman's writing—are linked to an interiority representative of the unconscious. This connection (see chapter 1) does not place Nin within the category of gender essentialist, however, for her formulating leans toward womb as secondary signifier rather than as the basis for a feminine consciousness. Nin's efforts to come to terms with her choice away from biological mothering intensifies and directs her thinking; she exploits a tradition of literary creation as a form of metaphorical parenting in order to create a positive alternative to bearing children, at the same time exonerating herself and separating from identification with the sacrificing model provided by her own mother. That Nin's Christian overtones point to a need for absolution in analysis and diary writing comes from Stuhlmann (G. S. to D. R-A., letter, 5/10/97).

9. Similarly, in Lacanian thought, the subject, as Juliet Mitchell points out, is

formed in the gap between an Imaginary wholeness and fragmentation and can only "conceptualise itself when it is mirrored back to itself from the position of another's desire" (*Feminine Sexuality* 5).

10. Freud was both baffled and intrigued by the artist's ability. He begins "Creative Writers and Day-Dreaming" by asking "from what sources that strange being, the creative writer, draws his material" (143). He goes on to hypothesize that the sources from which the artist draws are unconscious wishes or desires and that the artist's strangeness—or the difference between the artist and the nonartist—lies largely in the artist's lesser degree of repression. As he goes on, Freud gives essentially the same formula to explain the source of art as he does to explain the source of dream content, that is, "A strong experience in the present awakens in the creative writer [or dreamer] a memory of an earlier experience (usually belonging to his childhood) from which there now proceeds a wish which finds its fulfillment in the creative work [or dream]" (151).

11. I leave interpretation of Nin's relationship to her "transparent children," such as Gore Vidal, until it can be read in light of the unexpurgated diary volume of the same period.

12. But unlike the humanistic idea that people are masters of their fate, Nin's conception of self-making is based on an understanding with which Lacan credits Freud—that human subjects are formed through a cultural, linguistic, and social framework (Mitchell 4).

13. Bair's account indicates that Nin was seeing Clement Staff as her analyst during this period, an important omission in Nin's published account (Bair 311).

14. Nin's relation to a concept of *l'écriture féminine* (see chapter 1) places her outside the category of gender essentialism with which she has sometimes been associated. This significant distinction comes to fruition in Volume 7, particularly as Nin develops an attitude toward death that is similar to the concept of feminine artistry expressed in Volume 2 of the *Diary*, but which goes beyond gender as a primary determinant of artistic position. In her early work, feminine creativity hinges on the idea of a link between the corporality of language and a woman's relation to her own body. In *The Novel of the Future*, she uses the concept of form not to indicate something opposed to content, but to point to the embodiment of desire in language—the word made flesh. Nin's emphasis on writing from the basis of one's individual labyrinth leads her away from generalizations based on gender while it retains a concept of form based on identificatory structure. Her formulation of femininity—as a trait that allows or retains at least partially conscious acknowledgment of unconscious desire—stresses gender *specificity* (one's own relation to desire and law rather than to a gender category).

15. Nin's depictions mirror Lacan's characterization of feminine *jouissance* as a relation to identity that goes *through* and *beyond* the body, particularly the phallus as image of ego autonomy (*Feminine Sexuality* 147). This idea appears explicitly when Nin writes that, while she cannot explain the concept intellectually, she knows there is a way to go "*through* and *beyond* the self" (7: 289). Nin believed that it is "the *not going beyond*" the ego that has caused Western mentality to deny the unconscious and to remain trapped in a primitive egotism, manifested in Western literature (7: 289).

16. My friend Natalie Gilbert, a musician and dancer who teaches at Ohio State University, pointed out to me that tones of the gamelan were incorporated into several pieces by Debussy. It is quite possible that Nin, whose favorite musician was Debussy,

never identified the gamelan in that form but was immediately drawn to its tones when she heard them in isolation.

17. On *Henry and June's* unsuitability for literary study, see Bair (518).

18. Reactions to *Incest* range from Jong's wholehearted applause of Nin's triumph in beating her father at the seduction game to Miranda Seymour's "Truth Wasn't Sexy Enough" condemnation of what she, in her review of Fitch's *Anaïs: The Erotic Life of Anaïs Nin,* agrees are outright lies in Nin's earlier version.

19. Lacan named belief in the sexual relation as a natural and harmonious given and certainty about biological paternity as two impossibilities that give humans the most trouble. Similarly, the "cone of darkness" in Nin's writing is analogous to what Freud described as the "navel" of a dream, or that point at which the dreamer cannot reconstitute his dream consciously because its material slips into an inaccessible realm beyond the grasp of consciousness and unconsciousness, that which Lacan, in *Four Fundamental Concepts of Psychoanalysis,* named the Real (23). Such an element exists in every subject, and the effort to know the whole story of any person's life (including, and perhaps especially, one's own) is inevitably futile.

20. Phallic certainty comes under particular fire in Nin's ("I love to throw bombs"–inspired) structure. Scholar's hostility points to the quest for fixed meaning that Nin deconstructs. As I show throughout this chapter, Nin's texts do not deny meaning beyond language as literary deconstructionism does; rather, they disrupt the illusory wholeness to reveal a meaning beyond language. Similarly, Lacan depicted feminine *jouissance* as that kind of "knowing" that does not deny the body but, rather, goes through and beyond the body to that knowledge which lies beyond notions of autonomy embodied in language.

21. Bair, too, prefaces her account of Anaïs Nin's two-week "nonstop orgiastic frenzy" with Joaquín Nin y Castellanos with the words, "If Anaïs Nin the diarist is to be believed . . ." (174).

22. In her presentation entitled "Diary as Narrative" at the 1994 International Narrative Conference in Vancouver, B.C., on April 29, 1994, Susan Rubin Suleiman named both omission and chronological changes as violations of the implicit contract between a diarist and the readers of a diary assumed to be "real" (as opposed to a fictionalized diary acknowledged by the author as such). Readers who feel betrayed by Nin's withholding of facts might consider Gunther Stuhlmann's explicit acknowledgment, in the introduction to the first volume, that the *Diary* had been extensively edited—an effective refutation to the argument that Nin had failed to live up to her duty as diarist since she and Stuhlmann tell readers up front what they have done with the text.

23. Nin's references to lying, especially to her husbands and other lovers, are so numerous that they cannot be cited here. That this undermines the literary value of her work is doubtful, especially as she engages in the kind of self-questioning necessary to literary inquiry.

Selected Bibliography

Altieri, Charles. *Painterly Abstraction in Modernist American Poetry: The Contemporaneity of Modernism.* University Park: Pennsylvania State University Press, 1989.

Bair, Deirdre. *Anaïs Nin: A Biography.* New York: G. P. Putnam's Son, 1995.

Barron, Janet. "Equality Puzzle: Lawrence and Feminism." In *Rethinking Lawrence.* Ed. Keith Brown. 12–22. Milton Keynes, Pa.: Open University Press, 1990.

Blanchard, Lydia. "Love and Power: A Reconsideration of Sexual Politics in D. H. Lawrence." *Modern Fiction Studies* 21.3 (1975).

Bracher, Mark. *Lacan, Discourse, and Social Change: A Psychoanalytic Cultural Criticism.* Ithaca and London: Cornell University Press, 1993.

Brennan, Karen. "Anais Nin: Author(iz)ing the Erotic Body." *Genders* 14 (fall 1992): 66–86.

Caputi, Jane. *Gossips, Gorgons, and Crones: The Fates of the Earth.* Santa Fe: Bear & Co., 1994.

Chodorow, Nancy. *The Reproduction of Mothering: Psychoanalysis and the Sociology of Gender.* Berkeley and Los Angeles: University of California Press, 1978.

Cixous, Hélène. "The Laugh of the Medusa." In *New French Feminisms.* Ed. Elaine Marks and Isabelle de Courtivron. 245–64. New York: Schocken Books, 1981.

de Beauvoir, Simone. *The Second Sex.* Trans. H. M. Parshley. London: Jonathan Cape, 1953.

de Lauretis, Teresa. *Alice Doesn't: Feminism, Semiotics, Cinema.* Bloomington: Indiana University Press, 1984.

Denby, David. Film review of "Henry and June." *New York,* October 15, 1990, p. 66; cited in *Film Review Annual,* p. 662.

DuBow, Wendy M. "The Elusive Text: Reading 'The Diary of Anaïs Nin, Volume 1, 1931–1934.'" *Anaïs: An International Journal* 11 (1993): 22–36.

Edelstein, David. Review of "Henry and June." *New York Post,* October 5, 1990, p. 21; cited in *Film Review Annual,* p. 662.

Evans, Oliver. *Anaïs Nin.* Carbondale: Southern Illinois University Press, 1968.

Fitch, Noël Riley. *Anaïs: The Erotic Life of Anaïs Nin.* New York, Toronto, London: Little, Brown, 1993.

Freud, Sigmund. "Creative Writers and Day-Dreaming." In *The Standard Edition of the Complete Psychological Works of Sigmund Freud.* Trans. and ed. James Strachey, Anna Freud, Alix Strachey, and Alan Tyson. IX: 141–54. London: Hogarth, 1953–1975.

Franklin, Benjamin V., and Duane Schneider. *Anaïs Nin: An Introduction.* Athens: Ohio University Press, 1979.

Gallop, Jane. *The Daughter's Seduction: Feminism and Psychoanalysis.* Ithaca, N.Y.: Cornell University Press, 1982.

Gilbert, Sandra M., and Susan Gubar. *The Madwoman in the Attic: The Woman Writer and the Nineteenth-Century Literary Imagination.* New Haven and London: Yale University Press, 1979.

Henke, Suzette. "A Confessional Narrative: Maternal Anxiety and Daughter Loss in Anaïs Nin's *Journal of Love: Incest.*" *Anaïs: An International Journal* 14 (1996): 71–77.

———. "Lillian Beye's Labyrinth: A Freudian Exploration of *Cities of the Interior.*" *Anaïs: An International Journal* 2 (1984). Rpt. in *The Critical Response to Anaïs Nin.* Ed. Philip K. Jason. Critical Responses in Arts and Letters, No. 23. 133–45. Westport, Conn.: Greenwood Press, 1996.

Hinz, Evelyn J. *The Mirror and the Garden: Realism and Reality in the Writings of Anaïs Nin.* New York: Harcourt Brace Jovanovich, 1971.

Hutcheon, Linda. "Beginning to Theorize the Postmodern." In *A Postmodern Reader.* Ed. Joseph Natoli and Linda Hutcheon. 243–72. Albany: State University of New York Press, 1993.

Irigaray, Luce. "This Sex Which Is Not One." In *New French Feminisms.* Ed. Elaine Marks and Isabelle de Courtivron. 99–106. New York: Schocken Books, 1981.

Jason, Philip K. *Anaïs Nin and Her Critics.* Columbia, S.C.: Camden House, 1993. (Parenthetical citation of Jason's work refers to this entry unless otherwise noted.)

———. "Dropping Another Veil." *Anaïs: An International Journal* 6 (1988): 27–32.

Jones, Anne Rosalind. "Writing the Body: Toward an Understanding of *L'écriture féminine.*" In *The New Feminist Criticism.* Ed. Elaine Showalter. 361–77. New York: Pantheon, 1985.

Jong, Erica. "Donna Juana's Triumph." Review of *Incest: From "A Journal of Love."* *Times Literary Supplement,* June 25, 1993, pp. 3–4.

———. "A Story Never Told Before." *Anaïs: An International Journal* 12 (1994): 15–25.

Knapp, Bettina. *Anaïs Nin.* New York: Ungar, 1978.

Kristeva, Julia. "Oscillation between Power and Denial" and "Women Can Never Be Defined." In *New French Feminisms.* Ed. Elaine Marks and Isabelle de Courtivron. 165–67. New York: Schocken Books, 1981.

Lacan, Jacques. *Ecrits: A Selection.* Trans. Alan Sheridan. New York and London: W. W. Norton, 1977.

———. *Feminine Sexuality: Jacques Lacan and the école freudienne.* Ed. Juliet Mitchell and Jacqueline Rose, trans. Jacqueline Rose. New York and London: W. W. Norton, 1985.

———. *Four Fundamental Concepts of Psychoanalysis*. Ed. by Jacques-Alain Miller, trans. Alan Sheridan. New York and London: W. W. Norton, 1981.

LaCapra, Dominick. "Canons and Their Discontents." *Intellectual History Newsletter* 13 (1991): 3–14.

———. *Representing the Holocaust: History, Theory, Trauma*. Ithaca: Cornell University Press, 1994.

Leavis, F. R. *Thought, Words, and Creativity: Art and Thought in D. H. Lawrence*. New York: Oxford University Press, 1976.

Lee, Jonathan Scott. *Jacques Lacan*. Twayne Publishers, 1990.

Light, Alison. "Feminism and the Literary Critic." In *Feminist Literary Theory*. Ed. Mary Eagleton. London, 1986.

Millett, Kate. "Anaïs—A Mother to Us All: The Birth of the Artist as Woman." *Anaïs: An International Journal* 9 (1991): 3–8.

———. "D. H. Lawrence." In *Sexual Politics*. New York: Doubleday, 1970.

Mitchell, Juliet. Introduction—I to *Feminine Sexuality* by Lacan. 1–26.

Moore, Harry T. Introduction to *D. H. Lawrence: An Unprofessional Study*, by Anaïs Nin. 7–12. Chicago: Swallow Press, 1964.

———. *The Priest of Love: A Life of D. H. Lawrence*. Revised edition. New York: Farrar, Straus, and Giroux, 1974.

Morris, Daniel. "My Shoes: Charles Simic's Self-Portrait." *a/b: Auto/Biography Studies* 11.11 (spring 1996): 109–27.

Nalbantian, Suzanne. *Aesthetic Autobiography: From Life to Art in Marcel Proust, James Joyce, Virginia Woolf, and Anaïs Nin*. New York: St. Martin's, 1994.

Nin, Anaïs. *Children of the Albatross*. London: Peter Owen, 1959.

———. *Collages*. Denver: Swallow Press, 1964.

———. *D. H. Lawrence: An Unprofessional Study*. Introduction by Harry T. Moore. Denver: Swallow Press, 1964.

———. *Delta of Venus: Erotica*. New York: Harcourt Brace Jovanovich, 1977.

———. *The Diary of Anaïs Nin, Volume 1 (1931–1934)*. Ed. Gunther Stuhlmann. New York, San Diego, and London: Swallow Press and Harcourt Brace Jovanovich, 1966.

———. *The Diary of Anaïs Nin, Volume 2 (1934–1939)*. Ed. Gunther Stuhlmann. New York and London: Swallow Press and Harcourt Brace Jovanovich, 1967.

———. *The Diary of Anaïs Nin, Volume 3 (1939–1944)*. Ed. Gunther Stuhlmann. San Diego, New York, and London: Harcourt Brace Jovanovich, 1969.

———. *The Diary of Anaïs Nin, Volume 4 (1944–1947)*. Ed. Gunther Stuhlmann. New York: Harcourt Brace Jovanovich, 1971.

———. *The Diary of Anaïs Nin, Volume 5 (1947–1955)*. Ed. Gunther Stuhlmann. New York and London: Harcourt Brace Jovanovich, 1974.

———. *The Diary of Anaïs Nin, Volume 6 (1955–1966)*. Ed. Gunther Stuhlmann. New York and London: Harcourt Brace Jovanovich, 1976.

———. *The Diary of Anaïs Nin, Volume 7 (1966–1974)*. Ed. Gunther Stuhlmann. New York: Harcourt Brace Jovanovich, 1980.

———. *The Early Diary of Anaïs Nin*. Volume 1, Linotte—1914–1920; Volume 2,

1920–1923; Volume 3, 1923–1927; and *Volume 4, 1927–1931.* All volumes with prefaces by Joaquín Nin-Culmell. New York and London: Harcourt Brace Jovanovich, 1978, 1982, 1983, 1985.

———. *Fire: From "A Journal of Love"; The Unexpurgated Diary of Anaïs Nin, 1934–1937.* San Diego, New York, London: Harcourt Brace Jovanovich, 1995.

———. *The Four-Chambered Heart.* New York: Duell, Sloan, Pearce, 1950.

———. *Henry and June: From the Unexpurgated Diary of Anaïs Nin.* San Diego, New York, London: Harcourt Brace Jovanovich, 1986.

———. *House of Incest.* Chicago: Swallow Press, 1958.

———. *Incest: From "A Journal of Love"; The Unexpurgated Diary of Anaïs Nin, 1932–1934.* San Diego, New York, London: Harcourt Brace Jovanovich, 1992.

———. *In Favor of the Sensitive Man, and Other Essays.* New York: Harcourt Brace Jovanovich, 1976.

———. *Ladders to Fire.* Denver: Swallow Press, 1959.

———. *Little Birds, Erotica.* New York: Harcourt Brace Jovanovich, 1979.

———. *Nearer the Moon: From "A Journal of Love"; The Unexpurgated Diary of Anaïs Nin, 1937–1939.* San Diego, New York, London: Harcourt Brace Jovanovich, 1996.

———. *The Novel of the Future.* New York: Macmillan, 1968.

———. *Seduction of the Minotaur.* Denver: Swallow Press, 1961.

———. *A Spy in the House of Love.* Paris and New York: British Book Centre, 1954.

———. *This Hunger.* New York: Gemor Press, 1944.

———. *Under a Glass Bell and Other Stories.* Denver: Swallow Press, 1961.

———. *Winter of Artifice: Three Novelettes.* Denver: Swallow Press, 1961.

———. *A Woman Speaks: The Lectures, Seminars, and Interviews of Anaïs Nin.* Ed. Evelyn J. Hinz. Chicago: Swallow Press, 1975.

Ragland (-Sullivan), Ellie. "Dora and the Name-of-the-Father: The Structure of Hysteria." In *Discontented Discourses.* Ed. Marleen S. Barr and Richard Feldstein. 208–40. Urbana: University of Illinois Press, 1989.

———. *Jacques Lacan and the Philosophy of Psychoanalysis.* Urbana and Chicago: University of Illinois Press, 1986.

———. "Lacan's Seminars on James Joyce: Writing as 'Singular Solution.'" In *Compromise Formations: Current Directions in Literary Criticism.* Ed. Vera J. Camden, 61–85. Kent, Ohio: Kent State University Press, 1989.

———. "The Magnetism between Reader and Text: Prolegomena to a Lacanian Poetics." *Poetics* 13 (1984): 381–406.

Richard-Allerdyce, Diane. "Anaïs Nin's Mothering Metaphor: Toward a Lacanian View of Feminine Creativity." In *Compromise Formations: Current Directions in Psychoanalytic Criticism.* Ed. Vera J. Camden. 86–98. Kent, Ohio: Kent State University Press, 1989.

———. "Anaïs Nin's 'Poetic Porn': Subverting the Male Gaze." Paper presented at the Popular Culture Association/American Culture Association Annual Meeting, March 1990, in Toronto, Canada.

———. "*L'Écriture féminine* and Its Discontents: Anaïs Nin's Response to D. H. Lawrence." *D. H. Lawrence Review* 26 (1997): 1–27.

———. "Narrative and Authenticity (Strategies of Evasion in the Diaries of Anaïs Nin: Then and Now)." *Anaïs: An International Journal* 13 (1995): 79–94.

Rock, Joanne. "Her Father's Daughter." *Anaïs: An International Journal* 13 (1995): 29–38.

Scholar, Nancy. *Anaïs Nin.* Boston: Twayne, 1984.

Schwarz, Daniel R. *Narrative and Representation in the Poetry of Wallace Stevens.* New York: St. Martin's Press, 1993.

Seymour, Miranda. "Truth Wasn't Sexy Enough." Review of Noël Riley Fitch, *The Erotic Life of Anaïs Nin.* In *New York Times Book Review,* October 7, 1993, sec. 7, p. 18.

Showalter, Elaine. "Male Hysteria: W. H. R. Rivers and the Lessons of Shell Shock." In *The Female Malady: Women, Madness, and English Culture, 1830–1980.* 167–94. New York: Pantheon, 1985.

———. "Rivers and Sassoon: The Inscription of Male Gender Anxieties." In *Behind the Lines: Gender and the Two World Wars.* Ed. Margaret Higonnet et al. 61–69. New Haven: Yale University Press, 1987.

Siegel, Carol. *Lawrence among the Women: Wavering Boundaries in Women's Literary Traditions.* Charlottesville and London: University Press of Virginia, 1991.

Simpson, Hilary. *D. H. Lawrence and Feminism.* DeKalb: Northern Illinois University Press, 1982.

Spencer, Sharon. *Collage of Dreams.* New York: Harcourt Brace Jovanovich, 1981.

Steiner, Wendy. *Pictures of Romance: Form against Content in Painting and Literature.* Chicago and London: University of Chicago Press, 1988.

Williams, William Carlos. "'Men . . . Have No Tenderness': Anaïs Nin's 'Winter of Artifice.'" In *The Critical Response to Anaïs Nin.* Ed. Philip K. Jason. Critical Responses in Arts and Letters, No. 23. 70–75. Westport, Conn.: Greenwood Press, 1996.

Zaller, Robert, ed. *A Casebook on Anaïs Nin.* New York: New American Library, 1974.

Index

abortion, 97, 105; AN's in 1934, 6–7, 29, 55, 56, 62, 63, 66, 68, 71, 79, 82, 90, 95, 96, 105, 124, 136, 158, 161, 163, 167n.3, 183n.41, 184n.45; in "The Mouse," 79–83
Acapulco (*see* Mexico)
Adler, Alfred, 173n.16
Allendy, René, 21, 22, 29, 49–54, 55, 161, 173n.17, 180n.23; and countertransference, 46–47, 179n.13; and seduction by AN, 45–46, 47, 50, 55, 179n.8
Altieri, Charles, 10, 11, 13; copy models of reality (*see* Modernism); *Painterly Abstraction*, 9
American Academy of Arts and Letters, 146
American literature and culture, Nin's view of, 99, 133, 135, 142, 151–52, 155, 157
Architecture, 159
Armory Show, 123, 191n.29
art as source of comfort and transformation, 17, 38, 81, 100, 106–7, 108, 114, 120, 156 (*see also* Modernism)
art as transpersonal realm, 23, 27 (*see also* Modernism)

Artaud, Antonin, 15, 21, 29, 171n.2
authentic self, Nin's belief in, 9, 12, 49, 149, 150, 164
autobiographical authenticity, 6–8, 109, 114, 161–64, 197n.22
Avon Books, 100

Bair, Deirdre, 4, 16, 122, 168n.4, 181n.23, 181n.24, 182n.30, 182n.32, 184n.3, 189n.9, 192n.9, 195n.7, 196n.13, 197n.17, 197n.21; on Hugh Guiler, 172n.12; on *House of Incest*, 30; on AN's abortion, 183n.41, 186n.25, 187n.33; on AN's adolescence, 19; on AN's analysis with Clement Staff, 191n.3; on AN's attitude toward war, 87; on AN's cancer, 159; on AN's citizenship, 133; on AN's early adulthood and marriage, 20–21; on AN's early reading, 172n.11; on AN's erotica, 187n.31; on AN's feminism, 170n.18; on AN's flirtations, 21; on AN's fiction writing, 54, 95; on AN's houseboat experience, 72, 185n.11; on AN's incest, 29, 180n.17; on AN's lying,

of; Caputi, Jane; paternal wounding; trauma; wounded child;
wounded daughter; wounding);
AN's, with father (*see* Nin, Joaquín)
Incest, From "A Journal of Love," 6, 7, 29,
30, 46, 61, 96, 102, 161, 162,
168n.3, 180n.17, 183n.37,
197n.18
In Favor of the Sensitive Man, 170n.18

Jaeger, Martha, 52, 68, 93, 96, 115,
147–48
Jason, Philip, 90, 95, 127, 139, 146,
168n.6, 169n.9, 173n.21, 174n.22,
175n.29, 178n.3, 178n.4, 178n.5,
183n.34, 187n.34, 188n.2,
193n.11
Jong, Erica, 95, 197n.18
Joyce, James, 10, 13, 143, 169n.13,
173n.16, 189n.16
Jung, Carl, 173n.16
Jungian therapy, 68

Kahane, Jack, 176n.35, 178n.2
Kaufman, Philip, 168n.3, 172n.13,
189n.13
Knapp, Bettina, 139, 167n.2
Kristeva, Julia, 27

La Belle Aurore, 72
labyrinth imagery, 12, 13, 16, 18, 24,
32, 33, 37, 71, 89–90, 109, 110,
114, 123, 139, 148, 194n.20
Lacan, Jacques, 175n.30, 178n.47,
182n.31, 183n.43, 184n.44,
185n.16, 186n.23, 189n.14,
189n.15, 190n.21, 192n.5, 195n.9,
196n.12, 197n.19; analytic goals
of, 34, 104, 183n.36; and exile
theme, 71–72; and gender, 5, 27,
51, 170n.19, 188n.7; and hysteria,
175n.30, 190n.26; and identity
construction, 5, 46, 74, 177n.45;
and illusory nature of wholeness
concept, 36, 49, 51, 111, 181n.27;
and *jouissance,* 5, 23, 27, 51,

170n.19, 174n.24, 175n.30,
182n.31, 190n.25, 196n.15,
197n.20; and the materiality of language, 23, 174n.25; and the mirror
stage, 181n.27, 188n.8; and the
mystic, 175n.30, 181n.31; and the
"No" of the father's name, 74,
177n.44; and the Real, 170n.19;
and splitting, 5, 51; and the
woman as Other, 170n.19
LaCapra, Dominick: "Canons and their
Discontents," 14, 170n.21, 185n.15;
Representing the Holocaust, 16, 32
Ladders to Fire, 69, 99–112, 114, 124,
140–41, 143, 144, 151, 154, 155,
183n.42, 184n.6, 185n.17, 188n.4,
192n.5
Lawrence, D. H., 143
—absence of boundaries in, 28, 64, 78
—anxiety of, 28
—dream imagery of, 33
—as father figure for AN, 7, 21
—feminist response to, 26, 170–71n.1,
175n.29
—and gender relations, 170–71n.1
—and gender roles, 24, 25, 28, 115; and
gender theory, 25; and women's
perspectives, 25, 26
—as model for AN, 22, 28, 33, 42,
174n.22, 174n.24
—and mysticism, 27, 28, 78
—and paradox, 27, 36, 78
—scholarship on works by, 170n.1
—and somatic writing, 23, 30, 33, 37,
159
—and the "texture" of language, 16, 24,
25–27, 37, 42, 129, 131, 165
—and war, 28
—works by: *Lady Chatterley's Lover,* 26;
The Rainbow, 26; *Women in Love,*
21, 25
—writing style of, 16, 128
Lee, Jonathan Scott, 72, 179–80n.13,
181n.23, 181n.28, 185n.9,
185n.12, 185n.16, 186n.21,
189n.15, 190n.21

9 780875 802329